Palgrave Studies in European Political Sociology

Edited by
Carlo Ruzza, Department of Sociology, University of Leicester, UK
Hans-Jörg Trenz, University of Copenhagen, Denmark
Mauro Barisione, University of Milan, Italy
Neil Fligstein, University of California, US
Virginie Guiraudon, National Centre for Scientific Research (CNRS), France
Dietmar Loch, University of Grenoble, France
Chris Rumford, Department of Politics and International Relations, Royal Holloway, University of London, UK
Maarten P. Vink, University of Maastricht, The Netherlands

Palgrave Studies in European Political Sociology addresses contemporary themes in the field of Political Sociology. Over recent years, attention has turned increasingly to processes of Europeanization and globalization and the social and political spaces that are opened by them. These processes comprise both institutional-constitutional change and new dynamics of social transnationalism. Europeanization and globalization are also about changing power relations as they affect people's lives, social networks and forms of mobility.

The *Palgrave Studies in European Political Sociology* series addresses linkages between regulation, institution building and the full range of societal repercussions at local, regional, national, European and global level, and will sharpen understanding of changing patterns of attitudes and behaviours of individuals and groups, the political use of new rights and opportunities by citizens, new conflict lines and coalitions, societal interactions and networking, and shifting loyalties and solidarity within and across the European space. We welcome proposals from across the spectrum of Political Sociology including on dimensions of citizenship; political attitudes and values; political communication and public spheres; states, communities, governance structure and political institutions; forms of political participation; populism and the radical right; and democracy and democratization.

Titles include:

Luis Bouza Garcia
PARTICIPATORY DEMOCRACY AND CIVIL SOCIETY IN THE EU
Agenda-Setting and Institutionalisation 1997–2012

Matthias Kortmann and Kerstin Rosenow-Williams
ISLAMIC ORGANIZATIONS IN EUROPE AND THE USA
A Multidisciplinary Perspective

Andreas Müller
GOVERNING MOBILITY BEYOND THE STATE
Centre, Periphery and the EU's External Borders

Apostolis Papakostas
CIVILIZING THE PUBLIC SPHERE
Distrust, Trust and Corruption

Armando Salvatore, Oliver Schmidtke and Hans-Jörg Trenz (*editors*)
RETHINKING THE PUBLIC SPHERE THROUGH
TRANSNATIONALIZING PROCESSES
Europe and Beyond

Rosa Sanchez Salgado
EUROPEANIZING CIVIL SOCIETY
How the EU Shapes Civil Society Organizations

Palgrave Studies in European Political Sociology
Series Standing Order ISBN 978–1–137–28230–9 (Hardback)
978–1–137–28231–6
(*outside North America only*)

You can receive future titles in this series as they are published by placing a standing order. Please contact your bookseller or, in case of difficulty, write to us at the address below with your name and address, the title of the series and the ISBNs quoted above.

Customer Services Department, Macmillan Distribution Ltd, Houndmills, Basingstoke, Hampshire RG21 6XS, England

Europeanizing Civil Society
How the EU Shapes Civil Society Organizations

Rosa Sanchez Salgado
University of Amsterdam, The Netherlands

palgrave
macmillan

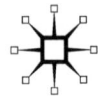

© Rosa Sanchez Salgado 2014

All rights reserved. No reproduction, copy or transmission of this publication may be made without written permission.

No portion of this publication may be reproduced, copied or transmitted save with written permission or in accordance with the provisions of the Copyright, Designs and Patents Act 1988, or under the terms of any licence permitting limited copying issued by the Copyright Licensing Agency, Saffron House, 6–10 Kirby Street, London EC1N 8TS.

Any person who does any unauthorized act in relation to this publication may be liable to criminal prosecution and civil claims for damages.

The author has asserted her right to be identified as the author of this work in accordance with the Copyright, Designs and Patents Act 1988.

First published 2014 by
PALGRAVE MACMILLAN

Palgrave Macmillan in the UK is an imprint of Macmillan Publishers Limited, registered in England, company number 785998, of Houndmills, Basingstoke, Hampshire RG21 6XS.

Palgrave Macmillan in the US is a division of St Martin's Press LLC, 175 Fifth Avenue, New York, NY 10010.

Palgrave Macmillan is the global academic imprint of the above companies and has companies and representatives throughout the world.

Palgrave® and Macmillan® are registered trademarks in the United States, the United Kingdom, Europe and other countries.

ISBN 978–1–137–35540–9

This book is printed on paper suitable for recycling and made from fully managed and sustained forest sources. Logging, pulping and manufacturing processes are expected to conform to the environmental regulations of the country of origin.

A catalogue record for this book is available from the British Library.

A catalog record for this book is available from the Library of Congress.

In loving memory of my father

Contents

List of Tables, Figures and Boxes — xii

Acknowledgments — xiv

List of Abbreviations — xv

Introduction — 1
1 The development of research on European CSOs: Fragmentary and unbalanced — 3
2 The EU's role in changing domestic CSOs: A sociologically informed analysis — 7
3 A sociological comparative approach — 9
4 Outline of the book: Europeanization of CSOs as a EU-driven process — 11

1 The Europeanization of CSOs—Institutional Impact or Strategic Action? — 14
1 Europeanization studies, including a sociological dimension? — 14
   1.1 Toward a sociologically informed concept of Europeanization? — 15
   1.2 A stimulating disagreement on the most relevant explanatory factors — 16
   1.3 An unfortunate dissociation of levels of analysis — 18
   1.4 Bridging divides in Europeanization studies between institutional analysis and a micro-sociology of the EU — 19
2 Combining approaches: The challenge of the research design — 21
   2.1 Analyzing EU impact: Combining top-down and bottom-up perspectives — 21
   2.2 The Europeanization of CSOs and the temporal dimension — 25
3 A sociological comparative approach — 28
   3.1 Diversity in the understanding of CSOs — 28

3.2 Justification of the selection of countries, policy areas and CSOs under analysis   30
3.3 An analysis based on a diversity of data collection   36

Part I Domestic Civil Society under EU Pressures

2 Domestic Civil Society: National or European?   41
1 The usages of European funds: A bottom-up perspective   41
   1.1 Strategies for Europeanization and main questions   42
   1.2 Methodological considerations   43
   1.3 National legal frameworks: An exclusive national pressure   45
2 The externalization of CSOs: Following the money   47
   2.1 Humanitarian CSOs: The most fancied   47
   2.2 EU funds and development and international human rights CSOs: A fair deal   50
   2.3 EU funds for domestically oriented CSOs: The national filter   52
   2.4 The Europeanization of consultation and direct presence in Brussels: An elite system?   56
3 Europeanization on the cheap: Transnationalization and internalization   59
   3.1 National CSOs in European peak associations: Present but not necessarily active   60
   3.2 The Internalization of Europe   63
4 CSOs' varying degrees of Europeanization   64

3 A European Policy for CSOs? Exploring European Political Opportunities   69
1 The absence of EU legal constraints   69
   1.1 EU treaties: An ex post facto recognition of civil society   70
   1.2 A single market for non-profit organizations?   71
2 Funding opportunities: Regulating activities through spending power?   72
   2.1 The rise and decline of EU funding opportunities   73
   2.2 European funding opportunities and EU member states   79
3 Access opportunities: From instrumental pragmatism to democratic opportunism?   83
   3.1 Regulating an increasingly overloaded interest group system   83

3.2	Access opportunities at the Commission: From pragmatism to high expectations	85
3.3	Promoting participation and consultation beyond the European Commission	88
3.4	A great diversity of national access opportunities	90

4 European Opportunities: Institutional Factors and Creative Usages — 94

1 CSOs' use of EU opportunities: Transforming the European civil society landscape? — 94
  1.1 Domestic funding opportunities: The prevalence of compensation strategies — 96
  1.2 Access and domestic opportunities — 99
  1.3 CSOs' lack of internal capacity: The positive persistence hypothesis reversed — 102
2 The usages by Europe: EU-driven shaping of CSOs — 103
  2.1 Shaping access through the creation of peak associations — 104
  2.2 How the EU has promoted the usages of EU funding opportunities — 108
  2.3 The Commission's limits in shaping powers — 110
3 The usages of Europe: Where there is a will, there is a way — 112
  3.1 The shaping of EU funding opportunities by CSOs — 112
  3.2 The shaping of access opportunities by CSOs: Creating new rights? — 113
  3.3 CSOs' bottom-up usages of EU opportunities — 115

Part II Europeanizing CSOs through European Opportunities

5 EU Funding of CSOs: From New Public to New Civic Management — 123

1 EU funding and the growth of CSOs — 124
  1.1 EU funding in the 1980s and 1990s: Boosting immoderate growth? — 124
  1.2 A moderate use of EU funding — 130
2 The EU role in the promotion of New Public Management among CSOs — 133
  2.1 From flexibility to New Public Management — 133
  2.2 NPM techniques and CSOs receptiveness: Toward convergence in Europe? — 136
  2.3 A widely promoted learning process — 138

x Contents

    2.4 Non-Europeanized CSOs: Old Public Management? 140
    2.5 From NPM to New Civic Management? 142

6 **CSOs and Identity Building: Cheerleaders for European Integration?** 147
  1 CSOs' potential contribution to identity building 148
    1.1 Promoting European values and European integration 148
    1.2 EU visibility and political advertising 150
    1.3 The invention and expansion of the EU transnationality principle 151
  2 The promotion of European values: Civic engagement or instrumentalization? 153
    2.1 How CSOs implemented European values and awareness-raising activities 153
    2.2 A bottom-up Europeanizing effect? 156
  3 Promoting EU visibility through CSOs: Mixed results 159
  4 Transnational cooperation: Europeanization as cross-loading 162
    4.1 Transnational cooperation and the transformation of CSOs 162
    4.2 Promoting a European identity? 164

Part III Europeanizing Civil Society through Participation

7 **The Europeanization of CSOs' Participation: Beyond the Brussels Consensus** 169
  1 Revisiting portrayals of the CSOs Brussels Consensus 170
    1.1 How the European Commission promotes a Brussels Consensus 170
    1.2 The EU's shaping of EU-based CSOs 172
    1.3 EU-based CSOs: Advocacy groups or consensus hunters? 175
  2 The Europeanization of CSOs beyond the Brussels complex 178
    2.1 Europeanization through national dialogue processes: The prevalence of diversity 178
    2.2 More Europeanized CSOs have less impact? 183
    2.3 Less Europeanized CSOs have more impact? 186

3 The Europeanization of advocacy activities from below	189
3.1 Beyond the Brussels Consensus: A bottom-up Europeanization of CSOs	189
3.2 Transnational cooperation beyond the Brussels Consensus	190
Conclusion: The Political Construction of European Civil Society: Legitimate and Democratic?	**197**
1 Integrating a sociological dimension in Europeanization studies	198
1.1 A diversity of interrelated EU pressures	198
1.2 Bringing together bottom-up and top-down approaches to Europeanization	200
1.3 The importance of the temporal dimension in Europeanization studies	202
2 The shaping of CSOs: Legitimate and democratic?	204
2.1 Addressing imbalances in the system of interest representation	205
2.2 The EU's shaping of CSOs: Putting their autonomy at risk?	207
2.3 Shaping CSOs, but not controlling them	210
2.4 The service delivery function and participatory democracy	212
2.5 Identity building through CSOs: A political system with multiple identities	214
Appendix 1: Interviews	218
Notes	220
References	232
Index	255

Tables, Figures and Boxes

Tables

1.1	Different conceptualizations of Europeanization	16
1.2	Europeanization and different explanatory variables	17
1.3	Different approaches for capturing the impact of Europe	20
1.4	Conceptions of the link between European integration and Europeanization	26
1.5	The process of Europeanization of CSOs	28
2.1	Platforms of CSOs selected for the website analysis	44
2.2	Humanitarian CSOs receiving EU funds	48
2.3	Grants given by DG ECHO in 2011	49
2.4	Development CSOs obtaining EU funds	50
2.5	Grants given by DG DEVCO/EuropeAid in 2011	51
2.6	Grants given by DG Employment in 2011	53
2.7	Grants given by DG Justice in 2011	56
2.8	Humanitarian and development CSOs directly involved in European peak associations	60
2.9	Types of CSOs and their varying degrees of Europeanization	65
2.10	Examples of exclusive CSOs	66
3.1	Examples of budget lines created in the 1980s and 1990s for development and human rights CSOs	75
5.1	The growth of CSOs: From exclusivism to pluralism	125
5.2	Resources of pluralist CSOs	130
7.1	EU networks engaged with Brussels (day one)	194
C.1	Values of some of the most EU-active CSOs	213
A.1	Interviews with CSOs and EU officials	219

Figures

2.1	DG ECHO funding for French CSOs (commitments for 2001 in euros)	49
2.2	DG DEVCO funding for French, UK and Spanish CSOs (commitments for 2001 in euros)	52

2.3 DG Employment funding for French, UK and Spanish
    CSOs (commitments for 2001 in euros) 54
2.4 DG ECHO funding for UK CSOs (commitments for 2001
    in euros) 58
3.1 Evolution of EU funding (in millions of ECUS/euros)
    during the expansion period 76
4.1 Evolution of public funding for French CSOs (in millions
    of French Francs) during the expansion period 97
4.2 Evolution of public funding for Spanish CSOs (in millions
    of pesetas) during the expansion period 98

Boxes

1 Humanitarian CSOs: From Neutrality and the Right of
  Intervention to the Responsibility to Protect 31
2 Development CSOs: From Self-Help to International
  Campaigning 33
3 Human Rights CSOs: Between Politics and Law 35
4 The Growth of MSF-France in the 1970s–1980s 127

Acknowledgments

This book could not have been completed without the help of some important and special people.

I would first like to thank the editors of the Palgrave series *Studies in European Political Sociology* for accepting this book for publication. I owe particular thanks to editor Carlo Ruzza for his thoughtful comments and for cheering me up during the most difficult moments of the publishing process. Thanks also to the anonymous reviewers for their useful remarks.

Thanks to my coworkers and colleagues at the University of Amsterdam (UvA), and at SciencesPo. During various phases of the writing process, I benefited from their stimulating remarks and ideas. Special thanks to Jonathan Zeitlin for his continuous feedback and advice and to Joost Berkhout for his tips on the figures.

Thanks also to the Political Economy and Transnational Governance Group (PETGOV) for their economic support and particularly to its codirector, Brian Burgoon, for his constant trust in my book project.

This book has also benefited from comments from discussants and participants in the conferences I have attended over the years. Thanks to all for the attention they gave to my research and for their inspiring remarks. Special thanks to Justin Greenwood for his interest and for his commentary on the back cover.

Sincerest thanks to all my interviewees—CSO representatives, public officials and experts—for making time for me in spite of their very busy schedules. I was often moved by their stories and impressed by the dedication and commitment that they put into their jobs.

For help with the onerous task of editing and proofreading, my thanks go to the expert eye of Mose Hayward. Great thanks also to all of the Palgrave editorial assistants for their help with the editing, marketing and production. I alone am responsible for any errors found in this book.

Finally, I wish to thank my friends and family, who sensed that something important was going on. Thanks for all of your excitement and enthusiasm!

Abbreviations

ACF	Action contre la faim (Action against Hunger)
ACH	Acción contra el Hambre (Action against Hunger)
ACPAHU	Action et Partage Humanitaire (Humanitarian Action and Sharing)
ACTA	Anti-Counterfeiting Trade Agreement
ACTED	Agency for Technical Cooperation and Development
AECI	Agencia Española de Cooperación International (Spanish Agency for International Development Cooperation)
AFD	Agence Française pour le Développement (French Agency for Development)
AI	Amnesty International
AIDCO	EuropeAid Cooperation Office
AIRE	Centre Advice on Individual Rights in Europe
ALAID	Association Laïque d'Aide et d'Initiatives au Développement (Secular Association for Aid and Development Initiatives)
ANSA	Association Agence Nouvelle des solidarités (New Agency for Active Solidarity)
ARE	Association of European Regions
ATTAC	Association for the Taxation of Financial Transactions for the Aid of Citizens
AUSAID	Australian Agency for International Development
BOND	British Overseas NGOs for Development
CAFOD	Catholic Agency for Overseas Development
CARE	Cooperative for American Relief in Europe
CCAA	Comunidades Autónomas (Autonomous Communities)
CCD	Comité de Coopération au Développement (Development Cooperation Committee)
CCFD	Comité Catholique Contre la Faim et pour le Développement (Catholic Committee against Hunger and for Development)
CEDAG	European Council of Non-profit Associations
CICDA	Centre International de Coopération pour le Développement Agricole (International Cooperation Center for Agricultural Development)

CIPIE	Centro de Investigaciones, Promoción y Cooperación Internacional (International Research, Promotion and Cooperation Center)
CLONG	Liaison Committee of Development NGOs to the European Union
CNVA	Conseil National de la vie Associative (National Council for Associative Life)
CODESPA	Cooperación al Desarrollo y Promoción de Actividades Asistenciales (Development Cooperation and Promotion of Social Activities)
CONCORD	European NGO Confederation for Relief and Development
CONECCS	Consultation, the European Commission and Civil Society
CONGDE	Coordinadora ONG para el Desarrollo España (NGO Coordination for Development of Spain)
CPCA	Conférence Permanente des Coordinations Associatives (Standing Conference for Associative Coordination)
CSCG	Civil Society Contact Group
CSO	Civil Society Organization
DFID	Department for International Development
DG	Directorate-General
EAPN	European Anti-Poverty Network
EEC	European Economic Community
ECHO	European Commission Humanitarian Office
ECOE	Equipo de Comunicación Educativa (Educational Communication Team)
EDF	European Disability Forum
EESC	European Economic and Social Committee
EIDHR	European Initiative for Democracy and Human Rights
EPAP	European Platform Against Poverty and Social Exclusion
EPPIE	Européanisation des Politiques publiques et Intégration européenne (Europeanization of Public Policies and European Integration)
EPHA	European Public Health Alliance
ERASMUS	European Community Action Scheme for the Mobility of University Students
ERDF	European Regional Development Fund

List of Abbreviations xvii

ERF	Enfants Refugiés du monde (Refugee Children in the World)
ESCODE	Estudios y Cooperación para el Desarrollo (Development Studies and Cooperation)
ESF	European Social Fund
ESF	European Social Forum
ESN	European Social Network
ETUC	European Trade Union Confederation
EU	European Union
EWL	European Women's Lobby
FAP	Framework Partnership Agreement
FEANTSA	European Federation of National Organizations Working with the Homeless
FIDH	International Federation for Human Rights
FIDH-AE	European Association for Human Rights
FNARS	Fédération nationale des associations d'accueil et de réinsertion sociale (National Federation of Social Rehabilitation Associations)
FSG	Fundación Secretariado Gitano (The Roma Secretariat Foundation)
FTS	Financial Transparency System
Groupe URD	Groupe Urgence, Réhabilitation, Développement (Group Emergency, Rehabilitation and Development)
HRDN	Human Rights and Democracy Network
ID	Initiative Développement
IMC	International Medical Corps UK
IMF	International Monetary Fund
IRC	International Rescue Committee
IRPF	Impuesto sobre la Renta de las Personas Físicas (Income Tax for Individuals)
LFA	Logical Framework Approach
MAG	Mines Advisory Group
MDM	Médecins du Monde (Doctors of the World)
MEDEL	European Magistrates for Democracy and Freedom
MER	Medical Emergency Relief
MPDL	Movimiento por la Paz, el Desarme y la Libertad (Movement for Peace, Disarmament and Freedom)
MSF	Médecins Sans Frontières (Doctors without Borders)
NGO	Non-Governmental Organization
NPM	New Public Management
ODA	Overseas Development Agency

OECD	Organization for Economic Cooperation and Development
OMC	Open Method of Coordination
ONCE	Organización Nacional de Ciegos Españoles (Spanish National Organization for the Blind)
PACO	Programme d'Appui au Co-Financement (Co-funding Support Program)
PCM	Project Cycle Management
PPA	Program Partnership Agreement
PROGRESS	Community Programme for Employment and Social Solidarity
PROYDE	Promoción y Desarrollo (Promotion and Development)
PU-AMI	Première Urgence-Aide Médicale Internationale (First Emergency – International Medical Aid)
RACINE	Réseau d' Appui et de Capitalization des Innovations européennes (Network for Support and Capitalization of European Innovations)
SADC	South African Development Community
SAG	Stakeholders Advisory Group
SEL	Service d'Entraide et de Liaison (Networking and Mutual Aid Service)
SODA	Strategic Organizational Development Approach
SOTERMUN	Solidaridad con el Tercer Mundo (Solidarity with the Third World)
SSCI	Social Sciences Citation Index
TACIS	Technical Assistance to the Commonwealth of Independent States
UAFSE	Unidad Administradora del Fondo Social Europeo (The Administrative Unit for the European Social Fund)
UK	United Kingdom
UNIOPPS	Union national interfédérale des oeuvres et organismes privés non lucratifs sanitaires et sociaux (National Inter-federal Union of Private Social and Welfare Charities and Organizations)
USAID	US Agency for International Development
VOICE	Voluntary Organizations in Cooperation in Emergencies
WSF	World Social Forum
WTO	World Trade Organization
WWF	World Wildlife Fund

Introduction

Ever since the end of the so-called 'permissive consensus' on European integration, civil society organizations (CSOs) have attracted widespread attention. The difficulty of applying traditional models of representative democracy at the European Union (EU) level has led policymakers and scholars alike to consider CSOs as one of the few remaining options to bring European citizens closer to European institutions and to bridge the legitimacy gap. CSOs have been central to many crucial debates on contemporary European politics, for instance in debates on the EU democratic deficit, European citizenship and welfare pluralism. Despite this growing interest, most recent studies in this field focus on the most visible dimension of this phenomenon, that is, the participation of CSOs in European policymaking and their democratic potential, particularly within the framework of new modes of governance.

As this study reveals, the treatment of this topic has been rather narrow until now. The shortcomings of current research are not accidental. Most research in this field has been completed within the framework of the literature on interest groups or new forms of governance. The theoretical and methodological choices typical of these approaches have significantly influenced the nature and scope of the research findings. Studies in this field suffer from an 'input fixation' since they only investigate the participation of societal actors in the decision-making process, neglecting other stages of the policy process (Pestoff 2009). They have established the importance of supply-side factors in understanding group mobilization, while demand-side pressures (including the external force of government) have been given less attention (Mahoney 2004). This change of focus calls attention to a new set of research questions. To what extent has EU governance generated identifiable changes in CSOs? How have CSOs seized European political opportunities? How have CSOs been affected by EU institutional requirements? What, if any, are the implications for CSOs' effectiveness and for their democratic potential? By emphasizing this overlooked dimension of the problem, this book sheds new light on current discussions on the role of civil society in Europe.

Furthermore, the great majority of existing studies focus largely on European-level organizations. To address these atypical questions appropriately, this study will broaden the research agenda of Europeanization studies to include the analysis of domestic CSOs. It will also contribute to the refinement of hypotheses and theoretical propositions within the Europeanization field of inquiry. The main purpose of mainstream Europeanization studies has been to trace the effects of EU policy on national bureaucratic structures and domestic public policies. The impacts of the EU on societal interests have been the least explored (Börzel and Risse 2006; Liebert 2009). Similarly, the concept of Europeanization has not yet been adjusted to appropriately cover this object of study. The EU has only been approached as a political construction, and, hence, the analysis of its visible institutions and policies remains largely ungrounded (Fligstein 2008). The political process is of utmost importance, but 'in the same way that policy cannot be understood without politics, politics cannot be understood without society' (Giraudon and Favell 2009: 552). For this to occur, the Europeanization studies agenda needs to not only focus on typically sociological objects of study, it must also include novel research designs that permit scholars to grasp the full range of the social effects of the EU (Giraudon and Favell 2009). The sociological approaches that have been adopted for the study of the EU are rather heterogeneous, but they all emphasize the role of strategic action (Saurugger 2008).[1]

The inclusion of a sociological dimension in Europeanization studies also contributes to the normalization of European studies. The EU today resembles a 'normal' political system, and this situation is increasingly reflected in academic research. Europeanization studies have been given credit for their contribution to the normalization of European studies (Exadaktylos and Radaelli 2009; Hassenteufel and Surel 2000). Since they focus on the EU impact on different member states, they often fall within the field of comparative politics. Europeanization studies work with theories and analytical tools that can also be applied to other political systems. Compared to previous studies on Europe, they have relied less on ad hoc theorizing (EPPIE 2007). This trend has been confirmed by quantitative analysis on EU research (Kreppel 2012). This book is on the subject of comparative state regulation of CSOs and, as such, it will take into consideration all other such studies. The focus on Europe, which is a multilevel system of governance, allows for both vertical and horizontal comparisons: up and down several levels (local, national and European) and across member states.

This book shows that the process of the transformation of CSOs has not been spontaneous and that, as general rule, CSOs have not been proactive in their process of adaptation to the EU. On the contrary, the adaptation of CSOs has mainly been EU-driven; without the *direct* intervention of European institutions and actors, the European dimension of domestic CSOs would still be very weak to this day. Most collective action at the EU level followed the transfer of power and competences to the EU (Balme and Chabanet 2008; Mahoney and Beckstrand 2011). To encourage the Europeanization of CSOs, the EU has offered a wide range of incentives, such as funding and access opportunities. This process should not only be seen as a strategic game, in which CSOs turn European in order to obtain specific benefits from the EU. Once CSOs decide to use European opportunities, they enter into dynamics of Europeanization that they cannot always control. The specific conditions related to the acquisition of EU funds and the prospects for effective participation in the policy process all affect the goals and strategies of CSOs in Europe. The study of the Europeanization of CSOs brings new insights to discussions on the democratic potential of CSOs in Europe and their role as service providers. The present study also argues that a primarily EU-driven process of transformation does not *necessarily* undermine the potential contribution of CSOs to democratic legitimacy.

This introduction is divided into three sections. First, a brief overview of current studies of CSOs in EU governance reveals that not much attention has yet been drawn to how EU governance architectures generate identifiable changes in CSOs. Second, the theoretical framework is introduced, combining institutional analysis and a micro-sociology of the EU. The challenges raised by such a combination are addressed through a comparative sociological approach. The case studies under analysis are then briefly introduced. Finally, the main argument—that the process of the Europeanization of CSOs has been mainly EU-driven—is presented, along with an outline of this book.

1 The development of research on European CSOs: Fragmentary and unbalanced

Interest groups were one of the most prominent objects of study during the initial years of the European integration process. According to the neo-functionalist perspective, interest groups were expected to turn their allegiances to the European level, and, in this way, significantly contribute to the process of European integration (Fligstein and Stone Sweet 2001; Haas 1968). During this period, sociological argumentation and claims were at the heart of European studies. But after the initial euphoria, the sociological objects of study and research methods became increasingly marginal (Giraudon and Favell 2009; Saurugger 2008).

Many years later, in the wake of the Single European Act and the Treaty of Maastricht, there was a renewed interest in societal actors at the EU level. The proliferation of interest groups during the early 1990s engaged the attention of scholars dealing with the most classical questions in the field of interest-group research. This field of inquiry was predominantly interested in the characteristics of the interest-group system and in the influence of interest groups on the policy process. The first wave of such studies has been criticized for being descriptive and monographic and for its excessive focus on economic interest groups (Saurugger 2002). The few articles on general interest groups dealt with environmental and consumer organizations, whose participation has always been most visible at the EU level (Pollack 1997; Webster 2000). Studies on the characteristics of the EU system of representation tend to conclude that an *imperfect* pluralist system of interest representation or an 'empowered pluralism' is emerging at the EU level (Coen 1998; Greenwood 2007; Mazey and Richardson 2002; Panebianco 2000; Schmidt 1999). Likewise, many studies have described the lobbying activities and the political practices of interest associations (Bouwen 2003; Coen 2007; Coen and Richardson 2009; Eising 2007; Greenwood 2007; Kollman 1998; Woll 2012) or have discussed the influence of interest groups in the policy process, which has proven to be a very tricky research question (Chalmers 2011; Dür 2009; Dür and De Bièvre 2007; Michalowitz 2007; Woll 2007). A few studies relying on quantitative research methods have offered an overview of the interest-group population (Wonka et al. 2010) or discussed the frequency with which different groups' strategies are used (Beyers 2002, 2004). All in all, while considering studies on interest groups, there is a substantial business bias and a focus on supply-side factors (Mahoney 2004).

All these studies have preferred to use concepts such as interest groups or collective action, which are usually employed by political scientists to refer to all kinds of interests represented in a pluralist society. It is worth noting the rare recourse to other concepts, such as non-profit organizations, the third sector or social economy (Kendall 2009). This reflects the weakness of the social dimension of the European integration process, and the lack of attention to these concepts by European policymakers.

Only a few articles have discussed the unsuccessful project that was the European Statute of Association (De Crombrugghe 1993; Kendall and Fraisse 2005; Vayssade 2001).

At the beginning of the 2000s, after the publication of the White Paper on European Governance (European Commission 2001a), attention shifted from interest groups to CSOs. European civil society has become a fashionable concept, since it 'promises better governance, improved legitimacy and citizens' participation in the relatively distant European polity' (Liebert and Trenz 2009: 2). While certain scholars include all kinds of interests in this concept, the majority restrict its use to organizations representing 'general interests' (Kohler-Koch 2010). In addition, this study also covers the category 'social movements', which until now has been widely neglected (Ruzza 2011). Empirical evidence on the Europeanization of social movements remains fragmentary and concludes that only a minority of social movements are active at the EU level (Della Porta and Caiani 2009; Kriesi et al. 2007; Imig and Tarrow 2001).

This newest strand of research focuses on CSOs' participation in the new European governance architectures (Armstrong 2002; Della Sala and Ruzza 2007; Finke 2007; Friedrich 2007; Kohler-Koch and Quittkat 2013; Ruzza 2004; Smismans 2006). The study of the different forms of participation in European policy processes has taken many different forms, reflecting the diversity of channels open at the EU level. Most studies deal with the new consultation procedures launched by the White Paper on European Governance. A few analyses focus on the participation of civil society in the Conventions for the Human Rights Charter or the Convention on the Future of Europe (De Schutter 2002; Lucarelli and Radaelli 2004; Perez-Solozarno Barragán 2007; Rüb 2002). While many authors have highlighted the inclusive character of new modes of governance and the significant place given to stakeholders, not many articles exclusively analyze the participation of CSOs in these processes. For the most part they refer to the Open Method of Coordination in the domain of social inclusion (Armstrong 2006; Brandsen et al. 2005; Davis 2009; Jacobsson and Johansson 2009; Johansson 2007). More recently, certain authors have also emphasized a 'social system approach', in which civil society is conceived of as an active factor in the development of a European political and social order (Liebert and Trenz 2010). As this brief review of the main literature reveals, most studies of non-state actors in the EU focus on participation in the policy process. Their main concern is the potential contribution of CSOs to the legitimation of European institutions and to the democratization of the EU polity. They have brought valuable insights on the possibilities and limits of the existing forms of participation. All in all, CSOs are considered to be rather ineffective, and to fall short of their legitimizing potential (Kohler-Koch and Quittkat 2013; Kröger and Friedrich 2012).

Only a few authors have raised the question of the influence of the European political system on societal actors (Cram 2011; Greenwood 2007; Kohler-Koch and Finke 2007; Mahoney 2004), but this research question has not been sufficiently developed until now. It is striking how few studies have used the term 'Europeanization' when discussing interest groups or CSOs. A search in the Social Sciences Citation Index (SSCI) shows that there are few articles on Europeanization combined with interest groups, social movements and/or civil society.[2] A review of these articles also reveals a clear confusion around the notion of Europeanization. Most articles do not refer to the impact of Europe on interest groups or to any identifiable process of change. They simply deal with the typical research questions previously presented and/or with the contribution of interest groups to the Europeanization process (for example, Warleigh 2001). Additionally, most articles are interested in the role of CSOs during the accession process or in Central and Eastern Europe,[3] while very little attention is paid to the transformation of CSOs in Western Europe.

Certain studies have analyzed the EU impact on business associations (Coen and Dannreuther 2003; Grande 2003; Grote and Lang 2003). Only a few authors have specifically drawn attention to the transformation of domestic CSOs. They have only understood Europeanization as synonymous with 'going European' (Balme et al. 2002; Beyers 2002; Beyers and Kerremans 2007; Císař and Vráblíková 2012; Imig and Tarrow 1999; McCauley 2011; Ward and Lowe 1998). Even if this research question is itself interesting, this approach only covers a very limited aspect of the process of Europeanization. This dimension is also the most ambiguous as it is sometimes unclear to what extent these evolutions could be covered just as well by classical theories of European integration, particularly neo-functionalism, rather than by theories that focus more specifically on the transformation of CSOs.

The few studies that have attempted to use the concept of Europeanization to analyze transformations of CSOs are rare and inconclusive. Even if their findings are not to be neglected, they are single-case studies. They focus on one sector and country and they cannot delve into the differential impacts of Europe. Likewise, the number of policy areas and countries covered until now is extremely low. The current studies focus on volunteer organizations helping immigrants in the United Kingdom (Gray and Statham 2005), Germany (Trenz 2007) and Sweden (Johansson 2007). Saurugger (2007) has also published an article on the Europeanization of interest groups in France, but unfortunately empirical data are rather limited.

2 The EU's role in changing domestic CSOs: A sociologically informed analysis

How do we know whether the EU has caused identifiable changes in domestic CSOs? The complexity of this research question is reflected in the controversies regarding the theoretical framework most appropriate for its study and the challenges related to its measurement.

In European studies, the impact of Europe is usually related to the concept of Europeanization. However, the top-down perspective predominant in this field of inquiry has been criticized on several occasions by proponents of research designs that place emphasis on domestic politics (Mastenbroek and Kaeding 2006; Graziano et al. 2011). This lack of agreement concerns not only the level of analysis but also the operationalization of the term and the most relevant explanatory variables. This book argues that both approaches can be combined, and, thus, the concept of Europeanization needs to be broadened to include a sociologically informed analysis. The added value of a sociological analysis is the emphasis it places on social practices and their social significance within any given institutional framework (Giraudon and Favell 2009). This analysis focuses not only on a set of institutions, it also aims to uncover social interactions that make the whole picture much more realistic and concrete.

At the midway point between state and society, CSOs are a very appropriate object of study to bridge the gap between institutional analysis and political sociology. Academic communication between mainstream institutional research and sociological analysis will provide many benefits to both strands of scholarship. Most institutional studies are often too distant from social realities to make practical sense, and sociological micro-analyses alone are too parochial to be relevant.

The analytical tools designed for the Europeanization of public policy are not necessarily appropriate for the analysis of societal actors. This book proposes a theoretical framework (detailed in Chapter 1) better adapted to the study of state–society relationships. CSOs and other societal actors are engaged in European and domestic politics, but they cannot be analyzed in the same way as public authorities or bureaucratic bodies. Their status as members of society (rather than as integrated parts of the political system) has not been taken into account sufficiently. First, CSOs are more broadly embedded in society, and, as such, they function according to a logic of their own. Second, with the current institutional configurations, CSOs cannot be *directly* affected by European institutions. The EU is not a 'regulatory framework' that places *direct* pressures on CSOs but is rather an entity that offers incentives. While studying non-state actors, it is essential to pay special attention to actor's agency. Europeanization only exists when actors perceive that their interests are better represented at the EU level or when they decide to seize European incentive structures (Coen and Dannreuther 2003).

Assessing the impact of Europe is also problematic, especially if the concept of Europeanization is broadened to include a sociological dimension. Institutional studies on the impact of Europe tend to focus on goal attainment and on the measurement of the performance of the implementers. Within this field of inquiry, Haverland (2005) criticizes the bias toward EU-level explanations and proposes that this could possibly be solved with counterfactual analysis and the inclusion of non-EU member states as case studies.

The micro-sociological approach to the study of the impact of Europe has not yet inspired a methodological discussion on measurement. A key element of the micro-sociological approach consists of analyzing European norms from a bottom-up perspective (Pasquier and Weisbein 2004). The emphasis is placed on domestic actors who are not officially involved in the decision-making process, but are subjected to European norms and constitute what has been called the 'social flesh' of the integration process. In order to grasp these dynamics, this approach relies on methodological tools from political sociology, and more specifically from studies on collective action or what in the French tradition is known as the 'sociology of public action' (Lascoumes and Le Galès 2007). One of the most challenging obstacles is that the micro-approach gives so much attention to context that it is confronted with a great number of potential explanatory variables. This approach runs the risk of understanding politics as the macro-aggregate consequences of individual actions or as a mere reflection of society (March and Olsen 2005). On top of this, given the small number of cases under study, the degree of generalizability is usually low.

This combination of approaches offers a wide range of possibilities for methodological pluralism and data triangulation. The research design—presented in detail in Chapter 1—has been specifically created to combine institutional analysis and a micro-sociology of the EU.

Thus, it adopts both the domestic and the EU level as starting points of the analysis; it includes the analysis of different time periods and a comparative dimension.

3 A sociological comparative approach

In this qualitative analysis, priority is given to providing an in-depth understanding of a complex process, taking into account national contexts and different policy sectors (Mahoney and Goertz 2006). A medium-*n* study has been considered to be more appropriate to mirror the diversity and complexity of CSOs in Europe. Thus, this analysis focuses on a relatively small number of CSOs.[4] The selection of these CSOs is based on the analysis of more than 400 CSOs active in three member states and different policy areas, presented in detail in Chapter 2. Given that this is a medium-*n* study, it has not been possible to dwell for long on the micro-dynamics within each one of the CSOs under analysis. A small-*n* study would have been more appropriate to explore the role of individual actors within specific organizations and the significance of social practices. Such a study would have been limited to two or three organizations, at the cost of generalizability.

In order to increase the prospects for generalization, this study also proposes a comparative analysis across policy sectors and countries. The countries and sectors under analysis vary across certain key variables relevant for this study. The consideration of these variations helps to grasp the relevance of contextual circumstances for the process and outcomes (Flyvbjerg 2006). More importantly, the similarities identified allow for some degree of generalization.

The policy fields selected are widely representative of very different forms of European governance. The Commission has established very different types of interaction with CSOs active in different fields. These CSOs are engaged in advocacy activities and in service delivery. Advocacy activities include activities such as lobbying efforts, litigation and information and awareness-raising activities. As service providers, CSOs tend to focus on particular human needs and involve the expression of civic engagement (Lewis 2001). Many CSOs studied perform both functions simultaneously and both functions are relevant in a democratic society. This study takes into account one policy area in which EU action toward CSOs has been particularly developed, that is, humanitarian aid. EU humanitarian aid totaled 1140 million euros in 2011, and at least 46.62 percent of this assistance was channeled through non-governmental organizations (CSOs) (European Commission 2012c: 24).

Additionally, the partnership between Directorate-General European Community Humanitarian Office (DG ECHO) and humanitarian CSOs has been viewed as an example of good practice that may be replicated by other DGs (VOICE 2004). The humanitarian sector is compared to other sectors that have received less support such as development and human rights in third countries, and to a sector where there were no identifiable European opportunities for CSOs, that is, human rights protection within the EU.[5] It is worth mentioning that the demarcation of policy fields can be rather problematic as the boundaries between the above-mentioned fields are not always identical in different member states. As is shown, the definition of different policy fields at the EU level is also part of the process of Europeanization of domestic CSOs.

While most DGs have engaged in a direct partnership with a large number of European and domestic CSOs, the opportunities offered to domestic CSOs active in the social field have always been channeled through member states. In this case, the provisions and rules of member states can also make a difference. To illustrate how member states have shaped EU opportunities, this book also includes examples of CSOs active in the social sector.

To grasp the axes of variation in domestic economic, social and political conditions, the comparison includes three member states, namely, France, Spain and the United Kingdom. These countries vary across a few crucial dimensions relevant for this study. First, since this book focuses on CSOs, the model of interest intermediation and state regulation regarding CSOs is very likely to affect their logics of Europeanization. The legal form of CSOs, the legal provisions regulating their activities and their functions within the welfare state are significantly different in the countries under analysis. The United Kingdom is usually identified as the most pluralist country within the EU, while France and Spain are often considered as 'statist models' (Grossman 2009). In statist models, participation by the private sector in decision making is often seen as an obstacle for the achievement of public interests.

This analysis also includes member states with different levels of economic development since CSOs may have fewer resources at their disposal in less wealthy member states. Spain has a lower level of economic development and is also a young democracy. The voluntary sector is much less developed than in the other two countries under analysis. Additionally, Spain has a decentralized system of territorial organization, and, thus, the role of local governments is expected to be more significant. Public attitudes toward the EU might also affect the willingness of CSOs to turn European and to dedicate time and effort to engage in European politics. This analysis compares one well-known euro-skeptic country, that is, the United Kingdom, to countries whose public opinion has been—at least until now—rather favorable to the process of European integration.

Even if the selection of countries includes cases that are most dissimilar in many aspects, it does not cover all the relevant axis of variation among the 28 member states. This extensive coverage would have been difficult to implement within the framework of a qualitative study. Such a study would indeed run the risk of a 'comparison at a distance' or a 'reductionist comparison' (Hassenteufel 2005). A comparison at a distance refers to comparative studies based exclusively on secondary literature, Internet websites and data that are not directly collected from the field by the researcher. A reductionist comparison refers to comparisons based on quantitative indicators, which cannot give a complete account of complex phenomena.

This study does not cover either new member states from Central and Eastern Europe or candidate countries. Groups based in Central and Eastern Europe receive significantly less funding from the Commission than those based in the old member states (Mahoney and Beckstrand 2011). The relations between the EU and CSOs in these countries were significantly different during the 1980s and 1990s, as they were set up within the framework of neighborhood and enlargement policies. Likewise, the EU contributes to the shaping of CSOs in third countries (Sanchez Salgado and Parthenay 2013), but the consideration of these developments is beyond the scope of this book. Chapter 1 offers a detailed account of the different countries and sectors under analysis and provides more details on the justification for the selection of cases.

4 Outline of the book: Europeanization of CSOs as a EU-driven process

Supranational actors and institutions have not only played a significant role in organizing civil society at the EU level, they have also played a prominent role in the process of Europeanization of domestic CSOs. When attention is directed to the moment at which the decision to go European is taken, the major dynamics at work is the usages *by* Europe. Opportunities for CSOs have been created by Commission officials because this served their own political agenda. The European Commission has played a very active role in this first stage of the Europeanization process, pushing for strategic decisions that otherwise would not have been necessarily taken. The Europeanization of domestic CSOs is more developed in those fields where European institutions are more active. In the absence of support or an EU impetus, the Europeanization of domestic CSOs has not been significantly developed. Thus, since the Commission has not been equally active across policy fields, the Europeanization of different policy areas is rather unbalanced. The degree of Europeanization also depends on the domestic context where CSOs operate, namely, existing domestic opportunities.

European requirements and rules have also generated identifiable changes in CSOs, inducing processes of absorption and transformation. Once specific CSOs decided to go European, European rules and requirements led to significant transformations. This study identifies changes in the organizational form, the strategies or repertoires of action and the introduction of European practices (for example, transnationality).

Chapter 1 gives a detailed account of the analytical framework of the book and the sociological comparative approach, including a detailed presentation and justification of the different policy fields and countries under analysis. Then the first part of this book focuses on the first sequence of the process of Europeanization, that is, Europeanization understood as 'going European'. Chapter 2 offers a descriptive overview of the frequency of uses of European opportunities at the domestic level taking the latter as its starting point (bottom-up perspective). Quite unexpectedly, this chapter shows that domestic CSOs in some policy areas are much more Europeanized than is currently assumed. If only economic resources were taken into account, many CSOs in Europe would be considered much more European than national. Chapter 3, based on a top-down perspective, presents the genesis and evolution of European political opportunities directed to CSOs since its origins in the 1970s. This analysis reveals that the role of European law is almost non-existent and that most European pressures and incentives come in the form of funding and access opportunities. In order to avoid a bias toward an EU-driven explanation, EU opportunities are systematically compared to domestic opportunities in the countries under analysis.

Once the domestic situation and the nature and significance of the institutional opportunities and constraints are clear, Chapter 4 proceeds to an analysis of the use of existing opportunities by EU officials and domestic CSOs. This chapter shows that European officials have played a very active role in the creation and development of European and domestic CSOs, contributing to the structuring of the civil society landscape in Europe.

The second part of the book focuses on the second sequence of the process of Europeanization, that is, Europeanization as transformation, through the analysis of a limited number of CSOs. Chapters 5 and 6 show that even if the effects of European requirements are far from homogeneous, the organizational structure of many domestic CSOs has been transformed. The actual changes concern not only organizational capacity but also values and goals, including well-known dynamics at the national level such as goal displacement. EU officials have also promoted European practices such as awareness raising, information and communication activities and transnational cooperation among domestic-based CSOs, in order to advance the European integration process. Chapter 7 turns the attention to Europeanization through access opportunities. It shows that the EU does not only promote an implicit Brussels consultation consensus on non-contentious strategies, as assumed by most contemporary research on this topic. The EU has also generated identifiable changes in social movements and protest groups. This chapter offers a complete picture of the situation, and it bridges the divide between academic studies on the participation of civil society in EU governance on the one hand and those dealing with contentious policies and the Europeanization of social movements on the other. The conclusion shows how bringing Europeanization theory closer to society has improved our understanding of the role of the EU in the shaping of CSOs. It first discusses the advantages of broadening the understanding of the concept of Europeanization. Second, it highlights the contributions of this volume to some of the most salient debates regarding the future of the voluntary sector, namely, its representativeness, its autonomy vis-à-vis of the state and its potential contribution to identity building and to democratic legitimacy.

1
The Europeanization of CSOs—Institutional Impact or Strategic Action?

Introduction

This chapter introduces a theoretical framework and a research design that broaden the notion of Europeanization to include a sociologically informed perspective. Drawing on previous literature on Europeanization, I propose a combination of institutional analysis with a micro-sociology of the European Union (EU). This combination will provide a better understanding of the impact of Europe on state–society relationships. The research design presented also addresses the challenges of this combination of approaches. It includes several levels of analysis as a starting point, the analysis of distinctive time periods and a comparative dimension. The last part of this chapter discusses and justifies the major methodological choices. The sociological comparative approach calls for a justification of the selection of the countries and policy fields under analysis. Detailed information on empirical data is also provided in the last section.

1 Europeanization studies, including a sociological dimension?

The catchy term 'Europeanization' has been employed in many different ways and for many different purposes. A victim of its own success, it can hardly be mentioned in any analysis without first discussing its many ambiguous and fluctuating meanings. But the absence of a common definition within the academic community does not necessarily make it useless. It rather offers a unique opportunity to clarify and develop our understanding of the impact of Europe. Few other terms in European studies have inspired so many efforts at definition and operationalization (Cowles et al. 2001; Featherstone and Radaelli 2003; Graziano and Vink 2007). The diversity of approaches is also an original contribution to the wider research design debate (Exadaktylos and Radaelli 2009; Haverland 2005). Given this diversity of views, Europeanization is hence considered 'something to be explained' (Radaelli 2006) rather than a theory to explain policy change at the domestic level. This section will discuss the shortcomings and advantages of the existing options, and it will be argued that the notion of Europeanization needs to be further developed to incorporate a sociological dimension.

1.1 Toward a sociologically informed concept of Europeanization?

The existing definitions of Europeanization cover a broad range of topics. Olsen (2002) has pointed out the many contrasting uses of this term. For example, it is used to describe changes in external territorial boundaries, the development of governance at the EU level, EU penetration in national and subnational systems of governance, the export of European forms of governance beyond the European territory and a political project aiming for a unified and politically strong Europe. Despite this variety, most efforts at conceptual clarification have considered Europeanization a device for capturing the impact of Europe (Börzel 2002; Closa 2001; Heritier et al. 2001; Schmidt 2004). Some of the most elaborate definitions also include processes of construction and the institutionalization of rules (Radaelli 2003) or the emergence of new modes of governance at the EU level (Cowles et al. 2001). The attempts to define Europeanization exclusively as uploading have not been very convincing. First, the process of transfer of competencies to the EU level is already satisfactorily covered by the concept of European integration. More importantly, studies defining Europeanization as uploading have not opted for a research design aimed at capturing uploading dynamics. Thus, there is an inconsistency between the definition of the term and the research designs that are later employed.

The two subsequent positions (presented in Table 1.1) reflect a trade-off between the analytical clarity of a given definition and its capacity to describe the complexity of the processes of change. Defining Europeanization exclusively as 'downloading' has the advantage of offering the most clear-cut approach to the term. This definition, in establishing a sharp separation between the process of European integration (uploading) and the process of Europeanization (downloading), preserves the analytical distinction between the dependent and the independent variables. The interrelation between European

Table 1.1 Different conceptualizations of Europeanization

	Europeanization as European integration	Europeanization as EU impact	Europeanization as interaction
Dependent variable	European level	Domestic level	European and domestic level
Major dynamics at work	Uploading (national bargaining)	Downloading (EU pressures)	Cross-loading (feedback loops)
Scholars	Cowles et al.	Börzel, Schmidt, Heritier	Radaelli, EPPIE

Note: Expansions for acronyms used in the table are available in the list of abbreviations.

integration and Europeanization is acknowledged, but it is considered that uploading dynamics should not be covered by the definition for the sake of analytical clarity (Dyson and Goetz 2004).

A few scholars have preferred a definition that accurately reflects the complexity of the dynamics at work. Europeanization is then defined as an interactive process in which dependent and independent variables cannot be clearly disentangled (EPPIE 2007; Radaelli 2003). This definition has the advantage of giving a broader picture, increasing the number of cases to be researched and uncovering the interactive character of the Europeanization process (for example, feedback loops). The definitions that place the emphasis on this interactive character highlight the explanatory variables of the process of change: institutions, strategic interests and shared beliefs (EPPIE 2007). This move has also the advantage of bringing European studies closer to mainstream comparative research (Hassenteufel and Surel 2000). However, the formulation of a research design that can capture uploading and downloading dynamics simultaneously is much more challenging. The conception of Europeanization as interaction is better adapted to capture the sociological dimension and thus is more appropriate for the study of civil society organizations (CSOs).

1.2 A stimulating disagreement on the most relevant explanatory factors

Studies that use the term 'Europeanization' have given weight to different variables, which has had significant effects on their research designs and on the scope of their findings. There is still an open and stimulating discussion on how different explanatory variables are to be connected and which ones should be considered the most relevant.

Scholars who conceive 'Europeanization' as downloading place greater emphasis on the significance of European institutions and rules as explanatory variables. This strand of research has developed into one of the most popular designs for the study of the impact of Europe, that is, the 'goodness of fit' model (Börzel and Risse 2003; Cowles et al. 2001). This model proposes an analysis in three stages: (1) the analysis of European norms and rules on the topic under study, (2) the assessment of the goodness of fit between European pressures and domestic practices and (3) the analysis of domestic mediating factors. Additional explanatory variables may be included in the research design, but only insofar as they are subsumed under the institutionalist framework. Thus, strategic interests and shared beliefs do not explain the transformation process itself; they only partially explain the final form it takes (Table 1.2).

As Europeanization is mainly concerned with the effects of European institutions and rules, it may seem reasonable that institutions are the most appropriate explanatory variable. The main assumption is that institutions are 'collections of structures, rules and standard operating procedures that have a partly autonomous role in political life (March and Olsen 2005: 4)'. As may be expected, the weaknesses usually associated with institutionalism apply, such as the excessive role assigned to institutions in shaping human behavior and the ambiguity of the term 'institution' (Schneider and Aspinwall 2001).

The institutional approach to the impact of Europe has been increasingly challenged by scholars who place more emphasis on the domestic level. The institutionalist approach is considered too rigid and

Table 1.2 Europeanization and different explanatory variables

	Top-down Europeanization	Challenging approaches
Major explanatory variable	Institutions	Political/strategic action
Major level of analysis	European level	Domestic level
Scholars	Cowles et al.	Mastenbroek and Kaeding Woll and Jacquot

deterministic, and, most importantly, it may overlook domestic politics and the political dimension of change. The 'goodness of fit' argument, understood hitherto as a 'theory that explains' and not as 'something to be explained', is not only criticized for its lack of parsimony; it is even considered to be logically flawed (Mastenbroek and Kaeding 2006). According to this view, rational choice theory and sociological institutionalism should be taken as the point of departure of any analysis in this field. The significance of EU institutional pressures has also been challenged from the perspective of social movements studies. The emphasis is then placed on bottom-up dynamics and alternative explanatory variables such as resource mobilization theory or the role of ideology and framing (Beyers and Kerremans 2007; McCauley 2011).

Last but not the least, the approach known as 'the usages of Europe' (Graziano et al. 2011; Woll and Jacquot 2009) focuses on domestic politics and political action. It proposes a more complex understanding of the combination of explanatory variables. 'Usages of Europe' are defined as 'social practices that seize the European Union as a set of opportunities' (Woll and Jacquot 2009: 116). Inspired by a sociology of the EU (Giraudon and Favell 2009; Saurugger 2008), these authors reject the mainstream methodological pattern that consists of isolating and confronting alternative explanatory variables. The sharp distinction between rational choice theory and constructivism is criticized, as well as the identification of sociological approaches with the constructivist turn in international relations. The distinction between shared beliefs and strategic action would be artificial at the micro level. However, more accurately reflecting the dynamics at work may often come at the expense of analytical clarity.

1.3 An unfortunate dissociation of levels of analysis

As Table 1.2 shows, the current positions do not only disagree on the relative significance of explanatory variables; they also place the emphasis on different levels of analysis. The dynamics of Europeanization concern the European and domestic levels simultaneously, but there is still a sharp disagreement on which level of governance is the most appropriate starting point for analysis. Studies that start from the European level tend to argue that the impact of Europe depends on the specific form of European governance (Andersen 2004; Bulmer and Radaelli 2004; Knill and Lehmkuhl 1999; Kohler-Koch and Eising 1999). A distinction is drawn between traditional hierarchical forms of governance, leading to the imposition of clear European rules and high levels of prescription and detail, and negative integration (or market-driven integration), in which the EU only alters the distribution of power and resources.

The impact of Europe is also expected to differ when European pressures are produced by new forms of governance, which are based on coordination, flexibility, openness and interaction.

Whenever the European level is taken as the starting point, domestic institutions are seen only as mediating factors (Börzel and Risse 2003). The domestic level is subsumed to European politics, and thus domestic actors are only expected to adapt their political processes and policies to European practices and rules. Even if the emphasis is placed on EU processes, it is worth noticing that most current research acknowledges the great diversity of results of the Europeanization process (Radaelli 2003). For example, the wide range of responses to European pressures include processes of interpretation, editing and transposition (Mörth 2003).

Studies on the usages of Europe or on bottom-up Europeanization opt for research designs that take the domestic level as a starting point. They first track major changes at the national level and then try to assess the contribution of the EU. The main advantage of this research design is that it controls for other possible causes that may account for the policy changes under scrutiny and thus avoids bias toward EU-level explanations.

These studies' attention is not directed to responses to European pressures but to how the EU is instrumentalized by domestic actors. Domestic actors use the EU to advance their own specific goals, to legitimate their political preferences, to gain support or to engage in blame avoidance or credit claiming strategies (Graziano et al. 2011). In this view, European rules and dispositions have no effects on their own; they only serve to accelerate, legitimate or obstruct certain domestic policy options (Palier et al. 2005). The motivations behind the different usages may be of different kinds: (1) *logic of influence*, in which actors try to shape the content of European policies; (2) *logic of positioning*, in which actors seek to improve their institutional position in the policy process; and (3) *logic of justification*, in which actors try to obtain support from other actors or the general public (Woll and Jacquot 2009: 117). This research design, taking a detour into the analysis of the impact of Europe, has uncovered interesting Europeanization mechanisms such as the leverage effect, which refers to the appropriation of European goals by domestic actors. The EU is considered therein as a selective amplifier rather than as the key driver of change.

1.4 Bridging divides in Europeanization studies between institutional analysis and a micro-sociology of the EU

As explained in the previous section (see also Table 1.3), research designs on the study of the impact of the EU differ along two dimensions:

the level of analysis (Europe versus the domestic level) and the type of analysis (institutional analysis versus a micro-sociology of the EU). Both alternatives offer ample opportunities to include a wide range of explanatory variables in the analysis, such as the role of resources, ideology and framing processes.

Up until now, most research on Europeanization has placed emphasis on the top-left and the bottom-right quadrants of Table 1.3; while the other quadrants of the table are underdeveloped. The top-right quadrant draws attention to usages *by* Europe. 'Usages by Europe' refers to strategic action carried out by European policy officials to promote the dynamics of Europeanization. The bottom-left quadrant captures the possibility of horizontal Europeanization. This kind of Europeanization refers to all processes in which there is no pressure to conform to EU policy models (Radaelli 2003). Studies on the 'usages of Europe' have not yet directed attention to the institutional dynamics that may take place in the absence of European pressures. However, Sabel and Zeitlin (2008) have shown that open-ended European goals can also be effectively promoted through experimentalist governance architectures, drawing attention to socialization and learning dynamics. Some examples of this are networked agencies, councils of regulators and open methods of coordination (OMC).

The confrontation of these two approaches not only gives a more complete picture of the multiple forms that European impact can take, it also helps explain change through an understanding of the connections between the different factors. Both institutional analysis and micro-sociological approaches have placed excessive emphasis on one single explanatory variable, that is, institutions and strategic action, respectively. As may be expected, strong and unambiguous European pressures and powerful supporting institutions give less leeway for European usages (top-down Europeanization) while more flexible provisions open more room for strategic creativity.

Table 1.3 Different approaches for capturing the impact of Europe

	Institutional analysis	Sociology of the EU
European level	Top-down Europeanization	Usages by Europe
Domestic level	Horizontal Europeanization	Usages of Europe
Main factors explaining change	Institutions	Strategic action

The micro-sociology of the EU emphasizes the other side of the coin. Institutional arrangements are considered to be empty shells that can only reach full form through individual and collective agency. Thus, they are only a potentiality, and they only matter if they are actualized. As the actual form and function of institutional arrangements depends on specific social practices, they cannot be analyzed as abstract entities. The ongoing debate fluctuates between these two extremes. While institutionalism argues that there are no strategic usages without institutions, the sociological approach says that institutions do not take concrete form in the absence of social practices. But these two approaches are not only complementary, they are the two sides of the same reality.

2 Combining approaches: The challenge of the research design

The research design presented herein has been conceived to address the challenges raised by the combination of institutional analysis and a micro-sociology of the EU. First, a top-down analysis of institutional opportunities is combined with the analysis of situations in which European opportunities are absent, and thus both the European and domestic levels are taken as starting points. Second, an analysis of different time periods gives a sharper view of the fluctuating role of explanatory variables in an unfolding process of Europeanization. Finally, a comparative analysis reduces the risk of a parochial, domestic-centered account of EU impact and, more importantly, provides some leverage for generalization.

2.1 Analyzing EU impact: Combining top-down and bottom-up perspectives

The concept of political opportunities is typically used for the study of social movements and collective action. It permits the study of the opportunities themselves (the top-down approach) and their uses by specific actors (the bottom-up approach). Even if the study of political opportunities is common currency in social movement research, there is still a 'need for a more careful and more explicit conceptualization and specification of political opportunities, variables and models, and for a broader and more nuanced understanding of the relationships among institutional politics, protest, and policy' (Meyer and Minkoff 2004: 1458). The concept of political opportunities is not always explicitly used by existing literature on interest groups in the EU but much of this literature could be understood in terms of the concept of opportunity structures (Princen and Kerremans 2008).

The premise underlying the political opportunity or policy process perspective is that political context affects activists' choices about goals, tactics and strategies (Meyer 2004). The political context (states and international organizations) can also lead to competition among CSOs for political space and access to resources (Cullen 2010).

The concept of political opportunities is not without its challenges. Its definition faces a trade-off: while a restricted definition of the term excludes a great number of cases from analysis, broadening the scope of the definition (including, for example, media and culture) runs the risk of concept stretching, and thus limits its heuristic potential (Goodwin and Jasper 2004). Political opportunities do not always produce changes even if they are objectively open. They also have to be visible and be perceived as opportunities (Princen and Kerremans 2008).

As this book aims to develop our understanding of the ways in which the EU affects CSOs, the specification of opportunity variables is adapted to the EU context. This study only focuses on two stable aspects of the regulative environment: access/consultation and funding opportunities. More volatile aspects (such as political alignments and changes in public policy) are also discussed but not systematically analyzed. This study observes the effects of these opportunities on three main dependent variables: the organizational form, the strategies or repertoires of action and the introduction of European practices (for example, transnationality). The incorporation of a sociological analysis allows one to take into account some important dimensions of the Europeanization process that are usually neglected. For example, domestic actors may have contrasting perceptions of political opportunities, which may affect the way in which these opportunities are translated into collective action.

Access and consultation opportunities

For a long time, studies on the participation of CSOs in European governance seldom aimed to establish any specific link between the political system and CSOs' strategies. Hilson showed that the strategies adopted by specific groups at the EU level depend on existing political opportunities (2002). He argued that the greater the number of opportunities to participate in the political process, the more interest groups will use conventional forms of participation. By the same token, the absence of appropriate channels for participation leads to more conflictual forms of collective action, such as public protests or lawsuits. The assumption that the EU promotes conventional forms of participation has been confirmed in several empirical terrains, such as with migrant groups (Geddes 2000), economic interest groups (Saurugger 2003), environmental organizations (Marks and McAdam 1999) and citizens' groups (Weisbein 2001). However, it is not clear to what extent this trend is specifically European, since it is also visible at the national level (Kriesi et al. 2007; Trenz 2007).

Quantitative analyses aiming to measure the relative significance of European protest at the EU level clearly conclude that conflictual strategies at this level are extremely rare (Beyers 2004; Imig and Tarrow 1999). Thus, it is generally assumed that the EU is not substantially shaping protest groups' agendas and repertoires of action. However, there are few qualitative studies analyzing how the EU shapes the activities and strategies of protest groups. It might be the case that the existence of a participatory regime at the EU level based on expertise could contribute to the emergence of a countermovement—an arena where symbolic protest and more or less populist arguments predominate (Eder 2001). In this view, CSOs unable or unwilling to fit within the model of the 'Brussels consensus' would be indirectly encouraged to deal with specific topics and/or pursue contentious action. There are also reasons to expect that contentious action in Europe is a necessary precondition for the democratization of the EU polity (Liebert 2009).

This study explores to what extent the EU promotes conflictual repertoires of action, and thus it offers a more complete picture of the situation. This approach also helps bridge divides between academic studies on the participation of civil society in EU governance and studies on contentious policies and the Europeanization of social movements. Even if my emphasis is on the role of access opportunities, other factors are also to be taken into account. Many scholars have emphasized the role of other explanatory variables, such as resources or types of interest groups (Dür and Mateo 2012).

Funding opportunities

In sharp contrast with the many studies on access and consultation opportunities, far too little attention has been paid to EU funding opportunities. In an article about cooperation among EU-level social non-governmental organizations (NGOs), Geyer (2001) describes the different EU funding opportunities and emphasizes the significant number of social NGOs supported by the EU. Greenwood (2007), Mahoney (2004), Ruzza (2011) and Sanchez Salgado (2014a) have also highlighted the importance of EU funds for EU-level citizens' groups. More recently, Mahoney and Beckstrand (2011) have presented a quantitative analysis aiming at identifying patterns behind the Commission's funding behavior. They show that the Commission primarily supports groups that promote a European identity and groups based in Western Europe. A few studies on this topic focus on Eastern European countries (Císař and Vráblíková 2012; Fagan 2005).

Most research on this topic concludes that the Commission has used relatively small pockets of money to support a constituency-building strategy (Cram 2011). The general perception is that EU-level groups strongly depend on EU funds, and that this situation is problematic for the autonomy and democratic potential of these groups (Cram 2011; Kutay 2012). However, these discussions have not gone very far until now due to a lack of detailed empirical evidence. Dependence and autonomy are still ill-defined concepts, and public funding is a much more complex process than is usually acknowledged. Many authors consider that far from leading to moderation and cooptation, public funds may empower CSOs, contributing to their ability to engage in advocacy activities and protest (Chaves et al. 2004; Císař and Vráblíková 2012). Dependency on government funds makes advocacy on behalf of clients less likely. The insider status and the focus on advocacy activities directed at increasing resources could also hinder CSOs' effectiveness as agents of change (Mosley 2012). On the other hand, the insider status can help to reach advocacy goals and, in practice, it is not always possible to disentangle self-interest from social change.

This book shows that domestic CSOs also receive substantial amounts of European funds, and they do so much more frequently than they participate in EU consultation processes (Chapter 2). Tracking down the effects of economic resources is an original way to analyze policy change (Sanchez Salgado 2007a, 2010). European funds, such as structural funds, have indeed been considered to affect domestic politics through their specific set of obligations (Kohler-Koch 2003).

Absence of opportunities

In the absence of access and funding opportunities, the process of Europeanization is expected to be much more proactive, creative and/or spontaneous. The simple transfer of competencies to the European level can, in an indirect way, potentially set domestic societal actors in motion. Since attention is also given to cases where there are no European opportunities, this research design uncovers the proactive dimension of the Europeanization process. Thus, it is flexible enough to take account of alternative explanations such as the roles of resources, ideologies and framing processes. When CSOs see the potential of

European politics, they may introduce organizational changes and develop strategies to create new opportunities in order to improve their institutional position in the policy process. Finally, it is also possible to observe whether CSOs that are not using EU opportunities have engaged in the same kind of transformational dynamics.

For the moment, there is little research on the transformation of CSOs in Europe in the absence of EU opportunities. Only a few research designs emphasize the interactive and bottom-up dimension of the Europeanization process, such as McCauley (2011) and Liebert (2009). Although inspiring and interesting, Liebert's study is exploratory and MacCauley's study uses a very narrow conception of Europeanization, in which this process is only understood as 'going European'.

2.2 The Europeanization of CSOs and the temporal dimension

The analysis of the Europeanization of CSOs requires a longitudinal analysis in which the process of Europeanization is divided into distinct periods, and the specifics of each one are taken into account. The distinction between time sequences also contributes to a better grasp of the complementarity between institutionalist accounts of the impact of Europe and the micro-sociological approach.

Europeanization as going European

This first time sequence focuses on the moment in which CSOs make the decision to use European opportunities. In this moment, the dynamics highlighted by the 'usages of Europe' approach seem to prevail. The EU cannot affect social practices if specific actors do not seize European opportunities, which is reflected in the motto 'no impact without usages' (Jacquot and Woll 2004).

Most current research on the Europeanization of non-state actors only investigates this first period. Europeanization is considered completed when non-state actors acquire a European dimension (Imig and Tarrow 1999). Balme and Chabanet (2002) have identified several possible outcomes of this first step in the process of Europeanization. If societal actors simply integrate European topics, the degree of Europeanization is considered to be lower, and is captured by the notion of internalization. Societal actors may also decide to use European opportunities; then they are engaging in the dynamics of externalization. In this typology, Europeanization is also seen as a horizontal process that can lead to transnationalization, in which societal actors decide to engage in transnational cooperation, or even to supranationalization, in which domestic societal actors decide to engage in an institutionalization process at the EU level (creating a new European actor).

This first period, while interesting, is the least clear from an analytical standpoint. At this stage there is no clear conceptual distinction between Europeanization and European integration. When analyzing European policies, it is conceptually possible to separate the moment in which the policy is transferred to the EU level from the moment in which this policy starts to have some impact. However, with CSOs this distinction becomes problematic even at the analytical level. In this first period, in which Europeanization is defined as going European, the transfer of allegiance to the EU level (CSOs becoming more European) cannot be separated from European impact if European pressures intend to give a European dimension to CSOs.

Table 1.4 gives an overview of the different forms in which the link between Europeanization and European integration has been seen. It adds this new possibility in the bottom-right quadrant. The most widespread conception of Europeanization (as downloading) sees it in terms of variables, and clearly separates Europeanization and European integration. This offers the most clearly schematized approach to the term, but also excludes many interesting cases. The Europeanization of CSOs cannot exclusively be thought of as uploading (the top-right quadrant), since CSOs often become European as a result of European pressures. When domestic CSOs decide to go European, European integration and Europeanization are not just interdependent processes (the bottom-left quadrant) (Dyson and Goetz 2003), they are the very same process. The Europeanization of CSOs is the last and most problematic quadrant of Table 1.4.

Since they focus on this first stage of the Europeanization process, the few studies of the Europeanization of non-state actors could have benefited from the insight of classical theories of European integration.

Table 1.4 Conceptions of the link between European integration and Europeanization

	Conceptual distinction	Conceptual fusion
Europeanization seen in terms of variables	Top-down Europeanization (downloading)	Bottom-up Europeanization (uploading)
Europeanization seen in terms of interactions	Interdependence between Europeanization and European integration	Bottom-up and top-down Europeanizations are blurred

However, up until now the focus on EU impact has diverted attention from some of the most interesting dynamics of the process of European integration, such as the mutually reinforcing interactions between European rules, European institutions and a transnational society (Stone Sweet and Sandholz 1997). If greater attention had been given to classical accounts of European integration, the role of supranational institutions would be more clearly understood today in the process of Europeanization of CSOs.

Europeanization as transformation

In the second time sequence, CSOs are confronted by institutional strings attached to EU opportunities, such as European requirements and EU-shared norms and beliefs. Once CSOs decide to use European opportunities, the situation changes significantly. The decision can be considered a *relatively* free choice, but once it has been taken, CSOs confront institutional dynamics beyond their control. When this occurs, actors enter a transformational process, as reflected in the motto 'no usages without impact'.

CSOs are affected by the EU in unpredictable ways. The costs of withdrawing from the European arena are expected to be high, in line with historical institutionalist views (Pierson 1996). In this period, institutional dynamics come to the fore. Europeanization is seen as downloading or cross-loading, and thus the concepts and frameworks developed by mainstream top-down Europeanization research can be helpful. An analysis of protest groups active in the European Social Forum uncovers an additional dynamic, that is, counterloading (Chapter 7). Certain CSOs may change their topics and strategies, but instead of downloading EU requirements and rules, they tend to shape their strategies using the EU as a countermodel (for example, if the EU promotes consensual forms of participation, as a reaction CSOs might engage in contentious actions).

Furthermore, the typology proposed by Radaelli (2003) is appropriate for grasping the possible outcomes of the process of Europeanization. It has the advantage of proposing a series of possible outcomes that cover both the magnitude of change and its direction. These outcomes are inertia, absorption, transformation and retrenchment. Inertia refers to a lack of change. While absorption and accommodation indicate adaptation, real transformation requires new ways of operating. Retrenchment is a rather contrary effect, since its outcomes reflect a move away from what was intended by European pressures.

Table 1.5 The process of Europeanization of CSOs

		H1. Access opportunities	H2. Funding opportunities	H3. Absence of opportunities
First period: Europeanization as going European	Major dynamics at work	Usages by Europe		Proaction Usages Rejection
	What changes?	Targets and topics		Topics
	Outcomes	Externalization		Internalization Inertia
Second period: Europeanization as transformation	Major dynamics at work	Downloading Cross-loading		Counter-loading
	What changes?	Goals and priorities	Goals and priorities	Topics, strategies
		Repertoire of action Strategies	Organizational size Management	
	Outcomes	Transformation, accommodation		Inertia, retrenchment

Table 1.5 sums up the potential relationships between the different concepts as they have been presented in the previous sections.

3 A sociological comparative approach

This section first clarifies the definition of CSOs. The selection of cases is then justified. Then the last paragraph detail the empirical data that will be used for the comparative analysis.

3.1 Diversity in the understanding of CSOs

Given its normative character, civil society is an essentially contested concept (Mair 2010). As a multidimensional concept, it has been employed in many different forms, creating great scholarly confusion. Its imprecision may have contributed to its current popularity among scholars, since imprecision allows for a promiscuous application (Jordan et al. 2004). In the present study, the expression CSOs is used for observational purposes. It refers to actors outside of the public sector, the informal sector and the market sector. The specificity of these actors is that they do not seek to form a government but they pursue public policy goals. This includes influencing policy outcomes and participating in policy implementation. CSOs are formally democratically accountable and involve some degree of voluntary participation. This definition includes a great range of organizations, such as public interest groups, NGOs, voluntary organizations and social movements.[1] In their traditional form, CSOs are a very old phenomenon, related to the Christian belief in charity and the humanistic philanthropic tradition. CSOs took on social action much earlier than the nation-state. Terms such as 'collective goods' and 'social rights' were originally formulated by social groups and adopted by nation-states much later (Piveteau 1998).

This definition is very close to definitions of non-profit groups, but not identical. The most popular definition of the non-profit sector pictures non-profit organizations as organized private groups that are non-profit distributing, self-governing and that involve some meaningful degree of voluntary participation (Salamon and Anheier 1997). This popular definition has been criticized for its emphasis on the non-profit constraint. This constraint excludes a great range of member serving organizations operating for a public purpose, such as cooperatives and friendly societies (Morris 2000).

To avoid this problem, I will use a definition that focuses on the public purpose. This focus on the public purpose only excludes from this definition market exchanges and profit-seeking organizations. For this reason, it differs from many other definitions of civil society including for-profit groups (Keane 1998; Walzer 1995). In this definition, it is not only the type of organization that counts but also its implied function. CSOs stand out for their normative dimension since they usually support values such as equality, justice and solidarity (Cohen and Arato 1992). However, my intention is not to suggest a normative approval of the ends of the groups studied. CSOs stand out for their intention to support the public interest. However, the definition of public interest at a given moment is problematic. What are now generally considered to be topics of public interest, such as the protection of human rights or of the environment, may be considered by a few (or by future generations) as limiting or alienating. This definition also differs from the strict interpretation of voluntary groups (Jordan et al. 2004). CSOs studied in this book are funded by a variety of supporters and patrons, including public donors. CSOs are a collective phenomenon but they are not always individually based; they can also be collective structures or organizations of organizations.[2] A definition restricted to individual membership is considered to be too narrow. Even if CSOs are generally democratically accountable, in practice, this criterion is often problematic. Sometimes the official mechanisms to ensure democratic accountability within CSOs are complex or indirect, and they may not always function effectively.

The relationship between the state and society has also been widely discussed (Sanchez Salgado 2011). The liberal tradition, placing the emphasis on individualism and equality, pictures civil society as a pluralist society detached from the state, which remains in a neutral position. In sharp contrast, the Hegelian tradition envisions civil society as an extension of the state. The universal values or general principles defended by civil society are only legitimate to the extent they are also endorsed by the state. On a more pessimistic note, the state would be instrumentalizing civil society to impose its own hegemony (Rumford 2002). Civil society is then seen as a means for social control, rather than a democratic force (Bowden 2005).

3.2 Justification of the selection of countries, policy areas and CSOs under analysis

CSOs have played very different roles in the development of domestic welfare systems in the countries studied (France, the United Kingdom, Spain). In countries such as France, voluntary organizations have taken a prominent role in the development of the welfare state, due to their role in service delivery. While in these countries voluntary organizations were recognized and received a lot of governmental support, in other countries, such as the United Kingdom, the nation-state monopolized public service delivery. As pointed out in reference to the construction of the welfare state in Britain, 'Voluntary agencies (...) were driven to the margins of social policy, tarnished with a Victorian authoritarianism and a Lady Bountiful image that took decades to wear off' (Glennerster 1995: 7).

In Spain, only limited welfare provisions were supplied under the dictatorship. And only a few social organizations, such as the Red Cross or the Spanish National Organization for the Blind, were supported or created during this period, following a corporatist ideology. After the process of democratization in the late 1970s, the development of the welfare state also contributed to the development of the voluntary sector. In sharp contrast with the other countries studied, Spain has welfare provided by several tiers of governance, namely, by the central state and the autonomous communities. Thus, the specific role of the voluntary sector in the provision of welfare is not identical across the whole country.

As is clear from the previous presentation and the boxes, the policy areas and countries under analysis vary across a few key variables relevant for this study. These variations demonstrate the relevance of contextual circumstances for processes and outcomes (Flyvbjerg 2006). Additionally, the common trends identified are likely to be present in other countries and similar policy fields.

Box 1: Humanitarian CSOs: From Neutrality and the Right of Intervention to the Responsibility to Protect

The principles of humanitarian aid were first defined by the Red Cross (founded in 1863), and later by the successive Geneva Conventions on Humanitarian Aid. These principles emphasize urgency, non-discrimination and neutrality. A first wave of humanitarian CSOs appeared during or just after the world wars. Such was the case of the biggest American humanitarian CSOs (Cooperative for American Relief in Europe 1945; International Rescue Committee 1940) as well as the biggest British CSOs (Save the Children 1919; Oxfam 1942). During the 1960s, the interest in emergency relief was progressively supplemented with developmental assistance and developmental aid.

At the beginning of the 1970s, in the wake of a new kind of conflict—such as that between Nigeria and Biafra—a new conception of humanitarian aid emerged in France, first seen in organizations such as Médecins Sans Frontières (1971) and Médecins du Monde (1980). The 'French Doctors', as they were known, emphasized the transgression of rules and borders, and vigorously supported the 'right to intervene' (Klingberg 1998). The French tradition also calls for public stances, which is in sharp contradiction to the principle of neutrality. These CSOs instead support the principle of 'impartiality'.

The right to intervene as supported by the French doctors has always been a matter of controversy. During the 1990s, systematic violations of human rights in Rwanda and Srebrenica reopened the question of the gap between legitimacy and legality.

> **Box 1 (Continued)**
>
> In response to these difficulties, the international community has now embraced the much more consensual concept of the 'responsibility to protect' (ICISS 2001). The underlying idea is that each state has the primary responsibility to protect its individuals. Whenever a state fails in this responsibility, the secondary responsibility falls on the international community (Evans 2006). In spite of its appeal and the detailed operationalization of the term, this concept has also proven difficult to implement in practice.

The countries analyzed have also developed contrasting traditions in the different policy areas under analysis. France and the United Kingdom hold opposite conceptions of humanitarian and development aid (Rieff 2002). In sharp contrast, Spain has not yet developed any specific tradition for any of these policy fields. France and the United Kingdom have also developed welfare systems that give contrasting functions to voluntary organizations. The inclusion of Spain allows for consideration of a state welfare system that is organized across different tiers of governance. More importantly, the countries under analysis have developed contrasting domestic opportunities for CSOs. The detailed analysis of these opportunities is an integral part of this book (Chapter 3).

The selected policy sectors (described in the boxes) are sufficiently distinct so as to be representative of a wide range of areas of study. They include CSOs involved in a wide range of activities, such as advocacy and awareness-raising activities, contentious action and service delivery. They receive very differentiated attention from EU institutions, which is another integral part of the analysis presented in Chapter 3. Comparison among these policy areas is not without challenges. Even if, at the EU level, there is a clear distinction between these policy sectors, this distinction is not always evident in practice. At present, CSOs are increasingly specialized in various policy areas, but their boundaries are often unclear or contested. On top of this, more often than not, specific CSOs are engaged in activities corresponding to different sectors. This raises some questions about the pertinence of comparison, which will be addressed in Chapter 2.

Box 2: Development CSOs: From Self-Help to International Campaigning

During the 1960s, some CSOs became more prominent as partners in development aid in the wake of the failure of big top-down state projects. Many development CSOs created during this period, especially in continental Europe, were inspired by the third world's ideology exemplified by the Conference of Bandung in 1955. On a completely different register, this new bottom-up conception of development also resonated quite well with the Catholic tradition, given its focus on communitarian and inclusive development (Hours 1998). That is why, in 1963, Pope Jean XXII, in his popular encyclical *Pacem in Terris*, called on the catholic community to promote development. Subsequently, many CSOs were created, such as the Catholic Committee against Hunger and for Development (CCFD) in France or Brot für die Welt in Germany (Ryfman 2004).

Some of the oldest humanitarian CSOs, such as Oxfam and CARE, adopted this new aid paradigm, captured in the motto 'from help to self-help'. They aimed to give to local populations the means to develop on their own. This was done through the implementation of small projects in close cooperation with the affected populations. During the 1980s, development CSOs lost much of their appeal due to the renewed popularity of humanitarian CSOs (Rieff 2002). In spite of this change in trends, many international CSOs such as Oxfam and Action Aid remained attached to the principles of development aid.

In the 2000s, it became clear that small-scale projects and help from population to population would not bring poverty to an end in the medium or short term. Development CSOs became increasingly aware of the need to influence the political agendas of states, international organizations and international donors (Degnbol-Martinussen and Engberg-Pedersen 2003). Since then, development CSOs have been increasingly involved in international discussions on development aid, especially within the Open Forum for CSO Development Effectiveness. On top of this, development CSOs became more involved in international campaigns to get the public's support, such as Jubilee 2000 and Make Poverty History.

To avoid an excessive focus on externally oriented CSOs, this book also analyzes the Europeanization of social CSOs. It is very difficult to precisely define the social field since it is broad enough to include most voluntary action. In spite of these difficulties, it is generally acknowledged that the core of social action includes fight against poverty and social exclusion and support for marginalized or discriminated-against groups. Some of the most typical issues are people with disabilities, employment, housing and the fight against poverty. However, scholars disagree on which activities to include in the social sector. For example, some authors consider health to be out of the social sector (Salamon and Anheier 1997), while for others health is definitely included (Ruiz Olabuénaga 1995).

Even if there is a clear distinction between social CSOs and humanitarian and development CSOs, in practice both kinds of CSOs share the same values and the general objective of fighting against poverty. The only difference is that while international CSOs focus on foreign countries, social organizations deal with poverty 'at home'. The inclusion of the social sector increases the prospects for generalization. Social CSOs, as many other CSOs operating within Europe, are subjected to different procedures and rules than CSOs engaged in external activities.

Human rights CSOs work both at the national and at the international level. They seem to be much more disciplined with respect to the boundaries of their sector of activity. Specific CSOs generally focus either on domestic or on international human rights violations. This analysis only covers non-specialized human rights groups that aim to promote all rights included in the International Declaration of Human Rights. As may be expected, many groups specialize in specific human rights, such as freedom of expression. At present, CSOs working with immigrant groups are often considered to be the closest to the human rights movement, at least at the domestic level. If specialized CSOs were to be considered, the delimitation of this sector would be rather complex since the definition of 'human rights' itself is not without controversy (Crettiez and Sommier 2006).

This study does not only compare sectors and countries, it also compares national CSOs at the meso level. The national CSOs under analysis have been selected on the basis of a preliminary overview of domestic CSOs, as presented in Chapter 2. Through descriptive statistics, this overview provides relevant information about the significance of Europe for domestic CSOs. It has been designed to create a descriptive classification of the relationships between CSOs and the EU, which will be used as the basis for a qualitative comparative analysis. Chapter 2 includes a more detailed presentation of criteria for the construction

Box 3: Human Rights CSOs: Between Politics and Law

The first human rights CSOs were created in continental Europe at the beginning of the 20th century under the label of leagues: the French Ligue des droits de l'Homme (1898), the Ligue Belge des droits de l'Homme (1901), the Liga española pro-derechos humanos (1913) and the Deutsche Liga für Menschenrechte (1922). In 1922, a few national leagues decided to set up an international organization, that is, the International Federation for Human Rights (FIDH). In the Anglo-American world, the emphasis was not placed on human rights, but rather on civil liberties. The American Civil Liberties Union was created in 1920, and British Liberty (at the time, the National Council for Civil Liberties) was set up in 1934.

International human rights CSOs were created much later, basically in the 1960s and 1970s, as a reaction to human rights violations around the world and other specific events. For example, Amnesty International (1961) was created following a press article by a British layer about two Portuguese students who had been imprisoned after a toast for freedom. The most popular American human rights CSO operating at the international level, Human Rights Watch, was created in 1978 only to monitor the agreement of Helsinki (it was first known as Helsinki Watch).

International CSOs initially based their action on the International Declaration of Human Rights, and later on successive international covenants on this topic. Human rightsfriendly international organizations, particularly the United Nations, often provided the forums to facilitate the emergence of transnational human rights coalitions and groups (Bandy and Smith 2005b). In sharp contrast with humanitarian principles and the Geneva Conventions, human rights CSOs emphasize the protection of civic and political rights in times of peace. Some of the frequently recurring topics dealt with by these CSOs are political prisoners, the death penalty and torture. Since their creation, international human rights CSOs have become much more popular and active than the traditional national human rights leagues. At present they benefit from much more support from international and national donors as well as from the public. The International Federation for Human Rights (FIDH), which was dormant during most of the 20th century, was renewed during the 1980s following the new popularity of international human rights CSOs.

of the taxonomy and discusses further methodological challenges in detail. Since CSOs belonging to each one of the categories in the classification is compared, the analysis includes both 'most likely' and 'less likely' cases (Flyvbjerg 2006). Thus, my conclusions may be representative of processes observable in other organizations belonging to the same category.

3.3 An analysis based on a diversity of data collection

A comparative study aiming to combine institutional analysis with a micro-sociology of the EU constitutes a methodological challenge. As may be expected, it requires not only a combination of methods but also triangulated data collection. Thus, empirical data come from a variety of sources: systematic web analysis, primary and secondary documentation and semi-structured interviews. The data come primarily from two levels of analysis: the European level and the domestic level.

Documentary analysis

At the EU level, the most relevant policy documents of each of the different policy sectors from 1970 to 2012 are analyzed. These include the treaties and legislation in force, communications and policy papers on the relations between the EU and domestic CSOs, calls for proposals and evaluation reports. At the domestic level, since there is much more data available, the present analysis also relies on secondary documentation. The current studies on this topic have been supplemented by the analysis of the most relevant regulations and policy papers. The reports of activities (and the financial reports when they are available) of the chosen CSOs from the 1990s until 2012 are systematically analyzed. Even if not all reports of activities for each year were systematically available, most of them give information about previous years and it is possible to fill in the gaps. This analysis was supplemented by the analysis of press releases, position papers and similar documents regularly published by the CSOs studied. The EU also provides some databases and reports with detailed information on CSOs.

Web analysis

The data for the first bottom-up descriptive overview of the significance of Europe to domestic CSOs come from a systematic analysis of around 100 organizations in each of the countries studied. To avoid an EU bias, these CSOs have been selected according to their participation in domestic umbrella organizations (see Chapter 2). These umbrella organizations are quite representative of the whole CSO population: they include the biggest CSOs such as Oxfam (with a total annual budget of around 280 million euros) as well as smaller ones like the Spanish CSO International Society for Development (Sociedad Internacional para el Desarrollo (SID)) with a total annual budget of less than 20,000 euros. The umbrella organizations under analysis only include a reduced number of CSOs in the social action policy sector and thus complementary documentary sources have been used to give a satisfactory overview of the situation of this sector in the member states. The data have been supplemented by information from national databases when they exist, as is the case in France and Spain.

Semi-structured interviews

To get an in-depth understanding of the dynamics at work, information is also drawn from 44 interviews with key informants in their fields. Semi-structured questionnaires were used in order to ensure that all relevant issues were covered. A total of 37 interviews have been carried out with policy officers at the Commission and representatives of CSOs at the domestic and EU levels between 2001 and 2013 specifically for this book (Appendix 1). Five interviews were carried out with domestic officials working on these topics and two interviews with an academic and a policy expert. This study also benefits from the insights of many other semi-structured interviews carried out with representatives of CSOs in France and in Spain within the framework of other research projects. Last but not the least, I have also worked as the research and program manager at the International Federation for Human Rights for five years. This gave me an insider's view of the topic, which has proven very useful.

Part I
Domestic Civil Society under EU Pressures

2
Domestic Civil Society: National or European?

Introduction

This chapter offers a descriptive overview of the frequency of uses of European opportunities. Is Europeanization of civil society organizations (CSOs) exceptional or the general rule? What Europeanization strategies are most widespread among national CSOs? Are there significant differences across countries and policy sectors?

A few quantitative studies have attempted to give an overview of the relationships between the European Union (EU) and national CSOs (Dür and Mateo 2012; Imig and Tarrow 1999; Mahoney and Beckstrand 2011). While interesting, these studies focus on lobbying and advocacy activities. Most of them analyze a broader category of interest groups and do not give specific attention to CSOs. Thus, they are not adapted to address the specific features of the CSO community. The present overview offers a much more complete picture since it considers several Europeanization strategies simultaneously. Taking the analysis of domestic CSOs as the starting point avoids an EU bias and helps identify relevant national pressures.

The degree of Europeanization varies greatly among CSOs in Europe. While some CSOs have developed strong direct links with the EU, most have developed softer Europeanization strategies. To sort out the different types of CSOs, the last section of this chapter puts forward a classification, distinguishing among three ideal types of Europeanized CSOs: exclusive, pluralist and sporadic.

1 The usages of European funds: A bottom-up perspective

This section introduces first a classification of Europeanization strategies and discusses the diversity of legal frameworks within the EU member states under analysis. The bottom-up analysis of the Europeanization of CSOs comes coupled with a considerable methodological challenge, which needs to be addressed.

1.1 Strategies for Europeanization and main questions

This study is inspired by Balme and Chabanet's (2002) classification of Europeanization strategies. The first strategy, *externalization*, refers to the establishment of direct contacts with EU institutions, namely, through the use of European opportunities. These opportunities include EU funds, consultation procedures and legal actions. The externalization strategy requires a high degree of Europeanization. In it, domestic actors turn to European targets and use European repertoires of action, which may lead to important transformations. The most relevant opportunities for CSOs are EU funding and access.

Existing studies focus primarily on lobbying and advocacy activities. They have concluded that a large number of groups engage in lobbying around EU legislation and that well-endowed interest groups find it easier to advocate for their interests at the EU level (Dür and Mateo 2012). However, the data presented so far do not clearly show to what extent citizen groups engage in lobbying and consultation with European institutions. A few articles show that social movements rarely engage in Europe-wide protest activities; for example, in one sample European mobilizations only represent 4.1 percent of the total mobilizations (Imig and Tarrow 1999).

Even if it has attracted less attention, the significant amount of EU funding available for CSOs has not been overlooked. Most commentators assume that the EU is just funding a few large EU-based CSOs or 'friends of the EU' (Boin and Marchesetti 2010). However, the EU is currently funding many CSOs beyond the EU level; 67 percent of all groups receiving EU funding from 2003 to 2007 are organized at the national or subnational level (Mahoney and Beckstrand 2011). In spite of the relevance of EU funds, there are currently no analyses of their effects on Western European CSOs.

Litigation is also an opportunity for engagement in public action but it is rarely used by EU-based interest groups (Kelemen 2003; Vanhala 2009). Seventy-one percent of interest groups registered in the European Database Consultation, the European Commission and Civil Society (CONECCS) were never (directly or indirectly) involved in litigation (Kelemen 2003). Groups often respond through litigation when other groups or domestic governing bodies fail to comply with EU regulations especially in the domains of the environment and women's rights

(Börzel 2003; Cichowski 2007). Most legal actions are launched by individual or collective applicants. From 1970 to 2003, the number of cases introduced by CSOs was rather low; there were only 18 cases (8 percent of the total) in the social arena and 13 (or 18 percent of the total) on environmental issues (Cichowsky 2007). Even if not too many national CSOs have directly engaged in this practice, litigation will also be considered in the qualitative part of this study.

The second strategy, *transnationalization*, also indicates a high degree of Europeanization. This strategy is adopted by actors involved in transnational activities who create transnational norms. In this analysis, this category will be interpreted broadly; it includes not just transnational CSOs but also national CSOs that engage in transnational peak associations.[1] I could not find any previous empirical study specifically on this topic. This is a crucial gap, since participation in European peak associations is a very relevant aspect of the process of Europeanization.

Finally, the softer strategy of Europeanization is *internalization*. This strategy implies low-profile Europeanization. CSOs engaged in this strategy include European issues in their daily activities. But they do not redefine their targets or repertoires of action, and they do not significantly alter their organizational structures. Since all types of national interest groups lobby much more frequently at the national level on EU legislation than at the European level (Dür and Mateo 2012: 979), one would expect that many groups have exclusively engaged in this strategy.

Balme and Chabanet (2002) also propose a fourth category, *supranationalization*, the strongest form of Europeanization. It refers to the institutionalization of certain actors at the EU level. This category includes European associations, such as the European Social Platform. These supranational actors only act at the EU level and will therefore not be directly included in this overview. They will, however, be indirectly taken into account, since most national CSOs engaging in transnational activities are among their members.

1.2 Methodological considerations

To avoid an EU bias, the CSOs in this overview have been selected on the basis of their membership in domestic peak organizations. These peak organizations do not include all CSOs operating in the policy sectors under analysis. However, there is no reason to assume that the selection of these national peak associations causes a serious bias in this study. There are indeed many CSOs that have engaged

Table 2.1 Platforms of CSOs selected for the website analysis

	Domestic platforms of CSOs	Number of members
United Kingdom	British Overseas NGOs for Development (BOND)	295 British members
France	Commission Cooperación Developpement	157 members
Spain	Coordinadora de Organizaciones no gubernamentales de cooperación para el desarrollo (CONGDE)	Around 100 members

Source: Elaborated by the author.

in Europeanization strategies that are currently not members of the domestic peak associations under analysis (Table 2.1).[2]

When data were not available in the reports published by national peak organizations, they were sought in the organizations' websites in 2003 and 2004.[3] As may be expected, many CSOs do not provide any relevant data in their websites. For the most part, these CSOs tend to be relatively small and they may even be non-operational. The lack of sufficient operational capacity is generally seen as an obstacle for obtaining EU funds and for participating effectively in EU peak organizations; thus, it is likely that these CSOs are not Europeanized. But small CSOs such as Espoire sans Frontières and Marins sans Frontières have obtained EU grants. This suggests that some CSOs with small budgets, or for which data are unavailable, may be Europeanized to some extent after all. A few of the smallest CSOs have ceased to exist since the analysis took place.[4] For the sake of data triangulation, the data from these websites have been complemented with data from the Financial Transparency System (FTS). The FTS provides the names of the beneficiaries of billions of euros in grants awarded by the European Commission since 2007.[5]

Each of the selected peak associations is active in one of the member states under analysis, and they are mainly composed of CSOs engaged in external action. There are also some social and human rights CSOs but they are not necessarily representative of the whole sector. Given the large number of CSOs working in the social arena and the variety in this policy sector, a bottom-up analysis was hardly feasible. In the social sector, there is no single national peak association that incorporates a manageable number of CSOs that could be used as a reference point for this analysis. Given the importance of including domestically oriented CSOs, data were attained through semi-structured interviews with representatives of national peak associations, of social CSOs and of general-purpose human rights CSOs. Analysis of internationally and domestically oriented CSOs will give us a more complete overview of CSOs' Europeanization strategies.

While the country in which each CSO is based is easily recognized, the distinction among CSOs belonging to different sectors is not always evident. Many CSOs engage in activities in different policy areas simultaneously. This is particularly the case for large CSOs such as the Red Cross or Oxfam. These CSOs are involved in humanitarian aid, development assistance and social action. They also tend to be fairly Europeanized. Most of the large multifunctional CSOs have contracts with DG ECHO and are actively engaged in the humanitarian peak umbrella organization Voluntary Organizations in Cooperation in Emergencies (VOICE). This shows that they seem to be mainly connected to the EU through their humanitarian activities. The predominance of humanitarian activities among the largest transnational CSOs has already been highlighted (Smillie 2000). The most reasonable choice to avoid counting these CSOs twice is to consider them primarily as humanitarian CSOs.

1.3 National legal frameworks: An exclusive national pressure

In strict legal terms, one should not expect much CSO Europeanization, since the legal status of CSOs remains national and is far from being harmonized. In the absence of an international or a regional legal basis, CSOs can only acquire legal recognition at the domestic level. As may be expected, different national legal frameworks are inspired by very different conceptions of the relationships between state and society. The diversity in this domain has already struck some observers. Archambault (1996: 56) noted that while each country specifies a legal status for non-profits, no two countries do so in exactly the same way. National divisions of international CSOs, such as Amnesty International or the Red Cross, implement similar activities but work in very different legal contexts. This diversity has been a great obstacle to the creation of international or regional legal statutes for voluntary organizations, for example, the European statute of association (see Chapter 3).

In France and Spain, CSOs can only be legally registered as non-profit associations and thus they share their legal status with actors pursuing a wide range of objectives. The legal status of associations is defined in France by the well-known Law of 1901 and in Spain by the Organic Law

1/2002. These two laws (articles 10 and 32, respectively) allow some CSOs to be recognized for acting for the benefit of the general interest (*utilité publique* or *utilidad pública*). The CSOs that attain this status have specific advantages, such as tax exemptions and the right to accept donations; the status also improves the reputation of these CSOs in these countries.

In France, the state has never granted a specific legal status for a few privileged CSOs. The preservation of equality among different groups can be explained by the republican tradition and by a pervasive state centralism (Ion 1997). In sharp contrast, in Spain there are a few favored CSOs that benefit from a specific legal status. Religious associations, including those in the policy sectors under analysis, are subjected to canon law, set down in an agreement between Spain and the Holy See in 1979 (Casado 1992). Some specific legal statuses are also a legacy of Franco's dictatorship. Such is the case of the Red Cross (Casado 1996) or the Spanish National Organization for the Blind (Organization national de ciegos españoles—ONCE).

In the United Kingdom, this analysis is limited to the legal framework in force in England and Wales. Since there is no general legal status for associations, the major distinction is between charities and friendly societies. According to the Charities Act (1960), a Charity Commission decides which groups can take this legal form. In the common law tradition, there are no strict criteria to define charities (Salamon and Anheier 1997). Charities also benefit from tax exceptions and many other advantages (Jas et al. 2002). Thus, a charity in the United Kingdom seems to be the equivalent of an association in Spain and France that has obtained recognition as acting for the general interest.

Thus, CSOs are registered under very different legal forms and are the object of very different administrative requirements and regulations. The national sections of a CSO such as Caritas have very different legal statuses depending on the country in question; in this case, it is a non-profit association *reconnue d'utilité publique* in France, a charity in England and an organization under double legal status in Spain (Caritas Spain is registered according to both civil and canon law). This diversity has important consequences for the functioning of CSOs, and it makes comparison difficult, but not impossible. The European Commission recognizes the different legal forms in force in different countries without worrying too much about the different juridical regimes. For example, EU funds are addressed to autonomous and non-profit non-governmental organizations (NGOs) that are registered in EU member states following their own specific legislations. It is noteworthy that

'NGO' or 'CSO', terms usually employed by the EU, are not used as legal terms in most member states.

2 The externalization of CSOs: Following the money

This section shows that the most widespread strategy of externalization is the receipt of EU funds. EU funding of national CSOs in some policy areas seems to be quite widespread. These findings challenge the position of some observers, arguing that the EU only supports elite European organizations at the expense of the majority of CSOs (Boin and Marchesetti 2010). Through its funding schemes, the EU can introduce distortions into the CSO system. The funds are indeed not distributed evenly across countries and policy areas. The EU is clearly contributing to the shaping of the European civil society landscape in one specific direction; it is enhancing the humanitarian sector at the expense of other sectors. EU money also tends to benefit CSOs based in certain countries.

If the receipt of funds and participation in European peak organizations seems to be quite widespread, other strategies—such as direct participation in consultations, dialogue processes or the establishment of an office in Brussels—are reserved to a few large CSOs or euro groups.

2.1 Humanitarian CSOs: The most fancied

It is not surprising that humanitarian aid is the most Europeanized policy area, as DG ECHO is the largest grantor of EU funds. And humanitarian CSOs also benefit from DG DEVCO grants. Most domestic humanitarian CSOs operating in Europe have at some point obtained funds from the EU. Table 2.2 shows that, at the time these data were collected, almost all humanitarian CSOs in France and the United Kingdom received EU funds (31 out of 36 in the United Kingdom and 25 out of 25 in France). In Spain, the number of CSOs that received EU grants is not as high, but in 1997 the EU still supported more than the half of the country's humanitarian CSOs (13 out of 21).

Unfunded CSOs are not necessarily being excluded from the system. They may not be willing and/or adapted to get EU funds. A few CSOs studied did not accept any kind of public support (for example, Doctors Worldwide, Muslim Aid and the Mothers' Union). And some of them were not very suited to apply for EU funds since they did not implement humanitarian activities directly. CSOs such as Engineers for Disaster Relief or Service d'Entreaide et de Liaison (SEL) were intermediaries that provided personnel to other humanitarian CSOs. Finally,

Table 2.2 Humanitarian CSOs receiving EU funds

	Total CSOs in this sample	CSOs with available funding data	Number of CSOs using EU funds (percent)	Examples of CSOs with EU funding	Examples of CSOs without EU funding
France	36	25	25 (100 percent)	Médecins du Monde; Aide médicale internationale; Inter Aide; Enfants réfugiés du Monde	Enfants du Monde; Association Hot Lua; La Gerbe
UK	50	36	31 (86.1 percent)	Action against Hunger UK; Aid International; Care International; CAFOD	Doctors Worldwide; Muslim Aid; The Mothers' Union; Christians Abroad
Spain	24 (1997) 43 (1999)	21 43	13 (61.9 percent) 21 (48.8 percent)	MPDL; Paz y tercer mundo; Acción contra el hambre; Asociación Nuevos Caminos	Alternativa solidaria Plenty; Ayuda en Acción; SOTERMUN; PROYDE

Note: Expansions for acronyms used in the table are available in the list of abbreviations.
Source: Original research (collected in 2003–2004, and in 1997 and 1999 for Spain).

some of the CSOs did not appear to be operational. Hôt Lua did not even have a website at the time of this analysis and Action et Partage Humanitaire (ACPAHU) had no hired staff. Only in Spain, where the number of non-EU-funded humanitarian CSOs was higher, is it more difficult to determine if a lack of EU support was related to a lack of willingness to apply or a de facto exclusion (see also Chapter 4).

Even if many humanitarian CSOs benefit from EU funds, most grants offered by DG ECHO are channeled through a small number of CSOs, as Table 2.3 shows. Seventy-seven out of the 246 ECHO grants allocated to French CSOs within the Framework Partnership Agreement in 2011 were given to three major recipients. The three major recipients in the United Kingdom got 95 grants out of the 201 that were awarded, and the two major recipients in Spain got 31 grants out of the total 69. The concentration of funds in a few CSOs is also clear in Figure 2.1.

Table 2.3 Grants given by DG ECHO in 2011

	Total amount in euros	Number of grants	Number of recipients	Major recipients
France	138,645,057	246	19 (average 12.9 grants/ organization)	Action contre la faim (34) ACTED (25) Croix Rouge (18)
UK	166,104,933	201	32 (average 6.3 grants/ organization)	Oxfam (38) Save the Children (38) International Rescue Committee (19)
Spain	39,772,234	69	13 (average 5.3 grants/ organization)	Acción contra el Hambre (22) Intermon Oxfam (9)

Note: Expansions for acronyms used in the table are available in the list of abbreviations.
Source: FTS.[6]

Many organizations that obtained a large amount of EU funding for humanitarian activities were not necessarily voluntary organizations in legal terms. They were legally foundations, which means that they were not required to be accountable to their members. However, in practice,

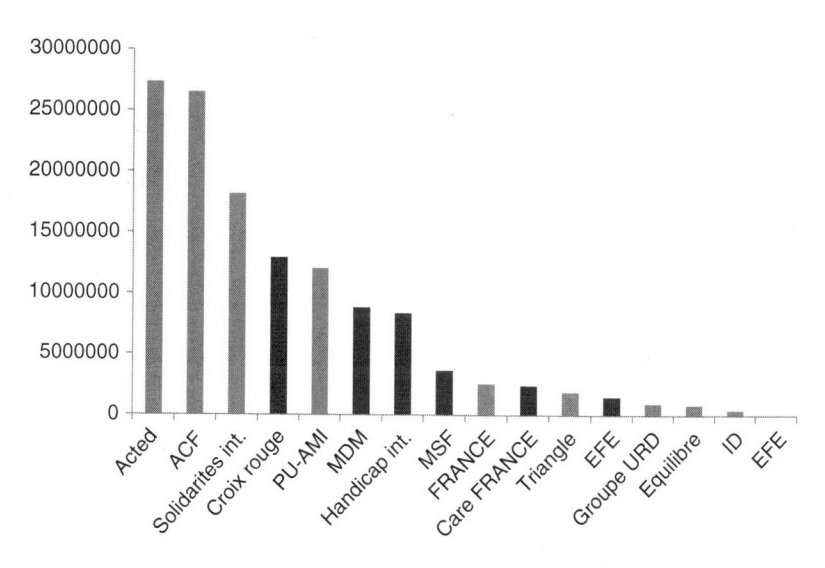

Figure 2.1 DG ECHO funding for French CSOs (commitments for 2001 in euros)
*CSOs with dark gray shaded columns have some kind of representation in Brussels.

the great majority of these CSOs have governing bodies that represent their members.

2.2 EU funds and development and international human rights CSOs: A fair deal

In the development sector, there are more CSOs competing for fewer EU funds and thus the percentage of development CSOs obtaining EU funds is smaller. However, there is still a remarkable number of development CSOs that at some point obtained funds from the EU (see Table 2.4). The CSOs obtaining more EU money were once again those based in France and the United Kingdom. It was hard to obtain data from most French CSOs, but it seems that a great number were supported by the EU. In the United Kingdom, more than half of the CSOs (with available data) reported that they obtained funds from the EU. In Spain, as was the case for humanitarian CSOs, the receipt of EU funds was less common.[7]

Most development CSOs that receive EU funds are quite large. They had budgets of about 600,000 euros or more. However, there were also

Table 2.4 Development CSOs obtaining EU funds

	Total CSOs in this sample	CSOs with available funding data	Number of CSOs using EU funds (percent)	Examples of CSOs with EU funding	Examples of CSOs without EU funding
France	109	40	33 (82.5 percent)	CCFD; Aide et Action; CICDA	La Chaine de l'Espoir; Foi Cooperante; ALAID
UK	214	117	58 (49.6 percent)	Farm Africa; Find your Feet; Health Unlimited	Action for Disability; Alliances for Africa; Christians Abroad
Spain	46 (1999) 60 (1997)	43 60	15 (34.9 percent) 16 (26.7 percent)	CIPIE; CODESPA; Associació Cooperació; ECOE	Ayuda, Desarrollo y Solidaridad; Educación sin Fronteras; Paz y Cooperación

Note: Expansions for acronyms used in the table are available in the list of abbreviations.
Source: Original research (collected in 2003–2004, and in 1997 and 1999 for Spain).[8]

a few small CSOs that reported funding from the EU, such as ECOE (Equipo de comunicacion educativa), which had a budget of only about 22,000 euros. In the development field there are also many CSOs that applied for EU funds and did not get them. The overall success rate for many of the 2011 calls for proposals in development was between 5 and 14 percent.[9] The present analysis only shows the number of CSOs that obtained funds from the EU. However, CSOs that failed to obtain EU funds may have also been affected by the EU to a certain extent.

Some funds from DG DEVCO/EuropeAid are also directed to international human rights CSOs working in third countries. There are not many such CSOs in the countries under analysis, but out of those that exist, many do benefit from EU funds. In the United Kingdom, 8 of the 14 international human rights CSO members of the peak association under analysis benefited from EU funds. In France and Spain, there are fewer international human rights CSOs. Only the International Federation for Human Rights (FIDH) seems to regularly obtain funds from the EU for its activities in third countries.

EU funds are distributed in a less concentrated way in the development and international human rights policy areas. The analysis of the FTS database shows that DG DEVCO grants are not given to a few large organizations, as is the case in the humanitarian policy sector. Most of the CSOs supported by DG DEVCO obtain only one or two grants, and thus, as Table 2.5 shows, more CSOs can be supported with fewer

Table 2.5 Grants given by DG DEVCO/EuropeAid in 2011

	Total amount in euros	Number of grants	Number of recipients	Major recipients
France	78,929,161.17 €	106	52 (average 2 grants/ organization)	Handicap International (12) PU-AMI (6)
UK	102,921,782.98 €	110	50 (average 2.2 grants/ organization)	Mercy Corps Scotland (10) Oxfam (7) Save the Children (7)
Spain	20,728,920.44 €	32	24 (average 1.3 grants/ organization)	Fundación Acción Contra el Hambre (3)

Note: Expansions for acronyms used in the table are available in the list of abbreviations.
Source: FTS, consulted 23 September 2013.[10]

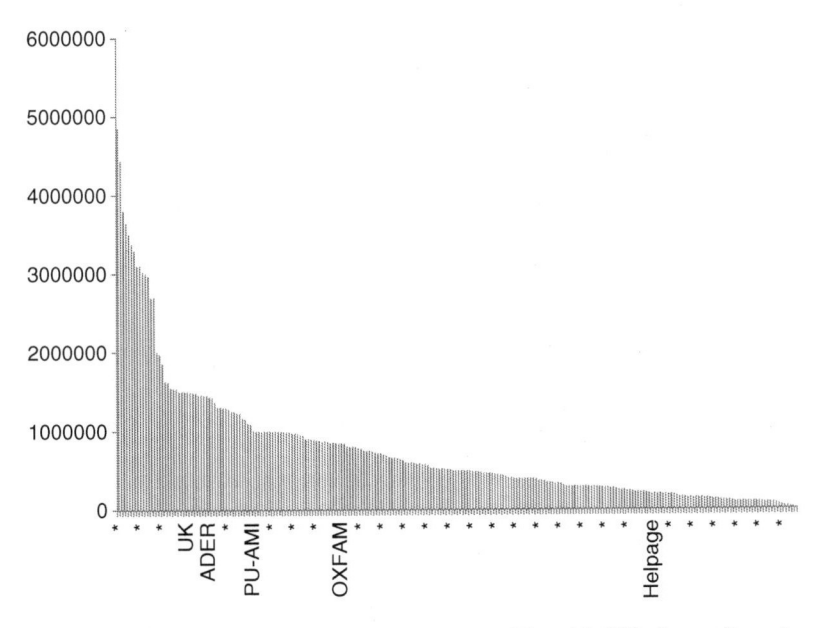

Figure 2.2 DG DEVCO funding for French, UK and Spanish CSOs (commitments for 2001 in euros)
*Save the Children's grant for 16 million euros is excluded from this list. The names on the table have been chosen by Excel at random.

resources. These CSOs obtain on average few grants, much less than the average number of ECHO grants obtained by CSOs. However, the proportion of EU money in their overall budgets can still be significant, as the budgets of development CSOs are generally smaller than the budgets of humanitarian CSOs.

DG DEVCO distributes grants to all kinds of non-profit groups and not necessarily just to CSOs. Some grants are given to universities, and even to radio and TV stations. The type of beneficiary also varies from country to country. For example, quite a few universities have been supported by DG DEVCO/EuropeAid in France and Spain, but not one has received support in the United Kingdom (Figure 2.2).

2.3 EU funds for domestically oriented CSOs: The national filter

The funding of domestically oriented CSOs is much more complex than the funding of external activities. In keeping with the principle of subsidiarity, there are only few grants directly supported by the EU

Table 2.6 Grants given by DG Employment in 2011

	Total amount in euros	Number of grants	Number of recipients	Major recipients
France	7,400,720	30	30	OECD French Republic
UK	5,417,754	17	17	University of Essex European Social Network
Spain	2,331,575	13	11	Kingdom of Spain

Note: Expansions for acronyms used in the table are available in the list of abbreviations.
Source: FTS, consulted 23 September 2013.

budget centrally administered by the Commission. While engaging in activities within EU borders, EU institutions are required to prove the European added value of their projects, which makes the whole process much more complex. Besides, most EU grants are not directly addressed to national CSOs, but rather to a great variety of operators, including governments, international organizations, consultancy firms and public authorities.

DG Employment only gave 60 grants to entities based in the three countries studied in 2011 (Table 2.6). Most of the funds went to public institutions such as the University of Essex or national governments. However, a few CSOs got a significant amount of funds, such as the European Social Network (ESN), Eurodiaconia or the Association agence nouvelle des solidarités (ANSA) and the Association of European Regions (ARE) (Figure 2.3).

Even if the Commission does not give much money directly to domestically oriented CSOs, these CSOs are not necessarily less Europeanized. For example, social CSOs can benefit from many other funding opportunities such as the European Social Fund (ESF) and the European Refugee Fund. These funding schemes are much more generous than the ones directly administered by the Commission available for externally oriented CSOs but, while European, they are administered by member states. Since the specific procedures for the disbursement of EU funds are left to member states, CSOs receiving funds are also shaped by national provisions and rules. Analysis of the Europeanization process is, in this case, much more complex, since it is not always easy to disentangle national and European pressures. Since most funding opportunities are distributed among different operators, the Europeanization of CSOs

54 *Domestic Civil Society under EU Pressures*

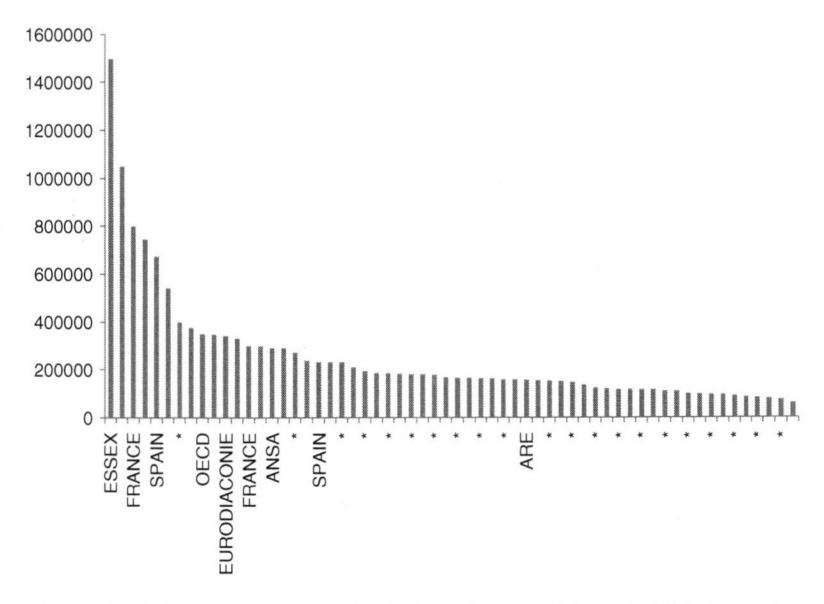

Figure 2.3 DG Employment funding for French, UK and Spanish CSOs (commitments for 2001 in euros)
*The names on the table have been chosen by Excel at random.

depends on the willingness of member states to include CSOs among their major grant recipients. As a general rule, applying for ESF grants requires a certain degree of technical capacity, and it is therefore unlikely that most small social CSOs benefit from these funds. As one representative of Union national interfédérale des oeuvres et organismes privés non lucratifs sanitaires et sociaux (UNIOPSS), a French peak association in the social arena, puts it:

> The social CSOs from UNIOPSS do not use much European funding since these funds are not very adapted to the reality of action. These funds are very tricky to manage. CSOs do not use them because they do not know how to use them. It is very difficult to build up a European project. Not many organizations can do that and it is very expensive. It's too complicated. Associations that apply for EU funds are very well structured and have an employee exclusively in charge of Europe, as for example with the FNARS, Famille Rurale, Coorace or the Association des Paralysés de France.[11]

The opinion that ESF grants are mainly received by CSOs with sufficient technical capacity is shared by many of those interviewed.[12] In countries like France, where the national rules for the administration of the ESF were very complex, CSOs experienced more difficulties. Small CSOs can also be involved in ESF projects, even if they are not directly responsible for management:

> Only the largest and most efficient organizations have access to EU funds. However, sometimes you see small entities using the ESF or EQUAL logo. This generally means that they are participating in a partnership. EU partnerships allow for diversity. There are not many CSOs directly responsible for management but there may be many more involved in partnerships.[13]

To improve participation by small CSOs in the ESF, the EU has encouraged the establishment of specific funding schemes for small CSOs, such as Measure 10b in France or Community Grants in the United Kingdom.[14] These small grants have benefited a great number of CSOs at the local level. For example, in the French region Pays de la Loire, the body in charge of Measure 10b funded 136 small projects from 2000 to 2007. There was a lot of demand for these grants and local CSOs would have been unable to do the funded activities in the absence of EU support.[15]

Since ESF implementation is the responsibility of member states, there is a lot of variation across member states. The countries under analysis here seem to do much better than the average member state. According to social inclusion CSOs, there are ESF funds available for their activities in less than two-thirds of member states (EAPN 2009). Only four member states (including France and the United Kingdom) have developed specific global grants to reach small CSOs.

As may be expected, not all domestically oriented CSOs are equally Europeanized. An example is human rights protection within EU borders; general purpose CSOs doing this work are not supported by EU funds for their main activities. In Spain, out of the 14 CSOs affiliated to the Spanish coordination of Human Rights CSOs, only one obtains funds from the EU: the MPDL (Movimiento por la Paz, el Desarme y la Libertad), which receives its EU funding for the implementation of humanitarian activities. In the other countries studied, the human rights CSOs identified such as the Ligue Française des Droits de l'Homme[16] or the British Liberty do not obtain funds from the EU. And, across the entire EU, only one CSO is supported by the EU to

Table 2.7 Grants given by DG Justice in 2011

	Total amount in euros	Number of grants	Number of recipients	Major recipients
France	7,725,504€	25	25	French Republic Euronews SA
UK	32,449,057€	69	83	Glasgow City Council Leeds City Council University of Salford
Spain	4,896,255€	18	23	Kingdom of Spain ESCODE

Note: Expansions for acronyms used in the table are available in the list of abbreviations.
Source: FTS, consulted 23 September 2013.[17]

defend citizen's rights: the Aire Center. Quite interestingly, the Aire Center is funded by DG Employment on a budget line for the promotion of the free movement of workers, and not by DG Justice.[18] This CSO's main goal is to promote awareness of European rights and to assist marginalized individuals in asserting these rights. According to one of its representatives, they are the only CSO to obtain EU funds for this kind of activity.[19]

As made clear in Table 2.7, there is not much EU money dedicated to general purpose human rights CSOs. A small amount of EU funding in this policy area is directed to very specific topics such as fighting racism, xenophobia, child abuse and domestic violence, and for the protection of refugees; this leaves much less room for CSOs to maneuver. One would expect that only those CSOs that work on these specific topics (or are willing to do so) will be eventually Europeanized. It is also worth noting that most of the funds presented in Table 2.7 are not given to CSOs, but rather to city councils, public authorities and professional organizations.

2.4 The Europeanization of consultation and direct presence in Brussels: An elite system?

Direct participation in consultation procedures and the establishment of an office in Brussels are also externalization strategies, since they involve the direct use of European opportunities and direct contact with EU institutions. Both strategies are correlated since having an office in

Brussels has a positive effect on CSOs' political activism at the EU level (Císař and Vráblíková 2012).

The establishment of an office in Brussels is rare, since it requires a significant investment. Smaller CSOs consider that a presence in Brussels is increasingly less important since they can acquire relevant information and contribute position papers directly through the Internet (Ruzza 2007). There are also interesting variations across policy fields. CSOs that have a tradition of lobbying international organizations were the first to establish offices in Brussels. Human rights CSOs are highly internationalized CSOs that already had offices for their international advocacy activities, mainly in Geneva. According to the census of the Yearbook of International Associations, most international associations focus on human rights (Bandy and Smith 2005a). The most popular international human rights CSOs, such as Amnesty International, Human Rights Watch and the FIDH, opened offices in Brussels in the 1980s or early 1990s.

CSOs without such a tradition of participation in international organizations have not been as quick to open offices in Brussels. That is the case for large CSOs such as Oxfam or Action Aid, which set up offices in Brussels in 1999 and 1998, respectively.[20] These CSOs took some time to become aware of the importance of their presence in Brussels. Further examples of UK CSOs that set up Brussels offices later on include Islamic Relief, Marie Stopes International, Medical Aid for Palestinians or People in Aid. Figure 2.4 shows that quite a few humanitarian CSOs that obtained ECHO funds have some kind of representation in Brussels.

It was difficult to find French humanitarian CSOs with offices in Brussels (see Figure 2.1), though this may be explained by the good train connection between the two capitals. Note that not all large humanitarian CSOs have established offices in Brussels, and that some of them have moved their international secretariat from Brussels to other cities in recent years (see Chapter 7). At the moment of this analysis, the MPDL was the only Spanish humanitarian CSO with an office in Brussels. The MPDL representative in Brussels affirmed that MPDL was the only Spanish CSO to have opened an office in Brussels at that time and explained the reasons for doing so. There was enough work to keep the office running and the follow-up of EU-funded projects was much easier. An office in Brussels facilitated involvement in Brussels' meetings and consultation processes, as well as their active participation in European peak associations. In the words of the MPDL representative, 'It was a way to be present.'[21] She also mentioned that for EU institutions it was easier to have a single contact.

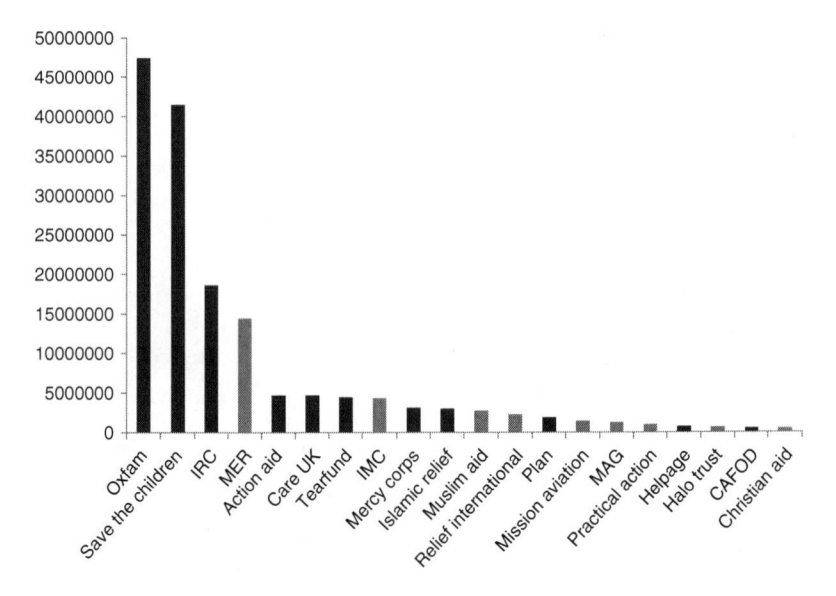

Figure 2.4 DG ECHO funding for UK CSOs (commitments for 2001 in euros)[22]
*CSOs with dark gray shaded columns have some kind of representation in Brussels.

In other policy fields, such as development or social action, it is even less common to find national CSOs with offices in Brussels. The failure to build direct connections with EU institutions may be due to the perceived cost of regularly lobbying them and to the complexity of the EU policy process (Ward and Lowe 1998). In these policy areas, CSOs also seem to rely much more on one another than in other policy areas. National CSOs may believe that EU peak associations are already taking charge of advocacy activities in a satisfactory way and see little need to open an office in Brussels.

In line with previous research on this topic, only a limited number of national CSOs appear to have established regular and direct connections with European institutions. EU-based CSOs are the groups best represented in European Committees and in consultations. EU-level peak associations or networks specialized in a specific topic have the highest participation rate in EU consultations (Quittkat 2011). For example, only a few CSOs (11 from France, 8 from Spain and 7 from the United Kingdom) participated in one of the last open consultations launched by DG DEVCO; it was on the role of CSOs in development cooperation (Sanz Corella and Van Goey 2012). There was more participation from CSOs from some outside countries such as Cameroon (16 contributions) and Madagascar (15 contributions). The largest number of contributions came from EU-based CSOs registered under Belgian law (17 contributions). The main reason for this lack of participation does not seem to be a lack of interest, but rather a lack of time and resources. The windows for submitting contributions to EU consultations are too brief for grassroots groups to engage, and even when the doors for civic participation are open, CSOs do not necessarily have the resources to step up (Quittkat 2011). Associations with a Brussels office or that are able to speak for a number of member countries are also likelier to be included in the Commission's consultative committees (Mahoney 2004). Most CSO-friendly DGs have launched specific initiatives to engage in regular exchanges with CSOs but these are mainly directed toward the Brussels CSO community; national CSOs rarely participate in these dialogues.

Even if EU peak associations often have a monopoly on representation in Brussels, they are not necessarily functioning in an elitist system. An alternative hypothesis is that within a complex system of multilevel governance, there is a distribution of tasks between CSOs operating at different levels (Eising 2009). While EU-based CSOs have direct dialogues with EU institutions, national CSOs engage with national authorities. The EU is also promoting participation at the national level in many policy areas, namely, in the social sector. National social CSOs can participate in EU-instigated consultation procedures organized by member states. Large national CSOs and national umbrella organizations are the most active in these national consultation processes even if, on occasion, member states also include a wider range of actors (see Chapter 7). Even if only few large CSOs are currently participating in national consultation processes, this situation may be improved in the future. The Commission is now encouraging much more pluralism in national partnerships, insisting on the need to include 'small innovative players' and 'the most vulnerable and marginalized' (European Commission 2012b: 5). The elitism of the system also depends on the degree of participation of national CSOs in European peak associations and networks, as discussed in the next section.

3 Europeanization on the cheap: Transnationalization and internalization

This section analyzes the remaining strategies of Europeanization: transnationalization and internalization. These strategies are the least time- and resource-consuming. The participation of CSOs in European umbrella organizations and networks is a bit less widespread than the acquisition of EU funds, but it remains significant. Membership in EU peak associations can also trigger identifiable changes in national CSOs, but the degree and importance of the changes depends on the type of peak associations (Chapter 7). Even if the softer strategy of Europeanization—internalization—implies few changes for CSOs, it is still significant for many of them, especially those that are advocacy-oriented.

3.1 National CSOs in European peak associations: Present but not necessarily active

European peak associations do not offer many incentives for the participation of domestic CSOs. They focus on the representation of interests and the provision of information, which as a general rule does not have a high impact on their members (Eising 2009). Given the lack of incentives and the absence of a strong neo-corporatist system in the countries studied, one should not expect much participation in European peak associations. But in fact European peak associations such as the Social Platform or the European NGO Confederation for Relief and Development (CONCORD) comprise an impressive number of national CSOs. Their participation in European peak associations is indirect, however, as they are only members of local and national peak associations that then represent them in European peak associations. Many small national CSOs may not even be aware that they count as members of EU peak associations.

Table 2.8 shows the number of CSOs that explicitly acknowledge their involvement in EU-based peak associations on their websites.[23] Since humanitarian CSOs are, as a general rule, highly Europeanized, it is not surprising that they often note their membership in EU peak associations. Development CSOs are much less inclined to make this membership public, but this may be because more development CSOs

Table 2.8 Humanitarian and development CSOs directly involved in European peak associations

	Humanitarian		Development	
	Total CSOs	Members of EU groups	Total CSOs	Members of EU groups
France	36	15 (41.7 percent)	109	21 (19.27 percent)
UK	50	20 (40 percent)	214	20 (10 percent)
Spain	24 (1997)	11 (52.4 percent)	46 (1997)	18 (39 percent)

Source: Original data collected in 2003 and 2004.

are small organizations, and so their websites do not provide much information.

All in all, CSOs active participation in EU affairs is not the general rule. For example, in 2003, there were only around eight large UK CSOs active in the Overseas NGOs for Development (BOND) European Policy Group. Only large CSOs such as Oxfam, ActionAid and Christian Aid seem to have the capacity to invest time and resources in this group.[24] However, instead of just dividing CSOs between active and non-active members, it would be more telling to distinguish between different degrees of activism. In the French Development Platform Coordination Sud, when it comes to actual work (for example, the definition of common positions) only five or six CSOs are involved in EU issues, whereas 20–30 participate in the European policy group on a regular basis. When the French Platform organizes ad hoc information meetings on EU issues, there are around 80 participants.[25] The degree of participation of social CSOs in the European activities of national networks seems to follow a similar pattern. As a representative of a French peak association in the social sector puts it:

> Not many organizations are interested in EU topics. Only 15 CSOs are regularly involved in the European policy group, out of around 30 that are officially registered. The other policy groups have a similar participation rate; they concern narrow issues. Only large CSOs are involved with the European policy group, such as Associations de Paralysés de France, Secours Populaire, FNARS, etc. These associations have direct contact with EU institutions but they do not have offices in Brussels. They are also involved in peak associations from their specific policy areas. They have a person in charge of EU topics and are very active. They organize seminars, they exchange best practices and they have partners in other countries.[26]

Even if national and local CSOs are not active participants in EU discussions, they may still be Europeanized to a certain extent. As general rule, when peak associations (whether their secretariats or particular members) decide to work on a European topic, the information is sent to all members and they can get involved in the discussion and/or in European advocacy if they are interested.[27]

The receipt of EU funds and membership in European peak associations tends to go hand in hand, which supports the hypothesis that EU funding for CSOs causes an increase in advocacy activities (Chaves et al. 2004, Mosley 2012). This trend is less evident in Spain.[28]

Participation in European peak organizations also seems to be more widespread (and less elitist) than participation in global networks. For example, in the external action area (which one would expect to be much more globalized), European peak organizations attract more members than global ones. However, this European orientation may vary among member states, as the trend is less pronounced in Spain. The number of humanitarian CSOs that only belong to European peak associations is higher (8 in Spain, 7 in the United Kingdom and 13 in France) than those only in non-European peak associations (5 in Spain, 3 in the United Kingdom and none in France). This is also the case for development CSOs. The numbers of French and British development CSOs that are exclusively engaged in non-European peak organizations (6 and 5, respectively) are smaller than the numbers in only European groups (17 and 8, respectively).[29] Spanish CSOs tend to get involved in Latin American and Mediterranean groups rather than in purely global peak organizations. Some CSOs based in the United Kingdom are members of American peak organizations such as InterAction.

In all, most CSOs participate indirectly in at least one EU peak association or coalition, even if their participation is not always very active. Only a few CSOs are reluctant to get involved in coalition work, which seems to be related to their size and to the value they place on their autonomy. Such is the case for the Red Cross and Médecins sans Frontières. These large CSOs sometimes engage in collective projects, but they prefer to act on a case-by-case basis since they do not always agree with the positions taken by peak organizations. They also fear that their own point of view could be watered down.[30] In the words of an MSF official:

> We are allergic to all kinds of political cooperation because it might not be what we consider is needed. We do not want our voice to be diluted. At VOICE we have guest status. We left the Spanish coordination since we are a humanitarian CSO and the CONGDE is more focused on development issues. Around 2002 or so we left because they started to take positions that we did not share. By default, we do not coordinate with others. But if in a specific case we consider that the coordination has added value, and it is not too costly to manage, then we will do it.[31]

International Human Rights CSOs also refuse to join peak organizations. For the moment, there is only an informal European CSO network: the Human Rights and Democracy Network (HRDN). It remains informal in order to keep costs down and to avoid bureaucracy. This seems to be particular to human rights CSOs, which may be more aware of the shifting rights and responsibilities when working under a peak association.[32]

3.2 The Internalization of Europe

Internalization, the softer form of Europeanization, occurs when CSOs integrate European topics in their daily activities without establishing direct relations with Europe or engaging in transnational dynamics. Thus, national CSOs that have already engaged in stronger forms of Europeanization are not concerned with this strategy. Internalization is much more common in policy areas where there are not many EU opportunities, and among small and medium-sized CSOs that cannot exploit EU opportunities due to a lack of resources or skills. CSOs that focus on the management or provision of information are also more likely to engage in the internalization strategy; their costs for integrating daily activities at the EU level are much lower than for others.

One would expect that many general purpose national human rights CSOs have engaged in internalization strategies, since they meet many of these characteristics. According to their websites, most national human rights CSOs have integrated European topics into their daily activities, even though they have no direct contact with the EU. Europe is a frequent topic in their activities, including press releases and position papers. Human rights CSOs refer to the European Court of Human Rights or to the Charter of Fundamental Rights of the EU. Some examples of CSOs that often cover EU issues are the British organization Liberty, Statewatch or the Ligue Francaise des Droits de l'Homme.[33] Most of their activities consist of symbolic action, legal advice, raising awareness or advocacy. Adding European topics to their agendas often makes sense and is not very costly.

Only a few development and social CSOs also deal with EU topics in their daily activities in spite of having no other direct link with the EU. But it seems logical that these CSOs would include the EU in their daily activities, given their goals. For example, CSOs such as OneWorld UK aim to provide online information on development issues, which obviously should require them to be as exhaustive as possible. Another example is Charities Evaluation Services, which offers training to other CSOs. If they want to offer attractive services, they obviously need to add Europe to their training programs.

CSOs that focus on the provision of social services become active on EU topics only on certain circumstances. This depends on the salience of EU topics to the CSOs, and whether they are directly affected by EU rules. In the words of a CSO representative:

> More and more CSOs are getting interested in EU issues, but this depends a lot on the news. CSOs were very interested in the Service Directive. They asked for information very frequently. The referendum also led to many discussions about Europe. Europe is not a priority for local CSOs. The social sector remains a national priority. The EU can propose new practices but social policy is still under the authority of the member states. Their main institutional partners are the national government and the Social Security Services (Caisse d'Assurance Maladie). The evolution is very slow. When CSOs are interested in Europe, it is always in order to get some money. They become interested in EU topics because they are looking for funds or for partners.[34]

4 CSOs' varying degrees of Europeanization

This section shifts attention to the contrasting degrees of Europeanization of individual CSOs, revealing three main ideal types: exclusive, pluralist and sporadic. This classification has been created purely for descriptive purposes. It informs the selection of CSOs for the qualitative analysis of the following chapters.

Exclusive CSOs are those that have fully engaged in the three strategies of Europeanization. They have frequent and almost exclusive contact with the EU and the majority of their public funds comes from the EU. They may also exclusively participate in European networks and, if they are large enough, have an office in Brussels.

Pluralist CSOs also have frequent contact with the EU, but it remains just one partner among many others. These CSOs obtain public funds from a wide variety of domestic and international sources, including private contributions. They also belong to a wide variety of European and global networks, and frequently consider European and international topics.

Sporadic CSOs do not have much direct contact with the EU. They do not use European opportunities (consultation procedures and funds) or they only use them in exceptional circumstances. They tend not to be engaged in European or international networks. Sporadic CSOs may still deal with European topics and thus they may engage in an internalization strategy.

Table 2.9 Types of CSOs and their varying degrees of Europeanization

	Exclusive CSOs	Pluralist CSOs	Sporadic CSOs
Externalization strategy (European opportunities)	Frequent and almost exclusive contact with the EU	Frequent contact with the EU and other international organizations	Absence of or very weak direct contact with the EU
Transnationalization/ supranationalization strategies (European networks)	Belong mainly to European networks	Belong to both European and global networks	One weak link or none
Internalization strategy	Deal very often with EU topics	Deal often with EU topics	Deal occasionally with EU topics

Even if the number of national CSOs that have engaged in Europeanization strategies is larger than expected, the type of Europeanization is highly dependent on the policy sector and to a lesser extent on the country under analysis. The degree of Europeanization of CSOs varies among the three strategies, as Table 2.9 shows. The examples of CSOs in each of the categories are to be considered with caution. CSOs do not always stay in the same category, and the lines between categories are often blurred. There will be more detail and a longitudinal perspective in the subsequent qualitative analysis.

Exclusive CSOs, the most likely cases, are the most interesting for the coming qualitative analysis. Since they exclusively have contact with EU institutions, the transformations that will be identified cannot be attributed to other levels of governance. Exclusive CSOs do sometimes receive funds and have direct contact with national agencies and ministries; however, for these CSOs, the national institutions are only secondary partners, and thus they are confronted with fewer domestic pressures. Since this analysis includes three different European countries, it will be possible to distinguish the effects of these domestic pressures.

As may be expected, the majority of CSOs are not exclusive. However, exclusive CSOs are still rather numerous, especially considering the strict criteria for this category. If the criteria were to be slightly softened (for example, to include CSOs obtaining substantial but not necessarily most of their funding from the EU), many more CSOs would slip into this category.

Most exclusive CSOs are humanitarian. A few development and social CSOs also come under this category, but there were no cases of human rights CSOs that clearly fitted. There also seems to be variation from country to country. While there were a few French CSOs that can be considered exclusive, it was much more difficult to identify such CSOs in the United Kingdom. UK CSOs obtained a great deal of funding from the EU, but they also obtained funds from Department for International Development (DFID) and many other donors. Thus, at that time, they tended to be much more pluralist than CSOs in other countries (Table 2.10).

Since pluralist CSOs have developed links with a range of partners, it is very interesting to compare them to exclusive CSOs. Pluralist CSOs obtain funds from many other sources and they are involved in a variety of consultation processes at different levels. Thus, it would be reasonable to expect some differences between pluralist and exclusive CSOs. The largest CSOs, such as Médecins Sans Frontieres (MSF), Oxfam and Save the Children, are pluralist. They have developed very strong relationships with the EU and often get most of their funding from the EU. However, they also have strong links with other international donors.

Most of these large, popular CSOs are involved in humanitarian, development and social activities simultaneously. Examples include Oxfam, the Red Cross, Caritas and MSF. Oxfam is one of the major recipients of EU grants but these funds only represented 12.9 percent of its total income for the year 2011–2012 (Oxfam 2012). The EU was Oxfam's largest public donor as it represented 31 percent of its income

Table 2.10 Examples of exclusive CSOs

	France	UK	Spain
CSO	Triangle	Afghanaid	Acción contra el Hambre
Percent of budget funded by the EU	48 percent in 2011	36 percent of restricted funds (which constitute most of its budget) in 2012	46 percent in 2012
Membership	VOICE	–	VOICE

Source: The activity reports of these CSOs.

from governments and other public authorities (its UK funds were only 7.9 percent of its public funding).[35] For MSF, resources from governments and other public authorities only represented 2 percent of its total budget in 2011. The EU was its largest public donor, providing 57 percent of its total public income.

Most if not all international human rights CSOs can be considered pluralist. Even if some of them, such as Amnesty International or Human Rights Watch, do not normally accept funds from public donors (including the EU), it seems reasonable to include them in this category since they have engaged actively in the externalization strategy by other means (such as an office in Brussels or direct contact with EU institutions). Their advocacy activities are often directed toward a variety of targets at several levels. Most international human rights CSOs have also developed strong relationships with other international organizations, including mainly the United Nations (UN) system.

Many medium-sized and small CSOs can also be considered pluralist even if they are quite different from those above. They tend not to have many international partners but they may have developed strong links with a plurality of local authorities and private bodies.

The number of CSOs that have developed only sporadic contacts with the EU is also quite significant. For these CSOs, the least likely cases, the European adaptive pressures are very low. In this category there are many CSOs that only occasionally receive small amounts of money from the EU. They do not participate actively in EU-based peak associations and they do not get involved in EU participation procedures. This analysis also includes CSOs that have not engaged in any Europeanization strategy, including protest groups. One would expect that CSOs that have not engaged in any Europeanization strategies would not be subject to European pressures.

Conclusion: The EU shaping of civil society landscapes

The Europeanization of CSOs is a process mainly driven by funding schemes rather than by new opportunities to influence policy outcomes. Humanitarian CSOs are by far the most supported by the EU. The EU has contributed to the development and reinforcement of the humanitarian sector to a greater extent than to the development of other sectors. While there are a lot of CSOs working in other policy areas, they have not received as much EU support. These policy areas remain composed of a few poorly resourced CSOs. While there are differences from country to country, they are not particularly striking.

Only a few large CSOs tend to get involved in direct dialogue with Brussels. At first glance, the transfer of power to the EU is not very likely to empower the weak (Dür and Mateo 2012). However, this conclusion should be tempered with two considerations. First, the receipt of EU funds and the operational capacity of CSOs are related. A few small and medium-sized CSOs may have been empowered by EU funds and thus they may have developed the capacity needed to engage in advocacy activities (Chapter 5).

Second, most lobbying and advocacy activities are carried out by European groups and peak organizations. Even if small and medium-sized CSOs are not very active members in these peak associations, this may not necessarily be a system monopolized by an elite to the detriment of the majority of CSOs; this could also be about the small exploiting the big (Olson 1965). That would mean that small CSOs are not ready or willing to bear the costs of collective action and thus they rely on large CSOs to represent their interests. The extent to which small CSOs are satisfactorily represented depends on how peak organizations work in practice. Even if at times there is friction between the preferences of peak organizations and small CSOs, there are also many examples in which peak organizations and small CSOs have cooperated successfully (Chapter 7).

It is remarkable that many CSOs that do not benefit from EU funds or get involved in EU consultations have still integrated European topics into their regular activities, such as press releases and position papers. Advocacy-oriented CSOs and CSOs that work with information include EU topics in their work much more frequently, since these topics are more related to their daily activities and doing so involves few costs. Service providers are much less likely to deal with EU topics on a daily basis, except if, for some reason, they are directly affected by EU rules.

Last but not the least, different degrees of Europeanization are expected to lead to different types of transformations. The following chapters provide a much more detailed analysis of how and why this happens. They focus on CSOs belonging to each of these categories, in order to see how the EU shapes CSOs. One would expect that the EU has significantly transformed humanitarian, exclusive CSOs, but had little or no influence on sporadic CSOs that have only engaged in internalization strategies.

3
A European Policy for CSOs? Exploring European Political Opportunities

Introduction

Before the establishment of the first European communities, only a group of civil society organizations (CSOs) created right after the Second World War were active in the promotion of European integration (Weisbein 2001). During its first years of existence, the European Economic Community (EEC) engaged in direct interaction with a few groups directly concerned by the European policies developed at that time, namely, agricultural and consumer groups (Meynaud and Sidjanski 1969). Already by this time, non-occupational interests faced sincere collective action problems (Eising 2009). At the beginning of the 1970s, the first European summits stressed the significance of the establishment of contacts with trade unions and youth organizations, revealing a nascent willingness to engage citizens in the integration process.

For a long time, treaties never referred to the—potential—role of civil society in the accomplishment of the objectives of the communities or in the promotion of the integration process (Kendall and Anheier 1999). The first funding and access opportunities for CSOs were set up during the 1970s and 1980s in an ad hoc manner and progressively unfolded into a full-fledged policy toward CSOs. After discussing the absence of significant legal constraints directly affecting CSOs, this chapter focuses on the most relevant European Union (EU) opportunities: funding and access. The potential EU bias is addressed through the analysis of equivalent opportunities at the national and global levels.

1 The absence of EU legal constraints

Legal provisions affecting CSOs are mainly defined at the national level (Chapter 2). Even if there has been some interesting evolution during the 2000s, current European rules do not confer any rights to CSOs and are not directly bringing any significant changes to their daily activities. This section shows first that there are no European regulations specifying minimum standards for the voluntary sector in Europe (positive integration). Current provisions have not changed the rules of the game for CSOs nor have they encouraged mutual recognition (negative integration). Non-profit organizations do not currently take advantage of (or face the potential damage from) the single market that is in place for most goods, services, capital and people.

1.1 EU treaties: An ex post facto recognition of civil society

The first EEC treaties only referred to CSOs indirectly through the creation of a European Economic and Social Committee (EESC). The EESC was composed of representatives from various facets of social and economic life, including the general interest.[1] EESC members were to be appointed by member states, limiting the bottom-up participation of CSOs.

While European institutions, particularly the Commission and Parliament, have developed significant relationships with CSOs from the 1970s onward, the first reference to CSOs in a treaty did not appear until the Treaty of Maastricht (1992). Thus, treaties have not really encouraged the development of relationships between EU institutions and CSOs, nor have they provided an appropriate framework for the development of a European policy toward CSOs. They have just provided an ex post facto legal basis for many practices that were already considered common currency in Brussels and beyond.

During the 1990s, a few references to CSOs or equivalent actors were incorporated into treaties in the form of declarations. These declarations were rather vague. They did not establish a full-fledged policy toward CSOs or even give any clear direction. Declaration 23 of the Maastricht Treaty, which concerns cooperation with charitable associations, is only applicable to the social policy objectives delineated in Article 117 of the Treaty. The adoption of this Declaration, championed by Germany, reduces the role of CSOs to the provision of social services (Kendall and Anheier 1999). Declaration 11 of the Treaty of Amsterdam is aimed at respecting the status of churches and non-confessional organizations. Declaration 38 on voluntary service activities justifies an active role for European institutions since it reads, 'The Community will encourage the European dimension of voluntary organizations with particular emphasis on the exchange of information and experiences as well as on the participation of the young and the elderly in voluntary work' (Treaty of Amsterdam 1997).[2]

During the 2000s the situation evolved in line with a new interest in filling the legitimacy gap between the EU and its citizens (see later in this chapter). The Treaty of Nice (2001) was the first to incorporate the notion of civil society. In it, Article 39 (modifying Article 257) on the EESC established that 'the Committee shall consist of representatives of the various economic and social components of *organized civil society*, and in particular representatives of producers, farmers, carriers, workers, dealers, craftsmen, professional occupations, consumers and the general interest'.[3] Going much further, the Treaty Establishing a Constitution for Europe and its replacement, the Treaty of Lisbon, refer explicitly to the participation of CSOs (Articles 11, 15, 300 and 302 of the Treaty of Lisbon). Article 11 of the Treaty of Lisbon states that EU institutions should maintain an 'open, transparent and regular dialogue with representative associations and civil society' (Treaty of Lisbon 2007: 21). These new articles provide a legal basis for the consultation of CSOs for the first time. Even if this will possibly contribute to the democratization of EU governance, the functioning of the Union is still mainly founded on representative democracy (Kohler-Koch 2013).

1.2 A single market for non-profit organizations?

At the beginning of the 1990s, the Commission proposed a statute for European associations with the purpose of extending the benefits of the single market to non-profit organizations. This project authorized the establishment of transnational associations with legal capacity in all member states. European associations with a European dimension (Article 3) would be able to receive donations and goods, hire staff and bring legal actions all across the Union (CEDAG 2003).

The Parliament, as well as the EESC, eagerly supported this Commission proposal, officially submitted in 1992. However, the statute for European Associations was never adopted, due to opposition from the United Kingdom and Germany. Both member states raised questions about the need to act in this area at the EU level. Many CSOs from several member states, particularly from Germany, also vigorously opposed this project, since they feared losing their national privileges (Kendall and Anheier 1999). In most member states the statute did not attract much public attention, even within the voluntary sector. According to Kendall and Fraisse, 'There is little evidence of concern for a subject which is understood very little or not at all, and whose relevance is hard to perceive' (2005: 9).

The single European market has never been open to CSOs, but it is not clear whether there is a good case for protection for this sector. Many would claim that protection is allowing organizations to survive without being as effective as they should be. They would argue that non-profits should be able to go after donations, public grants, contracts and staff and volunteers in every member state. However, given the diversity of the non-profit sector and the absence of a level playing field, non-profit organizations would not be able to compete on fair terms across the EU. The tax regimes for non-profits and for donors differ to such an extent that it seems unlikely that fair competition would take place if some degree of harmonization were not granted. In any case, a single market for non-profit organizations would significantly change the structure of the non-profit sector in Europe.

Even if the single market is currently not open to the third sector, in legal terms it is not very clear to what extent CSOs are protected from open competition by the current legal framework (Perri 1992). Certain practices of non-profit organizations could indeed be challenged under competition law. Article 92 of the Treaty of Rome could mean that grants to non-profits are incompatible with the common market wherever they affect trade or distort competition. Indeed, this Article uses the general term 'undertakings' and does not explicitly exclude non-profits. Non-profit organizations are also often monopolies and thus European anti-trust law could also—in theory—be applied to them (Perri 1992). The treaties only explicitly exclude non-profit-making legal persons from the benefits of the right of establishment (Article 58, Treaty of Maastricht). In any event, it seems unlikely that anyone would have sufficient interest in bringing an action against CSOs. That is why non-profits have been protected until now from indirect integration into the single market. The declarations attached to the treaties, especially the one aiming to protect the status of churches and charities (Declaration 23 mentioned above), could also be used by the Court of Justice of the EU to justify the authorization of grants, mergers and tax relief to non-profits.

Since there are currently no EU legal provisions directly regulating the role and activities of non-profit organizations, EU regulations can only affect CSOs indirectly. EU regulations can only be applicable to CSOs if they are involved in the implementation of European policies. For example, the service directive would have had many consequences for non-profits if it had been applied to social services, as proposed in a first draft.

2 Funding opportunities: Regulating activities through spending power?

As is clear from the previous section, the development of European policy toward CSOs does not follow a master plan set out in treaties or in European law. This section shows how the ad hoc establishment of budget lines supporting CSOs has evolved into a full-fledged system for EU funding of CSOs.

2.1 The rise and decline of EU funding opportunities

This section provides an overview of the evolution of the EU system of funding. Since funding opportunities have significantly changed over the past 30 years, one would expect that their effects on CSOs have as well.

CSOs' involvement: An innovation

During the 1970s, policymakers in Europe and beyond started to share the feeling that CSOs and their partners were better placed than government officials to address grassroots needs. Perceived benefits included the CSOs' lower costs, greater flexibility, heavier impacts and faster mobilization of resources (Clarke 2000).

The first budget lines specifically directed to CSOs were not set up with regular legislative procedures. They were created as a result of the entrepreneurship of the Commission and the Parliamentary Assembly, predecessor of the European Parliament (Carbone 2008). With the Treaty of Brussels of 22 July 1975, the European Parliamentary Assembly gained the power to approve the European budget and to decide on non-obligatory expenses (Brehon 1997). From this time on, the Commission could propose non-obligatory expenses on which the Assembly could decide alone. The Assembly, which has always been CSO-friendly, could also informally push the Commission to include new budget lines in the budget proposal. According to a report from the Commission, 'It seems that the European Parliament has been very active promoting an active role for CSOs for development aid within the EU, probably to ensure that EU aid helps those people that are most in need and it is managed efficiently' (South Research et al. 2000: 7). The Assembly's new powers resulted in a few innovations such as the European Community Action Scheme for the mobility of University Students (ERASMUS) program and the funding of CSOs.

More often than not, the Council of Ministers only approved these budget lines at a later stage of the policy process. For example, the first budget line specifically directed to CSOs was established in 1976 after being proposed by DG DEVCO and approved by the Assembly (budget line B7-5010, more commonly known under its later name B7-6000). The Council of Ministers on Development only discussed this budget line in a meeting held in November 1977 (European Commission 1994a).

In the absence of a common legal framework or of specific guidelines regulating the Commission's spending powers, each DG was left free to set up its own funding practices. This situation led to a great variety of funding practices within the Commission. For example, while externally oriented DGs created budget lines specifically directed to CSOs, DG Employment opted for programs addressed more generally to a variety of operators. Some examples include the first program against poverty (1975–1980) or the first program on handicapped people.

Social CSOs could also get access to the European Social Fund (ESF). Its first reform in 1971 allowed for the inclusion of non-state actors as recipients. Before that time, non-state actors could only apply for ESF projects if they were implemented in partnerships with public authorities. In sharp contrast with funding schemes directly administered by the Commission, the ESF has to this day been implemented by the member states according to their own national procedures and regulations. The involvement of CSOs in ESF implementation was only effective in those countries ready to involve non-state actors, such as Ireland, the United Kingdom and Germany. Many other member states were very reluctant. As the Commission put it, certain member states 'do not allow those associations and foundations over which they have authority to have access to specific European funding programs' (European Commission 1997: 13).[4]

The expansion of EU funding opportunities through bureaucratic politics

During the 1980s and 1990s there was a spectacular expansion of funding opportunities for CSOs. While in 1984 DG DEVCO only managed three budget lines totaling 174 MECUS,[5] in 1993 it managed more than 30 totaling more than 703.3 MECUS (European Commission 1994a). As Table 3.1 shows, most of these budget lines covered very specific issues. They were created in an ad hoc manner according to the priorities of the moment. The Commission units in charge of these budget lines tended to spend the totality of the allocated funds in order to get more generous amounts in the future (South Research et al. 2000). The swift expansion of EU budget lines can be understood as bureaucratic politics.

Most of the issue-specific budget lines in development and human rights only secured a limited amount of funding (each budget line was between 0.5 and 14 MECUS). However, the funding allocated to non-specialized budget lines also increased. The most popular budget line among development CSOs (known as B7-6000) was for 2.5 MECUS in 1976 and reached 200 MECUS in 1998 (110 MECUS in 1992). Most

Table 3.1 Examples of budget lines created in the 1980s and 1990s for development and human rights CSOs

Year of creation	Budget line	Topic
Development		
1986	B7-5073	CSOs working in Chile
1987	B7-5045	North–South cooperation in the domain of drugs
1986	B7-5070	Help to victims of apartheid
1988	B7-5071	Support to state members of SADC
1988	B7-406	Financial aid to Gaza and the West Bank
1991	B7-5074	Aid to CSOs working in Vietnam
1991	B/7-5075	Aid to CSOs in Cambodia
Human Rights and Democracy		
1992	B7-5210	Program TACIS for democracy
1994	B7-5201	Promotion of democracy and peace in Yugoslavia
1990	B7-523 (before B7-5078)	Democratization of Central America and Chile
1994	B7-527	Support to victims of torture and for organizations helping victims of human rights violations

Note: Expansions for acronyms used in the table are available in the list of abbreviations.
Source: Elaborated with information from the Commission (European Commission 1992a). This list is not exhaustive.

strikingly, funding for humanitarian CSOs increased to 764.1 million euros in 1994 (ECHO 2000). Unlike the cases with other budget lines, this line's increase was supported by the Council of Ministers. For example, in 1990 alone, the Council decided to increase budget line B7-5000 on humanitarian aid by 100 MECUS. The Council justified this decision by pointing to the increasing number of crisis situations in the world, particularly the gulf crisis (European Commission 1992a). Thus, the amount of funding available for different policy areas showed a wide variance. Figure 3.1 shows the evolution of EU funding by sector and the variance across policy fields.

As may be expected, this large-scale expansion of funding opportunities pushed the Commission to create a simpler and more rational framework for its spending decisions. At the initiative of the Parliament, all budget lines on human rights and democratization were combined in 1994 into the program European Initiative for Democracy and Human Rights (EIDHR), which had a total budget of 59.1 MECUS for that year

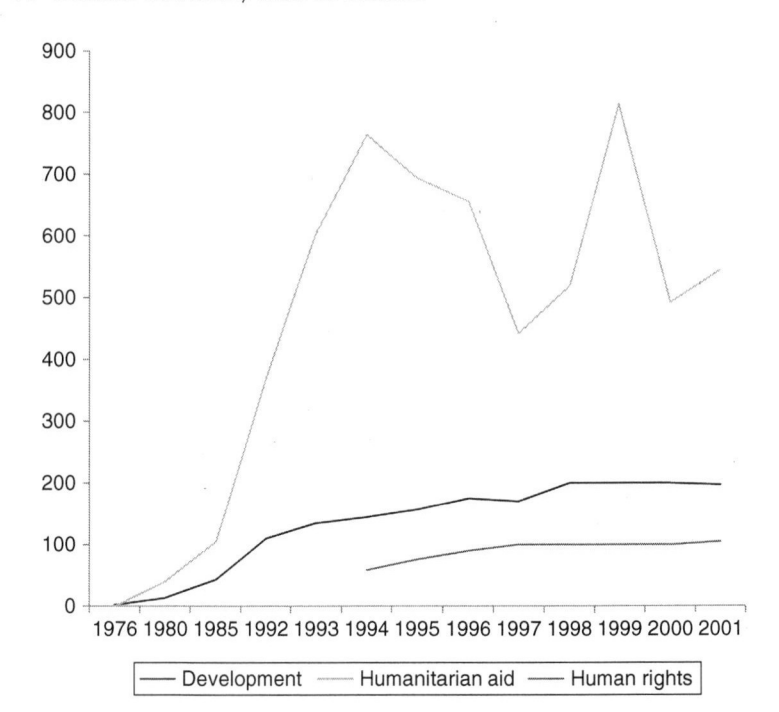

Figure 3.1 Evolution of EU funding (in millions of ECUS/euros) during the expansion period

(European Commission 1995). From that time on, EU funds for the promotion of human rights could only be dedicated to external activities. In 1998, most budget lines directed to development CSOs were placed under the program Co-Financing with European Development CSOs. In 2007, the funding of CSOs and public authorities came under the same budget line within the Development Cooperation instrument.

The strong preference for humanitarian aid was further enhanced by the creation, in 1992, of the European Commission Humanitarian Office (ECHO). According to the Commission, 'The Office will be responsible for administering humanitarian operations in non-Community countries to help the victims of natural disasters or exceptional events requiring a rapid response, and/or the implementation of expedited procedures' (European Commission 1991: 3). This pressing concern about the visibility and effectiveness of humanitarian operations is not found in other policy areas.

The expansion of budget lines directed to externally oriented CSOs was not an exception. During the 1980s and 1990s the amount of funds available for social CSOs also increased considerably. First, the Action Programs centrally administered by the Commission were given more resources. For example, the second (1985–1989) and third (1989–1993) programs against poverty totaled 29 and 55 million euros, respectively. Second, between 1989 and 1993 the ESF had its funding doubled. The rules governing structural funds also evolved favorably for CSOs during the reform of 1988. New rules introduced a partnership principle, and, from 1993 on, the presence of non-state actors in the partnerships was compulsory. Non-governmental organizations (NGOs) were explicitly mentioned after the reform in 1999 (Bache 2000). These reforms also established the so-called European Initiatives, which focused on topics of direct interest for social CSOs. For example, the European Initiatives aiming to promote employment, named, ADAPT and EMPLOYMENT, received 1638 million euros and 1849 million euros, respectively, for the period 1993–1999 (European Commission 1998c). Not all Commission DGs have followed the same time frame. DG Justice and Home Affairs established its first relationships with CSOs much later—at the end of the 1990s. DG Justice funding schemes only cover a very limited number of activities, such as the prevention of violence against women, children and young people; the fight against homophobia and combating racism and xenophobia.[6]

Funding opportunities: Stifled by success?

The quick growth of funding opportunities for CSOs was curtailed in the mid-1990s by two parallel processes: the negative reactions of certain member states to the uncontrolled extension of EU competencies and the decreasing capacity of the Commission to manage an ever-increasing amount of funding.

In the mid-1990s, the expansion of the Commission's spending powers was raising suspicions among a few member states. When the Council decided to use its power to cancel the Poverty IV Program, the Commission proposed a new budget line to cover the same type of activities under the new designation 'fight against social exclusion'. Given this situation, the United Kingdom, supported by Denmark, Germany and the Council, brought a legal action before the Court of Justice complaining of the Commission's decision to fund projects related to social exclusion. The Court of Justice concluded that the Commission had violated Article 4, stating that competences not conferred upon the Union in the treaties remain with the member states. This ruling established that the Commission cannot fund projects of 'significant importance' if they are not endorsed by a regulation from the Council of Ministers. The EU had to adopt new regulations to secure existing EU funding. They included comitology committees with supervisory powers over the Commission, in spite of the opposition from the Commission and several member states (European Commission 1998b). This decision of the Court can be interpreted as a non-negligible constraint on the expansionary politics of the Commission and the Parliament during the 1980s and 1990s. This seems to support the argument that the Commission currently lacks the support or capacity for an ambitious EU social policy (Cullen 2010).

The expansion of funding opportunities was also discontinued due to the decreasing management capacities of the Commission. The expansion of spending powers was never accompanied by an equivalent increase in resources or staff. The examination and attribution of grants was very demanding and the number of CSOs applying for funds was also growing steadily. Thus, the rate of proposals rejected by the Commission became extremely high (CLONG 2001). During the first years, the rate of approval for EU grants was 75 percent. In sharp contrast, in 2000 the rate of approval was only 40 percent. In 2001, the proposals submitted to the Commission by European CSOs under line B7-6000 totaled 1 billion euros, in contrast to the 200 million euros available. More importantly, at the end of the 1990s, the reputation of the Commission was tainted by cases of bad administration (delays in payments) and mismanagement (for example, the resignation of the Santer Commission). Thus, the Commission was also losing its credibility as a financial partner for CSOs. As the then-head of the civil society unit at DG DEVCO has since explained:

> Increasing criticism was leveled at the Commission by NGOs and several European institutions—notably the European Parliament and the European Court of Auditors. The dramatic expansion in NGO projects and programs managed by the Commission was taking its toll (more than 50 times the volume of funding compared with 20 years ago, with no equivalent expansion in human resources). Delays in processing project applications and payments were snarling up the system. Confidence and trust built up over two decades was being damaged.
>
> (Clarke 2000)

The rise and fall of funding opportunities was not unique to the EU. A similar evolution has been identified in Norway (Steen 1996). The pattern is this: after a first period, wherein the government struggles to bring CSOs into the aid arena, there is a second period in which the government operates as a controller and regulator. As the case of Norway illustrates, it is even possible that the government will end up in a situation where its most important role is to put the brakes on a process that it once initiated (Steen 1996: 157).

It is also worth noticing that not all Commission DGs have followed the same timing. The stabilization of spending only concerns those DGs that established funding opportunities during the 1980s and 1990s. Other DGs, such as DG Justice and Home Affairs, set up their first budget lines much later, at the end of the 1990s, and thus, the rise and fall of their spending powers has followed a different timing. Identifying the exact timing is more complicated for complex financial instruments such as the ESF. In that case, member states participate in the cofinancing and are in charge of the implementation; thus they can affect the rise and fall of EU spending.

2.2 European funding opportunities and EU member states

Are the funding opportunities offered by the Commission very different from the ones offered by member states? To better understand the relative significance of European funding opportunities, it is important to compare them to other funding practices, and more specifically, to the funding practices of the member states under analysis. Government funding of non-profit agencies has a long tradition in many countries. In continental Europe, non-profits have played a significant role in the building up of the welfare state. The funding of non-profits became even more widespread during the 1960s and 1970s with the rise of welfare pluralism and the contract state (Kramer and Grossman 1987).

European funding schemes: Taking the lead?

The EU did not create public funding of CSOs from scratch, but the Commission has often taken the lead in the promotion of funding opportunities for CSOs in Europe. This is clear, for example, in the domain of external relations.

In the early 1970s, the American government became one of the first to promote the role of private organizations in development aid. As Sommer points out,

It was a recognition of their special capability and role—and disillusionment with governmental foreign aid—that led the US public and the US Congress to reinforce the role of private organizations through proportionately larger monetary contributions and to give them a special place in the congressional foreign aid legislation of 1973 and 1975.

(Sommer 1977: 6)

The funding of CSOs was not widespread in Europe at that time. There were only a few special arrangements with privileged CSOs, which was in line with the neo-corporatist tradition. For example, since the creation of the German Federal Ministry for Economic Cooperation and Development (Bundesministerium für Wirtschaftliche Zusammenarbeit und Entwicklung—BMZ) in 1962, development aid has been channeled through a few political foundations and CSOs (Wohlfahrtsverbänden). Other pioneers in the establishment of funding schemes for CSOs were countries such as Sweden, Denmark and Norway (Steen 1996).

Most EU member states had not developed a system of funding for CSOs before the 1970s. According to the Organization for Economic Cooperation and Development (OECD), the launching of a funding system for development CSOs at the EU level encouraged many member states to create similar funding systems:

A lead was given in Europe by the Commission of the European Communities, which set up its co-financing program in 1975. Other countries followed soon: the United Kingdom, with its Joint Funding Scheme in 1975; Belgium in 1976; and the French Ministry of Cooperation, with its first Liaison Unit with NGOs in 1977.

(OECD 1988: 25)

The British Overseas Development Agency (ODA) did indeed institute a cofunding scheme for CSOs in 1975, right after the institution of such a system within the Commission (Smillie 1994). In France, a liaison office for CSOs was established soon after, in 1977 (Granda et al. 1987). New member states were also inspired by the EU model and created new funding opportunities for CSOs at the time of their accession. The establishment of a development policy in Spain likewise ran parallel to the process of accession to the EEC. The first guidelines for development cooperation, defined in 1987, already mentioned the role of CSOs as agents of cooperation (Baiges et al. 1996).[7]

At present, all old EU member states except Greece have developed a funding scheme for CSOs working in international development (DGCID 2001). Note that the new funding scheme introduced in Europe by the Commission also had some impact on those countries that already had funding schemes, such as Germany. The preexisting German schemes had been directed only to a few privileged CSOs. But at the beginning of the 1980s, Germany established a new budget line (budget line 68606) specifically directed to all kinds of CSOs (Privāte träger), which is much more in line with the more pluralist funding schemes that were being instituted in Europe during this period.

Diversity of funding schemes in the member states

EU member states, and, more broadly, all OECD members, have developed very different funding schemes for CSOs. The amount of funding channeled to CSOs and the procedures for their allocation vary greatly. To illustrate the diversity of funding schemes in the EU member states studied, this section will briefly present the evolution of funding opportunities in the development policy area. This variety is also characteristic of other policy areas such as social action.

France is one of the countries that offer the least money to CSOs in relative terms, since only 1 percent of its total public aid is channeled to CSOs. The amount of public funding directed to French development and humanitarian CSOs is considerably lower than in other European countries. During the 2000s, the total funding allocated to CSOs annually was around 50 million euros, and this was managed by the Mission for Nonprofit Cooperation (Mission pour la Cooperation Non-Gouvernementale—MCNG) (Senat 2005). Also, during this decade, the French government considered doubling the aid channeled through CSOs to reach the same levels as other OECD countries. However, this initiative was strongly opposed by the Court of Auditors and certain voices in the Senate. These people criticized CSOs for lacking transparency and rigor in their operations. The senator in charge of the report on this topic argued that since France—unlike other OECD countries—had a specific ministry for cooperation, there was no need to use CSOs for this purpose (Senat 2005). Since 2009, funds for CSOs have been channeled through the French Development Agency (Agence Française pour le Développement—AFD), but the amount of funds available has not increased very much. In 2011, 43.2 million euros were offered to CSOs for a total of 71 projects.[8] During his presidential campaign, François Hollande also promised that before the end of his mandate, public aid channeled through CSOs would double.[9] However, he has not yet taken any significant step in this direction.[10] French CSOs also obtain an indeterminate amount of funding from local authorities, but these local funding schemes have been heavily affected by the economic crisis.[11] Around 3800 local authorities are engaged in international cooperation. Many of them offer a small amount of funding for CSOs based in their territory of jurisdiction. For example, the richest French region, Ile de France, offered about 400,000 euros to CSOs for international development activities in 2003.[12]

In the United Kingdom, the Department for International Development (DFID) currently offers a variety of funding schemes for CSOs. DFID work with CSOs has expanded rapidly since the arrival of the Labour government in 1997; since then expenditure has more than doubled (National Audit Office 2006). In 2008–2009 the total spending on UK and international CSOs was 337 million pounds (422 million euros)[13] (James 2012). The main support mechanisms are currently the Program Partnership Agreements (PPA) and the Civil Society Challenge Fund.[14] The PPAs provide funding to international and UK CSOs for a period of three years. Under this program, DFID has funded 41 CSOs from 2011 to 2014, comprising a total commitment of 360 million pounds (451 million euros) for the whole period.[15] The Civil Society Challenge Fund is only addressed to small UK-based CSOs. The total amount of funding is around 40 million pounds (50 million euros) per year. Funding channeled to CSOs through these two mechanisms is significant, but a large share of it is channeled to a few CSOs with PPAs. For example, taken together Oxfam (33.5 million pounds), Save the Children (28 million pounds), the International Planned Parenthood Federation (25.8 million pounds) and Christian Aid (21.8 million pounds) secured almost one-third of total PPA funding for the whole period.

The amount of funds dedicated to CSOs by Spanish national and local governments considerably increased during the late 1990s and 2000s. The Spanish Agency for International Development (Agencia Española de Cooperación International, or AECI) annually offers between 200 and 300 million euros to CSOs. The total amount of EU funds channeled to Spanish CSOs in 2011 was 58 million euros, which is considerably less. However, after the economic crisis in 2008, national funds available for CSOs have been considerably reduced. The most drastic cuts came after the change of government in 2011[16] when funding for CSOs was reduced by 35 percent. In Spain, local authorities, especially autonomous communities and city councils, have also strongly supported the activities of humanitarian and development CSOs since the mid-1990s. But, due to the crisis, the future of local funding schemes is also uncertain. According to the Coordinadora de Organizationes no gubernamentales de cooperación para el desarrollo (CONGDE), local authorities owe 70 million euros to around 80 Spanish development CSOs. This situation does not apply to all autonomous communities. While nine Comunidades Autónomas (Autonomous Communities) (CCAA) are up to date with all of their payments, Andalusia and Catalonia owe 33 million euros and 13.5 million euros, respectively. In some cases, CSOs are suffering delays in payments going back more than five years. Some local authorities refuse to pay the second installments for projects that are currently being implemented or do not recognize contracted debts (Sanchez Salgado 2014b). The ups and downs of Spanish funding schemes permit an analysis over time, to see how evolving national opportunities affect CSOs' degrees of Europeanization (Chapter 4).

3 Access opportunities: From instrumental pragmatism to democratic opportunism?

Consultation arrangements with CSOs were also initiated during the 1970s, in the absence of any legal basis or informal general guidelines. This section first recounts efforts at the regulation of informal access, which had for a long time been the most widespread form of access at the Brussels complex. Attention is then turned to specific attempts to promote access to and consultation with EU institutions. This section also gives a brief overview of access opportunities in the member states analyzed, and thus contributes to the understanding of the significance of EU access opportunities by placing them in a broader context.

3.1 Regulating an increasingly overloaded interest group system

The first efforts to regulate interest groups at the EU level constitute a response to the significant increase of lobbying activities after the single European Act (Balme and Chabanet 2008; Mahoney 2004). The proliferation of lobbying activities led to certain misdemeanors such as lobbyists selling official documents for profit or misrepresenting themselves to the public by the use of Commission symbols (European Commission 1992b). The Commission and Parliament first adopted very different approaches to the regulation of interest representation, which are now tending to converge in the wake of the European Transparency initiative.

It is widely acknowledged that the Commission is the primary focus of lobbying activities (Coen 2007). Its first steps toward regulation at the beginning of the 1990s were directed at all kinds of non-state actors (European Commission 1992b). Aiming to clarify the relationships between the Commission and interest groups, a Commission communication proposed a set of guiding principles and encouraged the elaboration of self-regulatory codes of conduct by interest groups. Transparency was also addressed through the publication of a directory of interest groups active at the EU level (European Commission 1996a; Obradovic 2009).

The Parliament's regulatory strategy was slightly more demanding. The first discussions started in the late 1980s, but, given the sensitivity of this policy issue, the first norms for interest group representatives were not adopted until 1996 (Balme and Chabanet 2008; Vayssière 2002). The first parliamentary reports on interest group regulation (the MacGalle Report and, later, the Normand and Ford Report) were quite ambitious. They requested detailed information and included sanctions in case of non-compliance. However, the rules that were adopted in the end were considerably watered down. Access to the Parliament was restricted and conditioned on the signature of a code of conduct, but interest groups were not obliged to provide much detailed information. The system was compulsory but the only possible sanction was the loss of a EU pass.

After a few years without major revisions, the regulation of interest groups' participation in the policy process came back onto the policy agenda during the first Barroso Commission. In 2006, the Commission published a green paper titled Transparency Initiative that highlighted the need for a more structured framework for the activities of interest representatives (European Commission 2006). Its primary goal was to review the Commission's overall approach to transparency and, eventually, to build on existing transparency-related measures. A compulsory register and code of conduct, including detailed information on interest representatives, were finally discarded, given the strong opposition of certain interests, such as business groups, consultants and law firms (Billet 2007). The Register of Interest Representatives launched in 2008 contained many loopholes, and this was extensively criticized by CSOs active in the field (Alter-EU 2009, 2012).

That same year, the Parliament proposed a joint register that was much more ambitious (Stubb report). The Parliament called for a mandatory register including the provision of the names of lobbyists and full financial disclosure. An interinstitutional process ensued and lasted for several years, but for a long time it did not produce any clear results. The process regained new impetus after a bribery scandal at the European Parliament in 2011. A journalist from the *Sunday Times*, posing as a lobbyist, found that members of the European Parliament (MEPs) accepted offers of up to 100,000 euros per year in exchange for tabling amendments to legislation (Euractiv 2011). Following this episode, the Commission and Parliament concluded on an interinstitutional agreement for a common Transparency Register (European Parliament 2011). This new register does not introduce many innovations. It remains non-compulsory for groups seeking access to the Commission. Non-compliance with the code of conduct may only lead to suspension or removal from the register and the revoking of Parliament entrance badges. Even if the Transparency Register is an improvement in terms of transparency, it also has many irrelevant entries and some design faults that provide opportunities for miscategorization (Greenwood and Dreger 2013). In 2014 the Parliament approved a report adopting new rules to promote registration in the EU Transparency register. This report also called for the Commission to make such registration mandatory by 2017 (European Parliament 2014).

3.2 Access opportunities at the Commission: From pragmatism to high expectations

For many years, CSOs and interest groups have been involved in multiple committees and expert groups created by the Commission in an ad hoc manner. The first efforts to involve CSOs more systematically in the Commission policy process were not very successful, but that changed in the early 2000s, when the Commission started to see CSOs as potential sources of legitimation (Smismans 2006).

The ad hoc involvement of CSOs

A few DGs have highly institutionalized forms of dialogue with interest groups, according to their specific needs. Since there was no systematic attempt at coordination for many years, CSOs' participation has varied widely across the Commission. The most CSO-friendly DGs initiated formal consultation procedures with CSOs during the 1980s and 1990s. CSOs highly valued these ample opportunities to communicate (Dumon 1994). At this early time, CSOs were perceived in two different forms: as expert groups that could provide input and expertise for the policy process or as partners in policy implementation.

DGs considering CSOs as providers of expertise tended to develop pluralist access opportunities. Since it was useful to deal with a multiplicity of stakeholders, they tend not opt for a Neo-corporatist type of arrangement. They set up committees and expert groups open to a great variety of actors, including business groups, other private interests and member states. DG Environment is often presented as a leading example, since there is an EU regulation explicitly stating that environmental CSOs and other stakeholders should be involved in Commission committees and expert groups (European Parliament and Council 2002). DG Agriculture also authorizes the participation of environmental and consumer associations in most of its consultation committees.[17] These DGs seem to share the conception of CSOs including a wide range of actors adopted by the EESC and the Secretariat-General of the Commission.

In sharp contrast, DG Employment has established closed exclusive partnerships with CSOs more similar to a neo-corporatist arrangement. During the 1990s, this DG developed the concept of civil dialogue, considered to be complementary to social dialogue with social partners. From 1995 on, DG Employment engaged in an institutionalized dialogue with the Social Platform twice a year. More recently, after the creation of the European Platform against Poverty and Social Exclusion, DG Employment has regularly held institutionalized dialogues with EU stakeholders, including most EU-based CSOs interested in the social field.[18]

For other DGs, CSOs are partners not only in policy formulation but also in implementation. These DGs have tended to develop the closest consultation arrangements with CSOs. For example, consultations organized by DG ECHO have been considered an example of a best practice that could be replicated elsewhere within the Commission (VOICE 2004). The later revisions of the Framework Partnership Agreement (FPA) between ECHO and CSOs were preceded by a process of consultation with the FPA Watch Group, which was facilitated by the peak organization of humanitarian CSOs, Voluntary Organizations in Cooperation in Emergencies (VOICE). The Watch Group became a credible interlocutor and ECHO was willing to consult it in important matters (VOICE 2004). DG ECHO also established Annual Partners' Meetings and Strategic Dialogue Meetings with CSOs (see also Chapter 7).

While other DGs also involve CSOs in policy implementation, the partnerships are far less close, which is reflected in less-developed consultation procedures. For example, DG DEVCO used to hold regular annual meetings with Liaison Committee of Development NGOs to the European Union (CLONG) during the 1980s and 1990s (European Commission 1994a). A period of tense relations between the Commission and development CSOs during the late 1990s put an end to this customary CSO consultation. Ever since the publication of a Commission communication on the role of non-state actors in development (European Commission 2002b), development CSOs have been advocating for an institutionalized dialogue with EU institutions. There have been some attempts to promote dialogue during the 2000s, such as the Palermo process (2002–2003), and the Structured Dialogue process (2010–2011).[19] In 2005 DG DEVCO created the Stakeholders Advisory Group (SAG). In this group, a few CSO experts discussed participation and consultation of CSOs with DG DEVCO, with the participation of EuropeAid and DG External relations. However, the lack of political support from the Commissioner and the continuous restructuration of the Commission limited the impact of this advisory group (CONCORD 2011).

From pragmatism to high expectations

The first efforts to promote a generalized system of dialogue with CSOs at the Commission were rather unsuccessful. A few isolated DGs pushed for the establishment of a general policy toward CSOs but these efforts were never supported by most other services of the Commission. In 1994 the social economy unit within DG Enterprise proposed a white book on the role of associations and foundations in Europe. This proposal was adopted in 1997 in the form of a communication, and it had only the support of DG Employment (European Commission 1997). This document included many interesting recommendations that were for the most part disregarded. They included the introduction of a year for associations, the creation of an observatory for the third sector, the simplification of funding opportunities and the establishment of generalized consultation procedures.

At the end of the 1990s, DG DEVCO championed a new document titled 'The Commission and NGOs: Building a Stronger Partnership'. This discussion paper highlighted the existence of considerable differences in the relationships between the Commission and CSOs from one sector to another, and suggested ways to provide a more wide-ranging framework for cooperation across the Commission (European Commission 2000a). At the time of the publication of this paper, the Commission had already engaged in a reform process of European governance inspired by a different approach, and thus the above-mentioned suggestions were never given full consideration.

The Commission's new approach to European governance followed the resignation of the Santer Commission in 1998 and the crisis of legitimacy that ensued. Participatory governance was seen as one viable solution to the Commission's legitimacy problems and CSOs were perceived as the most obvious participatory agents. Emphasis was no longer on using CSOs for their expertise and ability to implement, but as a source of democratic legitimacy through participation (Greenwood and Halpin 2007). This new interest in the legitimation potential of CSOs runs parallel to the increasing popularity of CSOs within the international community. Some examples of this new visibility have been CSOs' mobilizations against the World Trade Organization (WTO) in Seattle in 1999 and the organization of periodic World Social Forums (WSF) since 2001. This new role attributed to CSOs is prominent in the White Paper on European Governance (European Commission 2001a), which proposes openness and improved involvement of citizens. The Commission committed itself to strengthening interaction with CSOs and other actors. The principles of this White Paper were again highlighted in a communication published in 2002, which adopted general principles and minimum standards for the consultation of interested parties (European Commission 2002a).

The introduction of this generalized system of consultation considerably increased the formal opportunities for access to the Commission. Even if the Commission often uses the notion of civil society, it is noteworthy that in practice it always employs a very broad definition of the term, which includes economic operators. Online consultations may have increased the access of some groups, but several problems persist, namely, the absence of any effective instrument to retrace whether or how consultation results are taken into account (Kohler-Koch and Quittkat 2013; Quittkat 2011).

3.3 Promoting participation and consultation beyond the European Commission

The Commission is not the only EU institution to provide access opportunities to CSOs. Most other EU institutions are less dependent on CSOs' expertise and implementation power, but they have also been affected by the legitimacy crisis. During the late 1990s and 2000s, the European Parliament and the Economic and Social Committee institutionalized their relationships with CSOs. There were even a few initiatives promoted by the Council, which is the EU institution most reluctant to provide access to CSOs.

The Parliament is now probably as open as the Commission to external input (Lehmann 2009) and benefits extensively from it. But the Parliament is directly elected by European citizens, and thus faces considerably fewer legitimacy challenges. So it is not surprising that there was no significant effort by the Parliament to *systematically* involve civil society until the late 2000s. The Parliament organized its first Agora on the Future of Europe in 2007 with the aim to provide room for open debate 'with a view to building consensus or revealing diverging opinions within civil society'.[20] At this point, four Agoras have been held (2007, 2008, 2011 and 2013).[21]

The Council and the European Council are usually considered the institutions least accessible to external input (Hayes-Renshaw 2009). They are characterized by a lack of transparency, which is evident in the Council's reluctance to join the Register for Interest representatives promoted by the Parliament and the Commission. According to a survey published by the Civil Society Contact Group (CSCG), the Council has not developed a strategy to provide access opportunities to CSOs and thus any involvement of CSOs with the Council is mainly due to the CSOs' own efforts.[22] Even if there is no general effort to engage CSOs in the policy process, some exceptions should be highlighted. Since 2000, the Social Platform has been invited to attend the trio meetings that bring together the EU presidencies. Since 2007, the Social Platform has also been able to participate in the informal Employment, Social Policy, Health and Consumer Affairs Council. Certain presidencies have organized conferences or used other policy tools to involve CSOs in the policy process. One interesting example is the web portal created by the Slovenian presidency in 2008 to promote the participation of Slovenian and international CSOs.[23]

The efforts during the 2000s to involve CSOs in the elaboration of EU treaties were also noteworthy. The Convention for the Charter of Human Rights and the Convention on the Future of Europe have provided CSOs with ample access opportunities (De Schutter 2002; Lucarelli and Radaelli 2004; Rüb 2002). However, given the failure of the Treaty Establishing a Constitution for Europe (the outcome of the Convention on the Future of Europe), it is unlikely that these consultation practices will be very popular in the future.

Even though the EESC is only a consultative body, it developed a full-fledged policy toward CSOs in the late 1990s. The EESC has not only published opinions about the most relevant Commission communications and policy papers related to civil society, which are mentioned above, it has also published own-initiative opinions on this issue.

Rangoni Maquiavelli, who was elected president of the EESC in 1998, believed that promoting dialogue with CSOs would be an excellent way to give the EESC new impetus (Smismans 2002). And so, in 1999 the EESC proclaimed itself the ideal venue for the development of a structured dialogue with CSOs (EESC 1999). Since then, a few initiatives to promote dialogue with civil society have been set up, such as the Liaison group. The Liaison group was created in 2004 as a liaison body and as a structure for political dialogue.

This level of enthusiasm has not been shared by the most popular CSOs active at the EU level. As Dick Oostings, the director of Amnesty International's EU office for many years, has pointed out, the EESC is not very well suited to develop a structured dialogue with CSOs since this body simply does not represent the vast majority of European CSOs and has only limited influence in the policy process (EESC and Notre Europe 2003). However, EESC policy papers and statements have often inspired the positions of other institutions. The EESC has provided a definition of organized civil society, which is quoted in most European policy documents (EESC 1999). It has also brought interesting ideas about CSOs onto the EU agenda. The last two own-initiative opinions on CSOs discuss the representativeness of CSOs in civil dialogue (EESC 2006) and the role of CSOs under EU council presidencies (EESC 2010).

3.4 A great diversity of national access opportunities

The EU is not the first nor the only system of governance providing CSOs with access opportunities. The EU has certainly been widely inspired by consultation practices already common in some countries and international organizations. In pluralist states, the government is usually expected to be open to external input, but this principle does not necessarily imply the existence of institutionalized forms of access. Only neo-corporatism stands for the establishment of far more official access opportunities in a highly institutionalized system of tripartite agreements between labor, business and the state (Schmitter 1979).

Inspired by neo-corporatism, many governments and international organizations, including the EEC, have set up economic and social consultative committees, with a variety of powers and attributions. More interestingly, right after the Second World War, a few international organizations established specific partnerships with CSOs. The Charter of the United Nations (UN) is the first official document that explicitly mentions NGOs. Within the UN system, CSOs can request consultative status at the Economic and Social Council. The Council of Europe has also granted consultative status to NGOs since 1952. This option has never been adopted by the EU, which has always been reticent about having any kind of accreditation system (Greenwood and Halpin 2007).

The participation of CSOs in global and domestic politics became widespread in the 1980s and 1990s. While the first Conference on Human Rights in Teheran only brought together around 10 CSOs, more than 1000 attended the Conference in Vienna in 1993 on the same topic (Soulet 2001). New systems for consultation with CSOs were set up by public authorities and international organizations. The World Bank set up its first consultative committee for CSOs in 1983 (World Bank 1996). The OECD also developed its first contacts with CSOs at the beginning of the 1990s (OECD 2002). Victims of their own success, international CSOs were soon challenged by prestigious publications. In the early 2000s, the *Financial Times* published several articles under the heading 'Series on Non-Governmental Organizations' that challenged the legitimacy and representativeness of CSOs. *The Economist* also published a few critical articles in which CSOs were dubbed 'government puppets' or 'secular missionaries' (The Economist 2000, 2004).

New partnerships were also established by Western democracies. Even if there has been a general tendency toward the inclusion of CSOs in the policy process, the countries analyzed created very different types of access opportunities. While France and Spain just followed the traditional model of consultative committees, the United Kingdom actively promoted online consultations among all of its government departments and agencies. In France, the establishment of systematic and generalized institutionalized relationships with CSOs was first promoted by the socialist government of Mitterrand at the beginning of the 1980s. The National Council for Voluntary Action (Conseil National de la vie Assocative—CNVA), created in 1984, was the first consultative body to bring together public authorities and CSO representatives. The main counterpart of the CNVA was the Permanent Conference of Associative Coordinations (Conference Permanente des Coordinations Associatives—CPCA), which brought together all relevant national peak associations. In 2011 the CNVA was replaced by the High Council on Associational Life (Haut Conseil à la Vie Associative), a new advisory group reporting directly to the prime minister.[24] This new instance currently has 25 members, and only a few large CSOs, such as the Red Cross, are represented.[25]

In Spain, formal consultation arrangements for non-specialized CSOs were created through laws on volunteer work. These laws were adopted by the autonomous communities and the central state during the 1980s and 1990s (Sanchez Salgado 2006). As it is quite decentralized, Spain has very different patterns of interaction with its CSOs depending on the region in question.

In the United Kingdom, the most interesting development was introduced by the Blair government in 1997, which established single-window access through both on- and offline consultations with government departments and agencies. Similar online systems were adopted by other governments at that time, such as the Canadian and Dutch governments.[26] In the United Kingdom, one of Blair's compacts with the non-profit sector specifically addressed consultation and policy appraisal.[27] The UK norms regulating online consultation have been detailed in several codes of practice, and share many features with the norms later established at the EU level. By the mid-2000s the UK online consultation system seemed to be much more open and efficient. For example, UK departments and agencies organized a total of 622 consultations in 2003 and most of them (77 percent) were carried out following the criteria of the UK codes of practice. However, the total number of consultations per year has since decreased (to around 400 consultations per year). This can be probably explained by the change of government. Different governments have different preferences concerning the promotion of dialogue with CSOs.

Conclusion

The Europeanization of CSOs should not come as a surprise. For more than 30 years, the EU has provided ample funding and access opportunities. The Europeanization of CSOs does not follow a European master plan designed by EU institutions or by the member states during the drafting of the treaties. The first opportunities for CSOs were access and funding opportunities facilitated by the Commission and Parliament in an ad hoc manner. Given the quick expansion of opportunities and the proliferation of CSOs, the existing practices became progressively institutionalized and sometimes even reflected in the treaties.

Analysis of EU legal, funding and access opportunities shows that it is of utmost importance to take into account how they change over time. Given their constant evolution, one should not expect EU opportunities to always have the same kinds of effects. In the 1980s and early 1990s the Commission struggled to bring CSOs into its funding schemes while in the late 1990s it became a much stricter regulator of a very competitive market. Access opportunities have radically changed after the rediscovery of CSOs as agents of democratic legitimation at the beginning of the 2000s. Legal opportunities have been absent for most of the period studied, but the recent legal basis for consultations included in the Treaty of Lisbon may have some effects in the future.

Interestingly, this chapter has shown that EU opportunities are sometimes more generous than national opportunities. In those cases, EU pressures are more important and thus, one should expect a higher level of Europeanization.

4
European Opportunities: Institutional Factors and Creative Usages

Introduction

The Europeanization of civil society organizations (CSOs) is a multi-faceted process in which both institutional factors and CSOs' choices are relevant. Variations in Europeanization can be explained by institutional factors, namely, European and domestic opportunities. This chapter's original contribution is in also looking at the agency of individuals, that is, uncovering the usages both *by* and *of* Europe. If the notion of usages *by* Europe prevails, one would expect that European opportunities are mainly created, promoted and shaped by European officials to serve their own interests. On the other hand, Europeanization from below or usages *of* Europe means that CSOs create and develop European opportunities to serve the purposes of self-organized citizenry.

The first section of this chapter examines CSO strategies toward European and domestic opportunities across countries and policy areas, relying on existing studies in the field. To fully grasp the interactive nature of the Europeanization process, attention is then turned to the effects of the agency of individuals. European Union (EU) opportunities have been strategically used by EU officials (usages *by* Europe) and by CSOs (usages *of* Europe). Empirical evidence for this chapter is drawn from policy documents and semi-structured interviews with key EU officials and CSO representatives.

1 CSOs' use of EU opportunities: Transforming the European civil society landscape?

The use of EU opportunities is affected by multiple factors at several levels. Previous research on this topic has highlighted the following:

national opportunities, the degree of fit between modes of interest intermediation at the national and European levels and resources (Beyers 2002; Eising 2007; Klüver 2010). Since all these factors are combined in different ways and vary widely across member states, the emergence of a uniform Europeanized civil society is very unlikely.

One would expect that CSOs are more affected by national factors since they are embedded in specific political cultures and face exclusively national legal constraints. If the degree of embeddedness of national CSOs were the most important factor, the advocacy strategies of CSOs would mainly be dictated by the degree of contraction or expansion of domestic opportunities. The relevance of domestic opportunities can be analyzed in light of four distinct hypotheses (Beyers 2002). First, the positive persistence hypothesis assumes that CSOs that benefit from favorable domestic opportunities will more frequently use European opportunities, since their capacity will carry over to the European level. Second, the negative persistence hypothesis predicts just the contrary, that favorable domestic opportunities will prevent domestic actors from turning to the European level. Third, another hypothesis (reverse positive persistence hypothesis) states that when domestic opportunities are not very well developed, CSOs may lack the capacity to effectively use European opportunities. In sharp contrast, the compensation hypothesis predicts that domestic actors have the capacity to bypass domestic opportunities. According to this last hypothesis, domestically weak CSOs may seek to compensate through funding opportunities at the EU level (Marks and McAdam 1996).

Previous research has concluded that higher levels of domestic access lead to a more Europeanized multilevel strategy (Beyers 2002). However, this positive relationship between domestic access and the development of a Europeanized multilevel strategy was not found to be so strong for groups representing diffuse interests, which are those closer to this book's definition of CSO. More recent research on the Europeanization strategies of territorial interests has shown that different hypotheses may be applied to different member states (Callanan 2011). In Denmark favorable access opportunities at the domestic level have carried over to the European level. While in Ireland poorly developed domestic access opportunities had resulted in poorly developed advocacy strategies at the EU level. In the United Kingdom the inverse was found: local governments engaged in an EU strategy in spite of poorly developed domestic opportunities (the bypassing strategy). Callanan's study suggests that it is unlikely that a general pattern will be found.

The present analysis assumes that the Europeanization strategy of CSOs is the result of a combination of multiple factors. The degree of national embeddedness is a very relevant factor (Beyers and Kerremans 2007) but it alone cannot explain the adoption of different strategies by CSOs from countries with equivalent national opportunities. The 'degree of fit' hypothesis can help explain variation across countries when CSOs employ different strategies in similar national contexts. Europeanization strategies also depend on the organizational resources and capacity of groups (McAdam et al. 1996; Princen and Kerremans 2008). Again, a resource-based perspective alone cannot fully explain Europeanization strategies (Beyers and Kerremans 2007), but organizational capacity and resources tend to have a positive impact on the Europeanization of lobbying activities (Klüver 2010). This analysis also takes into account an additional explanatory factor: the interrelatedness of different political opportunities. The use of public funds can be an empowering factor enabling the development of advocacy activities (Chaves et al. 2004; Císař and Vráblíková 2012; Mosley 2012). CSOs that have already established direct contact with the EU for funding purposes are likely to become more aware of EU policy developments, and thus get involved in the EU policy process.

1.1 Domestic funding opportunities: The prevalence of compensation strategies

CSOs tend to turn more frequently to EU funding opportunities in the absence of domestic funding opportunities, which gives some support to the compensation hypothesis (Attanasio 1994). However, this trend does not give an accurate overview of the diversity of Europeanization strategies across countries. The amount of funding available for national CSOs in the countries analyzed is very different, which presents an opportunity to observe this effect. French, Italian, German and EU-based CSOs generally obtain the most EU funding according to a sample of projects (Mahoney and Beckstrand 2011). The CSOs from these countries obtain 20–30 million euros per country. UK and Dutch CSOs are generally at a medium funding level of 10–20 million euros. Spanish CSOs obtain a very limited amount of money (3.8 million euros) considering the size and population of the country; they obtain less money than CSOs from Central European member states like Poland and the Czech Republic. In the following paragraphs, humanitarian and development aid is taken as an example to illustrate how the existence or absence of national funding opportunities affects CSOs' strategies.

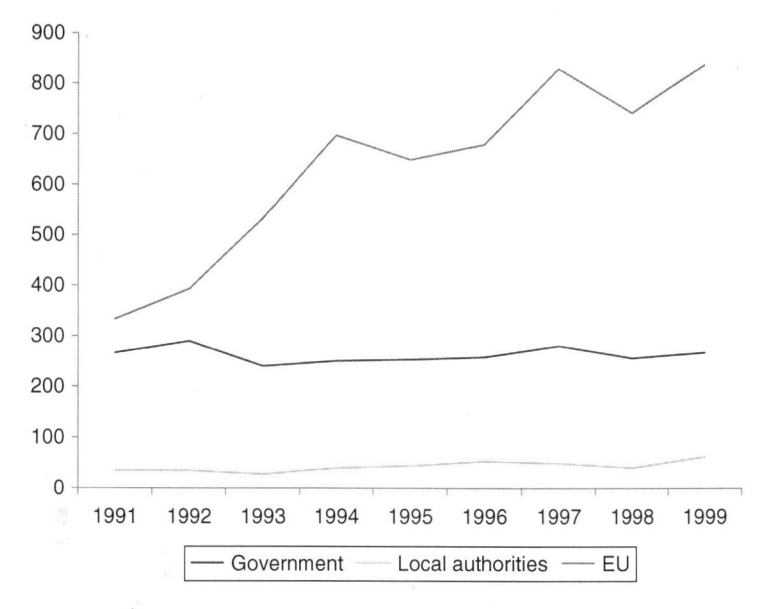

Figure 4.1 Evolution of public funding for French CSOs (in millions of French Francs) during the expansion period

As Figure 4.1 shows, French CSOs in the development policy area have clearly adopted a compensation strategy. In 1999, 49.5 percent of the total of public resources of French CSOs were of European origin while the public funds raised at the domestic level (from national and local authorities) were only 19 percent of the total (CCD 2000; CCD 2003). French CSOs would certainly be very weak if they had not bypassed the domestic level and applied directly for EU funding. In fact, if just economic resources were considered, it would be possible to conclude that French CSOs are actually more European than French. French funding opportunities have not changed drastically since the beginning of the 2000s (Chapter 3) and French CSOs continue to benefit substantially from EU funding opportunities (Chapter 2).

Spanish CSOs benefit from much more generous domestic funding opportunities in this policy area. Figure 4.2 shows that the relative importance of European public funds for Spanish CSOs has decreased as national funding opportunities expanded. European funds were quite important at the beginning of the 1990s, and even more important than national resources in certain years, such as 1994. In 1999, only 14 percent of the development and humanitarian CSOs' incomes

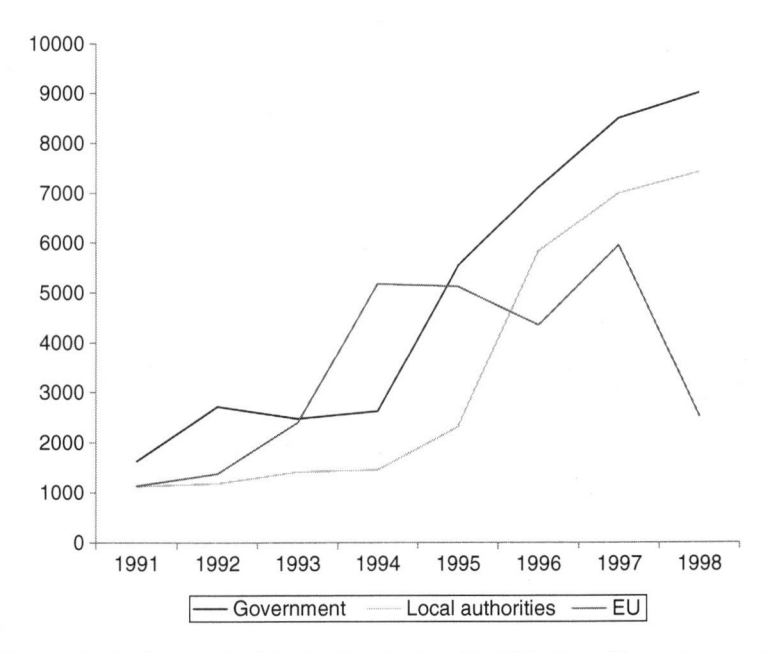

Figure 4.2 Evolution of public funding for Spanish CSOs (in millions of pesetas) during the expansion period

(including public and private funds) came from European institutions (CONGDE 2005).[1] The decrease in the use of EU funds coincided with the expansion of national funding opportunities during the late 1990s and 2000s. One could then infer that ample domestic funding opportunities have affected the choices made by Spanish CSOs, making them less prone to turn to EU funding opportunities. This scenario is in line with the negative persistence hypothesis, confirmed by interviews.[2] In the words of a CSO representative, 'There are many places to ask for funding in Spain, such as the projects funded by the Impuesto sobre la Renta de las Personas Físicas (IRPF) (Spanish income tax), city councils, etc. With so much on offer, Spanish CSOs do not bother to get entangled with Europe, because getting European money is much more complicated.'[3] Spanish funding schemes for development aid are currently being dismantled due to the economic crisis. Many Spanish CSOs have recently been turning to Europe, thus shifting to a compensation strategy (Sanchez Salgado 2014b).

The usages of EU funds by UK CSOs have also been affected by the contraction or expansion of domestic funding opportunities in the area of development and humanitarian aid. In this case the hypothesis that seems to hold more explanatory power is the positive persistence hypothesis. UK CSOs are obtaining a lot of funding from the EU, but also from the Department for International Development (DFID), the national agency. In the late 1990s, there was a considerable expansion of national funding opportunities due to the Blair government's third way policy. However, UK CSOs continued to apply for EU funds. UK CSOs are very close to DFID, but they also claim that EU funds are really important for them and that there is a lot of competition.[4] In absolute numbers, UK CSOs actually obtain even more EU funds for development and humanitarian aid than the French (Chapter 2). The 'goodness of fit' hypothesis can also be employed to understand this outcome. UK funding schemes are not very different from EU funding schemes and grants are written in the same language. UK CSOs' grant-seeking skills can be used at the EU level without further complication. There is no need to make any further substantial effort to apply for EU funds, which gives UK CSOs a comparative advantage.

It is worth noticing that variation is expected across policy fields. There can be some variation even within a specific policy field. Just to give an example, even if the positive persistence hypothesis seems to best explain the UK case, the compensation hypothesis explains the fund-raising behavior of UK CSOs toward awareness-raising activities during the Thatcher years. At this time, the British government did not fund awareness-raising activities on development issues and UK CSOs turned to EU funds to fill in this gap (South Research et al. 2000).

Analysis of the humanitarian and development policy field shows the great potential for diversity in Europe. One should expect that diversity also prevails in other policy areas with similar funding opportunities. In the social field, the situation is far more complex. Member states can determine the amount of EU funding that will be channeled to national CSOs, as well as their own domestic funding. Since they have control at both levels, they can try to shape CSOs' Europeanization strategies. For example, if a government wants to reduce its public spending for CSOs devoted to social activities, it can try to allocate more EU funds to this priority. In this situation, a compensation strategy is directly encouraged by the national government.

1.2 Access and domestic opportunities

On the subject of access opportunities, one would also expect that different hypotheses prevail in different national contexts. Additionally, access opportunities are more likely to be exploited by CSOs when they already have direct relationships with the EU due to EU funding. In this section, the humanitarian and development policy areas serve to illustrate how different national access opportunities shape CSOs' strategies.

Again, CSOs from the United Kingdom contribute to the Commission's online consultations more than those from any other nation (Quittkat 2011) and, as a general rule, they have a very good reputation in European circles.[5] The British Overseas NGOs for Development (BOND), the platform for development CSOs, considers itself the most active platform in Europe because it has more resources than the rest. Interestingly, it does not always work in cooperation with the European platform—the Confederation for Relief and Development (CONCORD). Sometimes it engages independently in EU advocacy activities or works in cooperation with other national platforms. In BOND's view, CONCORD does not work on every relevant issue.[6] To bring forward its own issues, BOND has developed direct contacts with the European Parliament and the Commission.

Since UK CSOs have a long tradition of consultation and lobbying at the national level, the positive persistence hypothesis seems the best fit. Development UK CSOs also have very good scores in all other intervening factors. UK CSOs generally have more resources than other European CSOs and the consultation system developed by the UK government is very similar to the EU system (Chapter 3). Development UK CSOs also get more EU funding than CSOs from most European countries, and this can carry over to political advocacy at the EU level. It is hard to precisely determine the relative importance of each factor, but it *is* possible to conclude that a combination of favorable conditions satisfactorily explains the successful Europeanization of UK CSOs. This success story is not necessarily transposable to other policy areas. For example, in social policy and, more specifically, social inclusion, national access opportunities have been mostly absent. The Europeanization strategies of UK CSOs in the social area seem to have been mainly EU-driven (Chapter 7).

In Spain, the conditions for successful Europeanization strategies in humanitarian and development aid are less present. As one would expect, Spanish CSOs are far from being the most active in EU consultations. For example, there hasn't been a single contribution from a Spanish CSO to the consultations concerning funding for external action since 2013.[7] The negative persistence scenario would likely be the best fit in this case. There is not a strong tradition of participation and the national and local governments do not offer online participation opportunities. In the words of a CSO representative:

Spanish civil society does not have a tradition of political lobbying. Civil society has no experience with this. The same is true in Portugal and Greece. CSOs are not used to taking on lobbying activities. (...) CSOs have never had a chance to get involved in politics. When has Spanish civil society had the opportunity to give its opinion? In other countries, CSO representatives are invited to participate in policy design. In Spain, nobody really thinks about CSOs.[8]

The lack of participation of Spanish CSOs at the EU level could also be explained by their smaller resources and less frequent use of EU funding schemes. In interviews, many Spanish CSO representatives reported that they had never thought about engaging in consultations or policy discussions with the Commission until they started to apply for EU funds.[9]

Also, the networking model at the national level—in which the monopoly of representation is given to peak associations—seems to be reproduced at the EU level. According to the details given in its activity report, Coordinadora de Organizationes no gubernamentales de cooperación para el desarrollo (CONGDE), the national peak association in the development policy field, has a monopoly on representation at both the domestic and EU levels (CONGDE 2012). In sharp contrast with the UK platform, CONGDE does not have direct contact with the Commission and emphasis is always placed on networking. All of their European activities go through the European peak association CONCORD. Whether this fact better supports the positive persistence hypothesis or the negative persistence hypothesis is open to discussion. On the one hand, strong domestic networking ensures indirect participation in European networks. On the other hand, strong domestic networking disincentivizes them from having *direct* participation with Brussels.

In the development field in France, there is currently no institutionalized procedure for CSOs to engage in dialogue with public authorities. To follow up on the promises of Hollande's electoral campaign, a new consultation council is currently being launched: the National Council for Development and Cooperation (Conseil National du Développement et de la Solidarité). However, its long-term viability is uncertain since previous ventures, such as the High Council for International Cooperation (Haut Conseil pour la Coopération Internationale), created after the arrival of Bernard Kouchner to the Ministry of Foreign Affairs in 2009, was only active for around one year.[10]

According to French development CSOs, advocacy activities directed toward the EU and domestic levels are complementary. Many French development CSOs have engaged in advocacy activities with EU institutions. The umbrella organization on development issues, Coordination Sud, has even represented the EU network CONCORD in some meetings (Coordination Sud 2012). This could be interpreted as a compensation strategy. Since Coordination Sud is not very satisfied with current access opportunities at the domestic level, it is quite active at the EU level. It could also be argued that French CSOs are very dependent on EU funds, and that the receipt of EU funds has encouraged their engagement in policy advocacy in this field. In France, consultation opportunities depend a lot on the policy field in question, and thus the conclusions for the development sector do not necessarily apply for other policy areas where access opportunities may be more developed.

1.3 CSOs' lack of internal capacity: The positive persistence hypothesis reversed

The choice of a few member states and the focus on one specific policy area may have given the impression that the compensation strategy and the positive and negative persistence hypotheses are more likely than the rest. In the cases analyzed, many domestic CSOs could actually make use of European opportunities. However, in many other EU member states, CSOs do not have the necessary capacity and skills to develop a successful European strategy; thus there the positive persistence hypothesis is reversed.

One would expect that for low-skilled CSOs, it is much more difficult to benefit from multilevel opportunities, especially funding opportunities. Chasing new funding streams is not an easy task and, more importantly, it costs money. CSOs need professionals, time and resources to put together competitive applications at the EU level. CSOs from many countries, especially from Central and Eastern Europe, are unable to develop viable proposals (Mahoney and Beckstrand 2011). The further lack of domestic opportunities results in a very weak CSO sector. Greek development and humanitarian CSOs do not apply for EU funds very often, even in the absence of domestic funding opportunities.

The lack of access to public funds by small and poorly resourced organizations is a well-known phenomenon:

> Grant seeking and grant management is especially burdensome for small nonprofit organizations. Ironically, the system of time-limited grants and contracts, intended to encourage community-based

services and local initiative, sometimes works against the interest of the local, single-program agencies and favors the larger, more bureaucratic organizations that have specialized staff with grant preparation and management skills and responsibilities.

(Kramer and Grossman 1987)

The obstacles for small organizations to effectively apply for public funds are increased in a market where sellers (public donors) are scarce. Thus, most small CSOs in Europe are certainly experiencing much more difficulties right now than during the 1980s and 1990s, when they could operate in a seller-dominated market.[11] For example, small and poorly resourced CSOs are hindered by the requirement for a bank endorsement. A new EU financial regulation tries to address this problem by offering many advantages to low-level grant recipients, such as an exception to the mandatory submission of prefinancing guarantees (European Parliament and Council 2012).

There are a lot of contrasts not only between the wealthiest and the poorest member states but also across policy sectors. As shown in Chapter 2, CSOs working in some policy areas, such as human rights within the EU, have considerably fewer resources. However, the great diversity of funding opportunities at the EU level makes it easier for small CSOs to have access to certain programs, especially those dedicated to awareness-raising activities. If the lack of organizational capacity and resources can be an important obstacle for the receipt of EU funds, these factors can also be countered. Where there's a will, there's a way. It is more difficult for small CSOs to get EU funds, and this may be a general trend, but it is not an impossible situation. There are some examples in which very small CSOs have managed to get EU funds against all odds. Small CSOs can establish alliances with larger CSOs to make sure they meet EU requirements. For example, a small organization based in Extremadura could have never obtained EU funds on its own because it could not obtain a bank endorsement. To overcome this obstacle, this CSO requested the support of the Spanish Red Cross, which signed the contract and served as an intermediary.[12]

2 The usages by Europe: EU-driven shaping of CSOs

The study of political opportunities sheds light on the general picture, but it does not really explain how these opportunities are actually realized. This section explores a neglected aspect of the transformation of Europe: the agency of individual actors. It shows how European opportunities are being perceived and used by EU officials and CSOs. The Commission has played the most active role in creating and developing European and domestic CSOs, and has thus contributed to the structuring of the civil society landscape in Europe.

2.1 Shaping access through the creation of peak associations

The involvement of all relevant stakeholders is often promoted as an ideal mode of governance by the Commission (Wolff 2013). Participation is more likely when policymakers provide appropriate information to potentially interested interest groups. More often than not, certain actions are required to involve those that are not represented in the process. The increase in interest representation activities at the EU level has generally been correlated to the transfer of competences to the EU (Balme and Chabanet 2008; Mahoney and Beckstrand 2011). However, not all groups decide to take advantage of EU access possibilities in reaction to new policy developments. The Commission's constituency-building strategy is well known and documented (Cram 1997; Harvey 1993; Mazey and Richardson 2006). The Commission has supported the creation of European groups to secure and expand its competencies and to promote the process of European integration. The first articles on this topic were written during the initial years of the integration process and were clearly inspired by the neo-functionalist perspective. According to Meynaud and Sidjanski, 'The Commission has tended to develop a social basis for political unification; it believes that private integration might help support general public integration' (1969: 271).[13] These ideas are supported in many passages from European policy documents, for example:

> By encouraging national non-governmental organizations (NGOs) to work together to achieve common goals, the European NGO networks are making an important contribution to the formation of a 'European public opinion' usually seen as a pre-requisite to the establishment of a true European political entity. At the same time this also contributes to promoting European integration in a practical way and often at grassroots level. Moreover, the ability of European NGO associations and networks to channel and focus the views of the various national NGOs is very useful for the Commission.
>
> (European Commission 2000a: 5)

Establishing new links with CSOs and, more generally, with interest groups was seen as a way to bypass member states. It is therefore not surprising that member states have not always been pleased with the efforts of the Commission to establish relationships with interest groups (Meynaud and Sidjanski 1969: 272). The Commission has tended to promote, more specifically, European peak associations (Buth and Kohler-Koch 2013). European peak associations are supranational actors with a clear European dimension. They aggregate the views and interests of domestic CSOs and provide the Commission with this key information (Ruzza 2004; Saurugger 2002; Wolff 2013). CSOs are valued for their expertise and for being able to provide information from the ground. CSOs can provide information about context, a deeper understanding of social phenomena and explanations of causal relationships. They can serve as lookouts for emerging or overlooked problems, and they have the experience to take such problems on (Wolff 2013: 137). There is also ample evidence that several DGs in the Commission have promoted the creation of CSOs at the EU level in order to expand their competencies:

> Much of the work of DGV* has been aimed at undermining the opposition of powerful governments and industries by creating a constituency of support for Union action, and inciting groups to cooperate, where there is little evidence that cooperation would have emerged of its own volition. Appealing to organizations and groups, often with a high level of moral credibility (if not political power), the activities of DG V have made the issue of EU social policy difficult for national governments to ignore.
>
> (Cram 1997: 165)

*DG V is now DG Employment

The constituency mobilization strategy has been pursued by some DGs within the Commission, such as DG Employment, DG Environment and DG DEVCO. There is a close similarity between the themes supported by EU peak associations and the main competences of a few Commission DGs (Buth and Kohler-Koch 2013). Support from CSOs gave these DGs the opportunity to maintain their status within the Commission and be on more equal footing when facing off with the most powerful DGs, such as DG External Relations, DG for Economic and Financial Affairs (ECFIN) and DG Competition.[14] This inter-DG rivalry has not only improved CSOs' access opportunities, it has also increased the access of business interests (Coen and Dannreuther 2003).

The constituency-building strategy has not only been discussed by scholars, but it is widely recognized in many EU policy documents (European Commission 1992a; European Commission 2001a) and by CSO representatives. For example, in the words of a CSO representative, 'DG Employment needed a common voice in a sector that was very heterogeneous, in order to have more legitimacy and to counterbalance other DGs, such as DG Enterprise.'[15]

CSOs have indeed efficiently supported certain Commission DGs. One recent example was CSO support of DG environment after the second Barroso Commission. The coordinating group for European environmental CSOs, the Green 10, has intensively lobbied for the strengthening of this DG. More specifically, they have called on the Parliament to support the maintenance of the units dealing with industry emissions, biotechnology, pesticides and health (Green 10 2009a). While the very existence of DG DEVCO has been challenged by many voices at DG External Relations, DG DEVCO has never been suppressed and this is also thanks to continuous CSO support.[16] CSO representatives even lobby in close cooperation with certain DGs against other European institutions or Commission services (Wolff 2013).[17] These alliances are based on not only common preferences but also a shared ideology. In the words of a CSO representative:

> The European integration process was already very advanced at that time and there was a willingness to create a social Europe. From my personal standpoint, I would say that there was a connection between the socialist European circles in Brussels. Even if EAPN is not a socialist voluntary organization, one of the first EAPN members was also a member of the socialist party in Brussels that had previously been an assistant at the EU Parliament. People from the Commission and the voluntary organizations are ideologically close.

Commission DGs often try to use CSOs to 'pursue their internal quarrels by other means'.[18] And they often use CSOs to improve their strategic position within the Commission. For example, EuropeAid initiated a consultation process with CSOs (the Palermo process) in 2002 in order to reinforce its own position within the Commission. The DGs that could actually decide on the topics under discussion (DG DEVCO and DG External Relations) were not invited to the discussions. As may be expected, such instrumentalization is reciprocal. CSOs also often try to exploit the differences between DGs in order to have more influence in policymaking. However, as a CSO representative bitterly pointed out,

Commission DGs have much more experience and skills in political infighting than most CSOs.[19]

At present, DGs are not only aiming to increase their power within the Commission, they are also concerned with their legitimacy deficit. CSOs have become an interesting way to raise the profile of Commission DGs. In this new context, it is not just the weakest but also some of the more powerful DGs that have developed an interest in consultation with CSOs; these include DG External Relations and DG Trade, as well as the Secretariat-General.

When CSOs are involved in service delivery, the support of peak associations runs parallel to the creation of budget lines. The opening of new funding opportunities has led to the development of consultation practices. Public funds have served as incentive to increase participation in the political process, rather than discourage it. For example, shortly after the establishment of budget line B7-6000 for development CSOs, the Commission promoted the creation of the Liaison Committee with CSOs (CLONG), in 1976. For each year until 1999, as much as 85 percent of CLONG's budget was provided by the Commission (Furtak 2001). Humanitarian and development CSOs were actively engaged with the CLONG. Right after the creation of the European Commission Humanitarian Office (ECHO) in 1992, humanitarian CSOs decided to establish their own specific umbrella group: Voluntary Organizations in Cooperation in Emergencies (VOICE).

The Commission also organized conferences to bring together domestic CSOs working in the same policy area. At the conferences, CSOs agreed to set up European umbrella groups that would count on the economic support from the Commission. Harvey (1993), Cram (1997) and Buth and Kohler-Koch (2013) gave many examples of peak associations created in this way with the support of the Commission, such as the European Federation of National Organizations Working with the Homeless (FEANTSA), the European Women's Lobby (EWL), Women in Poverty, Eurolink Age and EAPN.[20] The Commission is not the only EU institution that promotes the creation of peak associations (Cram 1997). The Parliament can also engage in usages by Europe, by promoting and reinforcing the advocacy activities of CSOs. This has been done mainly through intergroups, which can be coordinated by peak associations. The European Public Health Alliance (EPHA) is currently related to Working Party Public Health, which is part of Health Intergroup. AGE Platform Europe is closely linked to Intergroup Ageing. Intergroups can strengthen CSOs through their access to the Parliament's technical facilities, conference rooms and interpretation services.

2.2 How the EU has promoted the usages of EU funding opportunities

The process of contracting out external aid or other services is not automatic, and involves more complexity than one would expect (Kramer and Grossman 1987). In the event of a scarcity of non-profits that are willing to provide services (a seller-dominated market), government institutions have to persuade non-profits to participate. In situations like these, government agencies typically take the initiative and help establish an appropriate range of experienced and appropriate providers. They give incentives to potentially interested organizations and invest in technical assistance and provider development.

During the 1980s and 1990s, the Commission made considerable efforts to promote the usages of European funding opportunities in a seller-dominated market. EU requirements were not very demanding and the management of the applications and decision-making processes were very swift, which was very appreciated by the applicants (European Commission 1994b). CSO representatives have confirmed that at that time it was quite easy to get EU funding. Some even said that the conditions to obtain European funding were 'too easy' and that a stricter system would have been preferable.[21] This opinion was strongly shared by the Court of Auditors of the European Communities (Court of Auditors 1991).

EU funds were also more attractive because of their neutrality. At that time, budget line B7-6000 for development CSOs had no thematic and geographical focus and thus CSOs had the right of initiative. The first general conditions, published in 1988, stated that European aid 'stands out for the absence of any economic and political interests of the donor' (European Commission 1988). This was in sharp contrast with most member states, where public funding was subject to economic and political imperatives. Commission staff also played an active role in the promotion of the usages of European funding opportunities. They directly contacted some CSOs (through visits or phone calls) and suggested that they could get money to take action on specific crises. For example, the director of a well-known CSO, MSF-France, reported that the EEC contacted him to offer European funds for activities concerning the crisis in Cambodia. Thanks to this suggestion, this director created a grant proposal with a budget of 500,000 European Currency Units (ECU) in less than ten minutes that was later accepted (Vallaeys 2004: 364).

Commission officials also organized events to promote funding opportunities among the CSOs from their own country of origin. For example, Santiago Gomez Reino, a former director of ECHO from Spain, organized a meeting in April 1993 for the promotion of EU funds among Spanish CSOs. That same year, the percentage of funds obtained by Spanish CSOs multiplied tenfold (Gomez Gil 2005). This pattern has also been shown in interviews. In the words of an EU official, 'There were a lot of people from Spain working for ECHO, so Spanish CSOs submitted more projects. It was very difficult to understand the procedures. When there was someone to explain the procedures in their own language it was much easier to craft a proposal.'[22] The Commission has not only directly promoted the usage of EU funds, it has done this (and continues to do this) through EU-supported peak associations.

The promotion of the usages of European funding opportunities was quite common during the first years of expansion. But during the stagnating levels of EU funding of the late 1990s, applicant CSOs continued to increase, and thus the market situation changed to one of seller scarcity. Within this new market, there have still been ways that the Commission has been able to further its own organizational interests. One of the most common has been the limitation of competition by defining services narrowly or employing formal or informal mechanisms to support favored suppliers (Kramer and Grossman 1987). For example, in the late 1990s and 2000s the conditions for obtaining European funds became much more detailed and strict in terms of quality and sound management (see also Chapter 5). Under this new paradigm, if no compensatory measures are taken, smaller CSOs and newcomers will be especially handicapped.

In the social arena, the Commission cannot promote funding opportunities directly, but it has created a budget for technical assistance to be used by member states for this purpose. This support takes the form of workshops, training sessions, coordination and networking structures. The promotion of EU opportunities by national bodies in charge of technical assistance can also take on many different forms (Sanchez Salgado 2009; Sanchez Salgado 2013). During the programming period 2007–2014, in most member states, technical assistance was directly administered by a governmental department. Spain was a good example of this general trend. There, technical assistance was administered by a department within the Ministry of Social Affairs: the UAFSE (Unidad Administradora del Fondo Social Europeo). In only a few countries, such as France and the United Kingdom, was technical assistance managed directly by non-profit organizations. In France, technical assistance was managed for a long time by a non-profit independent body, Réseau d' Appui et de Capitalization des Innovations européennes (RACINE), which now seems to be out of business.[23] In the United Kingdom, technical assistance was basically used to support the cofinancing organizations that were responsible for 95 percent of program activity.[24] According to social CSOs, many member states have not used the funds allocated for capacity building in an appropriate way (EAPN 2009). They have sometimes not been enthusiastic about building the capacity of CSOs to engage with the European Social Fund (ESF) more effectively. The role of the Commission in the promotion of funding and access opportunities seems to be generally well received by CSOs. The example of the ESF is very clear in this respect:

> EAPN members are strongly against the re-nationalization of the structural funds. Such a move could make the funds even less transparent than they are at present and in some Member States open the door to more corruption. Instead, *they favour a strong supervisory role by the Commission,* as also proposed by the Barca Report.
> (EAPN 2009: 8) (Emphasis from original document)

2.3 The Commission's limits in shaping powers

The previous sections may have given the impression that the Commission has disproportionate power in the shaping of the EU civil society landscape. It is clear that most opportunities for CSOs have been directly created and shaped by EU officials because this served their political and legitimacy interests. However, it would be unrealistic to conclude that the Commission creates artificial European CSOs from scratch. CSOs are not necessarily receptive to European usages.

First, the Commission has been unable to withdraw its economic support for CSOs when they no longer served its own agenda. A few European peak associations have survived funding crises (Cullen 2009, 2010). For example, the Commission, following an external audit in 2000, blocked the funding that had been approved for CLONG and requested the reimbursement of around one million euros under the claim of mismanaged funds. CLONG was never formally accused of fraud; it was only suggested that it was not properly able to use EU funding (European Commission 2000b). In Brussels CSO circles, this audit was perceived as part of a hostile strategy by the Commission toward the increased activism of CSOs (Carbone 2008). CLONG had been in existence for 20 years, and was a powerful peak association composed of around 900 development CSOs working through 15 national platforms all across Europe. After an intense advocacy campaign, it was not very difficult for its members to get various actors (such as the European Parliament, many member states, etc.) to help put pressure on the Commission. The Commission had to back down and continue to fund this European umbrella. Since this episode, the CLONG has been dissolved, but its members have created a new umbrella: the European NGO Confederation for Relief and Development (CONCORD). CONCORD currently receives an annual 700,000 euros as grant from the Commission, which represents slightly more than half of its total budget (around 1.3 million euros) (CONCORD 2012). If the Commission's intention in blocking funding was to tame this EU peak association, the strategy clearly backfired. Instead of getting broken down, it got an opportunity to show its strength.

The Commission has only been able to dismantle peak associations with considerably less support. After 16 years of existence, EuronAid ceased all operational activities in 2007 due to a decision by the Commission to change the contracting mode for food aid and food security programs (EuronAid 2007). The dissolution of this peak association seems much more related to restructuring processes within the Commission and, in any case, its advocacy activities are widely covered by CONCORD and VOICE. EuronAid was less representative than the other peak associations in this policy area since it only had 38 member organizations in 2007. For all these reasons, it may have been harder for EuronAid to plead its cause and to get enough support to justify its survival.

Another limitation to keep in mind is that the Commission has not always been able to create peak associations according to its own designs. For example, at the end of the 1990s, DG External Relations promoted the creation of a peak association that would bring together international human rights CSOs. After some conversations between DG External Relations and CSOs, the selection of CSOs that would be involved in this peak association appeared to be problematic.[25] Human rights is a very broad concept and there were too many CSOs potentially interested in the topic. Two of the most popular CSOs in this policy area, Amnesty International and Human Rights Watch, were reluctant to participate, since they already had quite a good access to EU institutions. A group of human rights CSOs made a proposal but it was not considered representative and legitimate by the Commission.[26] In brief, the Commission would have preferred a peak association made up of the most popular and professionalized CSOs based in Brussels, but these CSOs did not feel any need.

Instead of a fully operational EU-based peak association in this policy area, there is currently only an informal group of CSOs: the Human Rights and Democracy Network (HRDN), which exists only as a virtual organization (Buth and Kohler-Koch 2013). The Commission has had difficulties in shaping interest groups on other occasions, for example, in setting up EU representation for small and medium enterprises (SME). Although the Commission supported such representation much more than it supported other business groups, the small business sector ultimately failed to organize itself in a way that the Commission and EU policymaking community saw as legitimate (Coen and Dannreuther 2003: 264).

3 The usages of Europe: Where there is a will, there is a way

There is not much evidence to suggest that EU opportunities were actively created from below to serve the purposes of a self-organized citizenry.[27] CSOs were clearly followers rather than instigators in the Europeanization process. They sometimes reacted to specific EU developments, but they did not create proactively European opportunities. However, today many CSOs are experienced players in the EU political arena, and are increasingly able to shape opportunities according to their goals (usages of Europe).

3.1 The shaping of EU funding opportunities by CSOs

Certain observers, in arguing that European CSOs have too much power in Brussels, have developed a 'circle of convenience' thesis (Boin and Marchesetti 2010). According to it, CSOs looking for more funding tend to lobby for increases in the EU budget, which meshes with the bureaucratic interests of EU officials. The EU funding of CSOs leads to a vicious circle in which the interests of CSOs and EU officials are satisfied at the expense of the general interest. In this interesting hypothesis, usages by Europe and usages of Europe are not necessarily opposed. Following this logic, Boin and Marchesetti (2010) conclude that CSOs might be exploiting the democratic process for their own purposes.

As one would expect, there are many examples in which CSOs have contributed to the shaping of EU funding schemes. The current financial regulation (European Parliament and Council 2012) makes access easier and less administratively burdensome for CSOs (EUCLID 2012). Examples of CSO demands that have been honored are the recognition of value-added tax (VAT) as an eligible cost, setting time limits for funding processes, and including some extra advantages for low-value grants. CSOs have also successfully advocated for the suppression of the principle of degressivity regarding operating grants (according to this principle, all renewed operating grants were gradually decreased).

Even if CSOs are systematically pushing for an increase of several EU budgets and for favorable rules, they are far from getting everything they want. This is clear from looking at the same evidence provided by Boin and Marchesetti (2010). Their analysis shows that EU-based environmental CSOs failed to green the cohesion fund for the programming period 2007–2013. More importantly, even if EU-based CSOs may have contributed to an increase in the EU budget and a change of rules now and then, they have systematically failed to bring about cross-sector minimum standards for the EU funding of CSOs. CSOs are constantly calling for unified application formats and for more standardized grant management.[28] The current system is extremely complex, and, according to CSOs, this benefits private consultancy companies and public authorities (Social Platform 2010b).

All in all, CSOs' demands regarding EU funding schemes have been, more often than not, ignored. Unheeded demands include the reduction of administrative burdens and red tape for the management of EU grants, the recognition of the work of volunteers as eligible costs for all types of grants and the suppression of the requirement for bank endorsements. Note that the current funding practices vary widely across different sectors and that not all CSOs are equally satisfied with the current funding schemes. Development and environmental CSOs seem pretty satisfied with the systems for calls for proposals of EuropeAid and DG Environment, respectively (CONCORD 2009; Green 10 2009b). In sharp contrast, social CSOs are quite dissatisfied with the format of the structural funds, which have been inaccessible to most CSOs during the programming period 2007–2014 (EAPN 2009).

3.2 The shaping of access opportunities by CSOs: Creating new rights?

CSOs have tried assiduously, but not necessarily successfully, to shape access opportunities. While the Commission and other European institutions amply provide such opportunities, they tend to avoid formal commitments. Up to the Treaty of Lisbon, the Commission was consulting CSOs without any regulations or any legal basis for doing so in treaties. Consultation procedures were very fragile and could have been challenged by member states on the basis that such competencies were not conferred in the treaties. The Commission has always rejected accreditation systems, a consultation status or any other scheme conferring specific consultation rights to CSOs:

> The Commission remains convinced that a legally binding approach to consultation is to be avoided, for two reasons: First, a clear dividing line must be drawn between consultations launched on the Commission's own initiative prior to the adoption of a proposal, and the subsequent formalized and compulsory decision-making process according to the Treaties. Second, a situation must be avoided in which a Commission proposal could be challenged in the Court on the grounds of alleged lack of consultation of interested parties. Such an over-legalistic approach would be incompatible with the need for timely delivery of policy, and with the expectations of the citizens that the European Institutions should deliver on substance rather than concentrating on procedures.
> (European Commission 2002a: 10)

EU-based CSOs such as the Social Platform, the Civil Society Contact Group (CSCG) and the European Council of Non-profit Associations (CEDAG) have long been campaigning for the inclusion of a legal basis in the treaties and for regulations that cover dialogue with CSOs. One of the greatest successes for EU-based CSOs was the inclusion in the Treaty of Lisbon of a legal basis for the consultation of CSOs. Article 11.1 of the Treaty indeed provided that 'institutions shall, by appropriate means, give citizens and representative associations the opportunity to make known and publicly exchange their views in all areas of Union action'. According to CSOs, this Article institutes civil dialogue (dialogue with CSOs) as something different from social dialogue and lobbying practices.

However, European CSOs have been far less successful in achieving regulation to specifically address civil dialogue or, in UK terminology, the 'civic compact'. Even if labels change over time, the underlying idea is to promote a set of rules or a code of practice to ensure that consultations are held under the best conditions. More recently, organizations such as the Social Platform have been advocating the signature of an interinstitutional agreement on civil dialogue, as proposed by the Parliament (Social Platform 2010a).

All in all, CSOs do not seem to have been very successful in shaping the regulation of interest representation. Another good example is the Transparency Register for interest representatives. Since the launch of the Transparency initiative in 2008, CSOs have been pleading for specific treatment and for a compulsory register. However, the current Transparency Register is not compulsory or sufficiently detailed and the sanction mechanisms are weak and ineffective. CSOs also obtained some concessions; the Commission agreed to periodically review the register with an eye to making it compulsory if it proved ineffective. CSOs have extensively used this window of opportunity. Alter-EU is currently monitoring the register. It regularly publishes evaluation reports signaling questionable practices. This CSO has also written up detailed transparency guidelines and promoted their use among interest representatives. This may lead to regulation in this policy area in the future.

As may be expected, CSOs do not try to gain access for the sake of access. They want to use EU opportunities to bring about changes in public policy. CSOs that could not bring about changes at the domestic level have engaged in venue shopping and even in the political construction of scales (Princen and Kerremans 2008). One good example is the binding Code of Conduct on Arms Exports, adopted by the EU in 2008 (Jutta and Dembinski 2012). A group of UK CSOs, including Safeworld, the World Development Movement and the British branch of Amnesty International, after realizing that the British government was not very open to the regulation of arms exports, advocated an EU code of conduct.[29] They based their actions on the Luxembourg criteria on national arms exports adopted by the Council between 1991 and 1992. The group of mainly British CSOs promoted this issue among the members of the Parliament and the Commission, who were mostly receptive and cooperative.

3.3 CSOs' bottom-up usages of EU opportunities

There is no reason why CSOs should stick to the access opportunities that are offered to them. The EU system offers many possibilities that, while not specifically addressed to CSOs, could be exploited. Occasionally, CSOs get creative and use these opportunities to advance their policy objectives on their own initiative, which is a clear example of bottom-up Europeanization.[30] This requires a lot of effort, time and resources, but it can have a significant impact in the policy process, provided that the CSOs have sufficient citizen support. Examples in this section include CSOs' use of litigation, complaints over bad administration, petitions, and Citizens' Initiatives.

The great majority of CSOs (89.8 percent) prefer to avoid the use of litigation (Kelemen 2003). This can be explained firstly by the limited legal opportunities for CSOs at the EU level (Harlow 1992; Shapiro 1998). A claim to protection of public interest is generally not possible before the Court of Justice of the EU since cases can only be submitted if applicants are individually concerned. This doctrine has been very restrictive in several policy areas of interest to CSOs (European Commission 2012a). It is almost impossible for associations to ever succeed in showing individual concern. In spite of these difficulties, several CSOs, such as Greenpeace or World Wildlife Fund-UK, tried to bring cases before the Court of Justice. These cases were considered inadmissible on the grounds that the applicants were not individually affected by the decisions.[31]

The interpretation of the principle of individual concern has not been as strict in other areas, namely, certain economic policy areas (European Commission 2012a). The requirement of individual concern was also not compatible with several articles of the Aarhus Convention that grant 'wide access to justice in environmental matters' and it may not comply with Article 6 of the European Convention on Human Rights. And in fact, a 2011 ruling of the European Court of Justice has significantly increased the legal standing of environmental CSOs, which can now bring claims that purely protect the public interest, but only in the areas covered by the Aarhus Convention.[32]

Given their lack of direct access to the Court of Justice of the EU, CSOs have been using the preliminary ruling procedure and their ability to submit complaints to the Commission when EU law is not being applied. However, it is doubtful that these procedures effectively grant the right to justice (European Commission 2012a). The preliminary ruling procedure allows applicants to raise questions regarding the interpretation of the treaties or the validity of EU acts before courts of an EU member state. These national courts may then bring the cases to the Court of Justice of the EU for interpretation. The possibility of bringing a legal action that is purely in the public interest is also limited in most EU member states. CSOs are usually—but not always—authorized to pursue the interests of their members collectively, and thus domestic judicial systems are more open to litigation by CSOs. However, there is no guarantee that a domestic court will consider it appropriate to raise a question before the Court of Justice of the EU.

CSOs have also used the right to submit a complaint to the Commission for non-application of EU law. The Commission has the obligation to ensure the application of EU law on any matter under its competence (Article 258 of the Treaty on the functioning of the EU). The extent to which CSOs can make use of this opportunity is clearly up to the Commission's discretion. These procedures have been used by many CSOs, especially CSOs defending women's rights (Cichowski

2007; Pollack 1997) and for the protection of the environment (Börzel 2003; Dehousse 1997). However, these opportunities have not been used very frequently by humanitarian, development and human rights CSOs, which do not generally have complaints about the non-application of EU law in member states.

Human rights CSOs could have extensively used the Court of Justice of the EU, as some business groups have already done. Paradoxically, the first recognition of human rights by the Court of Justice did not come out of a procedure launched by CSOs, but rather out of a procedure initiated by private companies to defend the right to private property. Human rights CSOs' lack of activism at the EU can be explained by the weakness of these CSOs; as previously explained, they have not yet developed direct links at the EU level. The only human rights CSO active on this topic seems to be Advise on Individual Rights in Europe (AIRE) centre. According to this UK-based CSO, there are many important gaps in the application of EU law related to the protection of human rights. The director of the AIRE Centre believes that human rights CSOs do not engage in litigation due to a lack of resources.[33]

CSOs are also currently submitting complaints before the European ombudsman for bad administration. Most of the complaints introduced by CSOs are related to transparency issues, including the lack of publication of documents by EU institutions, and the unbalanced representation of interest at the EU level. One example was the complaint launched by Greenpeace and the Corporate Europe Observatory. The complaint, filed in October 2012, denounced the failure of the Commission to adequately implement the 'revolving door' rules. As a result of this 51-page complaint, which included detailed cases, the European ombudsman has launched an investigation into conflicts of interest within the Commission.

The right of petition to the Parliament is granted by Article 227 of the Treaty on the functioning of the EU. The Parliament receives 1000–2000 petitions per year (1414 in 2011). CSOs usually use this petition mechanism to complain about non-compliance by member states with EU law, but citizens in general remain uninformed about these access opportunities (European Parliament 2013). Most cases are related to the environment and human rights (16.1 percent and 8.7 percent, respectively, in 2011). These petitions often refer to NIMBY (not in my backyard) cases. For example, residents complained about the effects on the environment and public health of projects such as the Lyon–Turin rail tunnel, the M30 motorway project in Madrid and the airport at Notre-Dame-des-Landes (European Parliament 2012).

A few petitions have been introduced by CSOs to pursue their general interest goals. For example, the Open Society Foundation Mental Health Initiative issued a petition with some other CSOs against the misuse of structural funds for institutions for people with disabilities in Central and Eastern Europe. It was alleged that these institutions had become places of confinement that deprived people of their basic rights.[34]

In 2012, the Parliament received a formal petition with over 2.5 million signatures that opposed the Anti-Counterfeiting Trade Agreement (ACTA) on the grounds that it violated the rights of citizens with regard to their privacy and freedom of expression (European Parliament 2013). The members of the Committee of Petitions met several citizen representatives and relayed their position to the respective legislative committees. As is widely known, the full Parliament rejected ACTA with 478 votes against and only 39 in favor.

The European Citizens' Initiatives instituted by the Treaty of Lisbon can also be used by CSOs to promote their own priorities (Greenwood 2012). In May 2013, there were 14 ongoing Citizens' Initiatives, according to the Commission's website. Citizens' Initiatives are formally submitted by a Citizens' Committee. However, to be viable, Citizens' Initiatives need CSOs' support. For example, the Citizens' Initiative 'Water and Sanitation Are a Human Right' (1,437,459 signatures as of May 2013) is supported by nine European and international CSOs including the Social Platform, the European Anti-Poverty Network, the European Environmental Bureau and the European Trade Union Confederation. European and domestic CSOs supporting Citizens' Initiatives have organized awareness-raising activities aimed at collecting signatures.[35]

Conclusion

The Europeanization of CSOs is a multifaceted process, shaped by EU and domestic institutional arrangements and by EU officians and CSO choices. Looking at things from these two angles offers a more complete view of the Europeanization process and brings some new elements into current discussions. When attention is drawn to the impact of opportunities, institutional and national factors are very relevant (see also Beyers 2002; Beyers and Kerremans 2007; Callanan 2011). When attention is turned to strategic action, the Europeanization of CSOs appears as essentially EU-driven, since 'usages of Europe' is the major dynamic at work. EU policy officers have promoted the use of EU opportunities across Europe but the effects of their actions do not need to be identical in every member state. EU officials have created new opportunities to serve their own strategic goals but the effectiveness of their actions is mediated by institutional factors at the national level.

Identifying the EU's shaping of CSOs as an essentially EU-driven process also raises questions about the artifactuality of European civil society. Even if the Europeanization of CSOs has been mainly initiated from the top, the EU actually has little capacity to create a civil society from scratch and, more often than not, it cannot directly use CSOs for its own purposes. The empowering of CSOs has created a new situation in which the Commission is not always able to instrumentalize CSOs. Once CSOs gain in experience, expertise and reputation, they become more successful at defending legitimate causes, sometimes to the detriment of Commission policy preferences.

Part II
Europeanizing CSOs through European Opportunities

5
EU Funding of CSOs: From New Public to New Civic Management

Introduction

Once civil society organizations (CSOs) have decided to go European, they are confronted with the restrictions that come with funding opportunities. In this second sequence of the Europeanization process, emphasis is on the effects of the usage of European Union (EU) money. Since institutional impact is more relevant at this stage of the policy process, Europeanization can be understood as downloading and cross-loading; the motto is 'no usages without impact'. The relevance of EU funding has been highlighted by academics and practitioners alike. As Rony Brauman, the Médecins sans Frontières (MSF) president from 1982 to 1994, states:

> Over the last 10 years there has been a growth in funding that has provided humanitarian CSOs with resources that they could never have dreamed of before! (...) This money comes from international institutions, primarily the European Economic Community (EEC).[1]

In spite of the importance of EU funding, there have not been many studies focusing on its impact on CSOs. A few scholars have, however, analyzed the effects of public funding on organizational capacity and advocacy activities at the national level (Harris and Rochester 2001; Queinnec and Ingalens 2004; Mosley 2012; Smith and Lipsky 1993). They conclude that the public funding of CSOs leads to a professionalization process that is usually considered a natural evolution for CSOs within the framework of a political system (Grossman and Saurugger 2006). Professionalization is generally defined in a very broad and ambiguous way. The concept takes different forms: the regulation of a specific profession, a bureaucratization process and the concentration of power among professionals (Eberwein and Saurugger 2009). The changes discussed in this chapter are related to the so-called process of professionalization, but, for the sake of clarity, this concept will often be replaced by more specific terms.

The EU's impact through public spending comes in two forms. First, the increase in public spending and the allocation of funding to specific policy fields imply a distribution of resources that can significantly alter CSOs' capacities and internal structures. Second, EU funding programs and calls for proposals include requirements for specific management techniques, namely, New Public Management (NPM). The data used in this chapter are derived from internal policy documents and semi-structured interviews with key representatives of CSOs from each of the three categories identified in Chapter 2 (exclusive, pluralist and sporadic CSOs).

1 EU funding and the growth of CSOs

The previous chapters showed how EU funding has contributed to the expansion of the voluntary sector in some policy fields strongly supported by the Commission, such as humanitarian aid. But what happened to individual CSOs that were active in these policy fields? How have they been transformed by this newfound wealth?

This comparative study gives an overview of the variations across countries and policy fields. One would expect that the CSOs that have grown the most with EU funds are those whose primary partner is the EU (exclusive CSOs). French humanitarian CSOs frequently fall into this category (see Chapter 2). In countries where national funding is more relevant than EU funding, one would expect that the EU has not had the same effects. This analysis also looks at effects at various points over a long timeframe. An EU-instigated expansion process among humanitarian CSOs is more relevant at times when EU funding opportunities are more generous.

1.1 EU funding in the 1980s and 1990s: Boosting immoderate growth?

During the 1980s and 1990s, the EU supported an extraordinary growth process for national CSOs, particularly, but not exclusively, humanitarian CSOs. Table 5.1 presents data from a few CSOs that were relatively small during the 1970s and early 1980s; these CSOs grew significantly

Table 5.1 The growth of CSOs: From exclusivism to pluralism

	Before EU funding	1980s–1990s	2000s	2011
MSF-France (1971)	Budget: 1.1 (1979) First contract with the EU in 1979	Budget: 34.3 (1990) 68.76% of public funding from the EU	Budget: 146 (2006) 43.88% of public funding from the EU (0.47% of total funding)	Budget: 221.2 57% of public funding from the EU (1.26% of total funding)
MDM-France (1980)	Budget: 15.24 (1990)	Budget: 45.73 (1999) 69% of public funding from the EU	Budget: 53 (2006) 29% of public funding from the EU (9% of total budget)	Budget: 57.3 49.1% of public funding from the EU (15.15% of total funding)
MSF-Spain (1986)	Budget: 0.16 (1988)	Budget: 8.6 (1993) 68.5% of public funding from the EU	Budget: 45 (2005) 22.47% of public funding from the EU (3% of total budget)	Budget: 110.66 26.6% of public funding from the EU (2.5% of total funding)
MPDL-Spain (1983)	Budget: 0.6 (1990) First contract with ECHO in 1993.	Budget: 12.7 (1998) 64% of public funding from the EU	Budget: 12.6 (2006) 94.5% of international funding from the EU (12.17% of total funding)	Budget: 12.6 5.37% of public funding from the EU (4.8% of total funding)

Note: Elaborated by the author with data from the CSOs' activity reports. All amounts are in million euros.

during the 1980s and early 1990s thanks to EU funding. For example, Médecins du Monde (MDM) had a rather small total budget at the beginning of the 1990s (15.24 million euros). In the 1990s, the EU became MDM's first institutional donor. Thanks to EU funding, MDM began to grow, and its budget reached 53.2 million euros in 2006.

Certain CSOs created during this period of expansion of EU funding opportunities, such as Aide Médicale d'Urgence or Équilibre, were sometimes dubbed 'ECHO babies' (Freyss 2004). As Table 5.1 shows, the EU has not just supported exclusive CSOs. Many CSOs that today are clearly pluralist were at that time strongly supported by the EU. During the 2000s, EU funding stagnated and thus these CSOs could no longer support such continued growth.

Looking at the amounts of funding provided helps in assessing the potential transformative effect of the EU. During the 1980s and early 1990s, the expansion of funding opportunities resulted in a situation in which the Commission was willing to promote the usages of EU funding (a seller-dominated market). However, during the late 1990s and 2000s, funding opportunities showed little change while the number of applicants continued to increase (a market characterized by seller scarcity). In some cases, this resulted in granting privileged support to a few suppliers (Kramer and Grossman 1987). During this new period, the EU promoted growth only for a lucky few.

EU-supported growth is more likely when certain conditions are met. First, small CSOs are more likely to engage in disproportionate growth. EU-instigated growth is also more likely in the absence of easy funding alternatives from public donors or from other patrons such as churches and political parties. Finally, growth also depends on the willingness of CSOs. Though a detailed description of CSOs' internal processes is beyond the scope of this book, the cases investigated suggest that the decision to extensively use institutional funding usually entails intense discussions within CSOs.

Even if the CSOs in Table 5.1 were very dependent on EU funding during the 1990s, many of them successfully diversified their funding during the late 1990s. The EU has contributed considerably to the development of many CSOs at an early stage in their growth, but once these CSOs attained a certain budget level, they became masters of their own destiny. The diversification of resources for these CSOs was facilitated by an increase in funding from other international donors and from national agencies during the 2000s.

Different CSOs have followed different trajectories depending on internal choices. Even if, for many CSOs, private donations have become as important as public funding, it is much more difficult to launch a process of quick growth from private sources alone. Fund-raising techniques for the acquisition of private funding (such as public marketing techniques) require a substantial investment (Vallaeys 2004). One successful example of funding diversification was shown by MSF-France. After a growth process clearly facilitated by EU institutional funding, this organization continued and consolidated its growth during the 2000s, basically through public marketing techniques (see Table 5.1 and Box 4 for details).

Box 4: The Growth of MSF-France in the 1970s–1980s

During its first years, MSF-France had a very limited budget. Its few resources mainly came from its members (for example, 10,000 French francs {1524 euros} from its 146 members in 1972) and from public campaigns. Even if MSF-France was growing steadily during the 1970s, this growth was very slow. For example, the most successful public campaign during this period only brought in around 80,000 French francs (12.196 euros). The turning point was in 1979, following the Cambodian crisis. The MSF budget multiplied tenfold during the last three months of that year. According to Rony Brauman, its president at the time, 'The embassies started jostling each other. They implored us to take their checks for 20,000, 50,000 or even 10,000 dollars. Then there was the Urgent Aid Fund from the EEC, whose existence we had been unaware of until that moment; they began offering us money. I remember quickly writing, in less than 10 minutes, a budget for the 500,000 ECUs that we obtained' (Vallaeys 2004: 361).

Thanks to this newfound affluence, MSF-France was able to hire its first two employees. During the 1980s and early 1990s, MSF-France supplemented its institutional funding (mainly from the EU, but also from the High Commissioner for Refugees) with public campaigns. Thanks to this combined approach, the budget of MSF-France hit 342 million FF in 1993, and, from that time on, institutional funding has represented only a very small portion of its total income.

Many other CSOs expanded their activities without diversifying their sources of income or making administrative changes that would allow them to handle greater resources. When the EU became more demanding in the mid-1990s, such CSOs were the most likely to collapse—as was the case of the French humanitarian CSO Équilibre. After reaching a budget of around 180 million FF (27,44 million euros) in 1994–1995, Équilibre had to file for bankruptcy on 8 June 1998, with a budgetary gap of 22 million FF (3.35 million euros).[2] According to the leaders of this CSO, their failure was related to the extremely fast growth encouraged by the European Communities and to the abrupt change in regulations. As one leader of this organization complained, 'After having been encouraged to grow so quickly, we should have benefited from more leniency from Europe.'[3]

Even if it was not as drastic for development CSOs, a few were also caught up in rapid growth. A good example is the British development CSO War on Want. After receiving EU funding throughout the 1980s, it had to file for bankruptcy in the early 1990s. According to the Court of Auditors, War on Want, 'having received a large increase in its financial resources, expanded its activities without making the necessary arrangements for proper administrative monitoring. Consequently, it became insolvent and had to suspend its activities' (1991: 6). In spite of these difficulties, both Équilibre and War on Want continue to exist today with the same names.

Many social CSOs experienced similar developments. However, since the rules for the funding of social CSOs depend on member states, the extent to which growth is promoted depends much more on national rules and provisions. In Spain, the European Social Fund (ESF) is distributed only among a few operators. Since 2000, five large CSOs have been in charge of a large program to fight against discrimination (Fundacion Vives 2006). In 2007 alone, 48 million euros were channeled to these CSOs, and these lucky few are more likely to have engaged in growth. That's the case, for example, with the Fundación Secretariado Gitano (FSG). Its total budget was around 5.6 million euros in 2000 and already at that time around 20 percent of that came from the EU. In 2001, FSG legally became a foundation and started to directly obtain ESF funding.[4] In 2006, its budget reached 18 million euros, of which 55 percent came from the EU.[5] In 2011, its budget was about 22 million euros, and primarily composed of funding from the ESF and the European Regional Development Fund (ERDF). In other countries, such as France, the situation is different. Most ESF money is distributed among a lot of intermediary bodies and participants (Sanchez Salgado 2009, 2013). Since funding is less concentrated, it cannot spark so much CSO growth.

The drastic growth experienced by all the above-mentioned CSOs cannot just be seen as adaptation; it did not merely entail the implementation of more activities, but also involved cognitive development (Radaelli 2003). There was a clear shift away from small organizations focused on symbolic action to medium-sized or large organizations engaged in effective action. This change, often referred to as professionalization, includes processes such as goal displacement, the transfer of power from voluntary leaders to permanent employees, the concentration of power among professionals and a less active implication of employees in the associative life (Harris et al. 2001; Roberts 2007; Salinas Ramos 2001; Smith and Lipsky 1993). Professionalization is also thought to hinder the prospects for comprehensive changes in policy-making (Mosley 2012; Saurugger 2006). This turn toward efficiency and accomplished action may also mean a loss of authenticity (Vedelago et al. 1996:134). Such transformations concern not only EU-based CSOs but also their partners based in third countries. In the words of a CSO representative:

> EU funding requirements are not adapted to small and medium-sized CSOs because the grants are too large for single projects. This also means that such CSOs' partner organizations in third world countries have to modify their administrative capacities. These CSOs are not used to implementing budgets or to functioning in a very formal way. We work with CSOs that are much more political and they do not have technical staff.[6]

The process of goal displacement should not be seen as an EU-imposed change of priorities. The EU simply makes money available, and CSOs with differing priorities just become more active in topics where it is easier to gain funding. A detailed account of the organizational changes within CSOs is beyond the scope of this study. The following examples of goal displacement illustrate how the priorities of CSOs are affected by increases in EU funding. The Movimiento por la Paz, el Desarme y la Libertad (MPDL), was originally a peace movement created in the wake of the peace-building processes in Central America. At the beginning of the 1990s, its focus shifted to humanitarian activities, as these were mostly funded by the EU.

The FSG, created in 1982, at first prioritized the promotion of employment, education, health and training. Before EU funding, each priority was allocated equal resources. After FSG started to manage the ESF-supported program ACCEDER, the largest portion of its budget was directed to fighting unemployment, as per EU priorities. Other priorities, such as education, got even less resources than before (FSG gave out 82 scholarships in 2000 and only 77 in 2006). A recent FSG slogan (used in their awareness campaign against discrimination) was 'Employment makes us equal'.[7] However, employment as promoted by the FSG does not make Roma equal; they have only access to certain technical professions such as auto repair, cooking and carpentry. An emphasis on education would enable the Spanish Roma population to have access to university degrees and, eventually, to jobs with greater qualifications.

1.2 A moderate use of EU funding

The redistribution of EU funding does not always lead to immoderate growth or to the sprouting up of new CSOs. To get a more complete view and avoid the typical EU bias of Europeanization studies, this section focuses on cases wherein the conditions that lead to fast growth are lacking.

The absorption of EU funding

Many CSOs, especially pluralist CSOs, were already quite large in the early 1980s and thus their growth was not instigated by the EU but rather by other donors and patrons. Public support for CSOs is common at the national level in many countries and policy areas. And many CSOs, such as Christian Aid, Caritas or the Comité Catholique contre la Faim et pour le Développement (CCFD), obtain most of their resources from churches or directly from worshippers. For example, most of CCFD's funding is collected at Mass. Every year during Lent, each diocese collects money for the CCFD for one or two days. With this strong support from worshipers, religious CSOs are much less dependent on public funding. As Table 5.2 shows, in 2012, only 4.7 percent of CCFD's total resources came from public grants (CCFD 2013).

Table 5.2 Resources of pluralist CSOs

	First years	1980s	2000s	2012
CCFD	27 million FF (4 million euros) (1976)	116 million FF (18 million euros)	37 million euros, public funding was 7.9% of total budget	40 million euros, public funding are 4.7% of total budget
Oxfam	100,000 pounds (1950)	16 million pounds (1982), EU and UK funding was 10% of total resources	189 million pounds	385 million pounds (2011–2012), around 41% from public donors (31% of public funding from the EU)

A third group of CSOs has generated significant income from private sources through extensive fund-raising and/or commercial activities. That's the case, for example, of Oxfam, whose private funding comes primarily through direct marketing techniques and fair trade shops. Interestingly, Oxfam's budget has also expanded during the 2000s, mainly due to an increase in public funding (Oxfam 2012). While in the 1980s public funding only represented a very small portion of its total budget, in 2012 it represented 41 percent. Oxfam is one of the lucky few that has benefited from privileged access to European Commission Humanitarian Office (ECHO) grants during the 2000s (as well as from the Department for International Development (DFID)). The example of Oxfam also shows that the boundary between exclusive and pluralist CSOs is constantly moving.

Even if the EU has contributed to the growth of the above-mentioned CSOs, such growth can be better understood as an adaptation rather than a radical transformation. Pluralist CSOs get a great deal of EU funding. It is also very likely that they have developed their activities in areas strongly supported by the EU. However, it would be difficult to conclude that this funding has radically altered their basic organizational structure. Quite interestingly, the use of EU funding hasn't contributed to 'a race to the bottom' (Smith and Lipsky 1993), a phenomenon in which relatively large CSOs reduce the quality of their services or target beneficiaries in order to have a better chance at obtaining public funding. This effect, which has been identified in social CSOs in the United States, has also been observed in Europe, but it does not seem to be directly related to the use of public funding. Rather, it is related to the introduction of cost efficiency in social services delivery.

Even if it is less common, pluralist CSOs can also become quite large in the absence of public support. One good example is Amnesty International (AI) (Besset 1991). In 1961, the budget of AI's British section was about 7359 pounds, which came mainly from membership dues. Today AI's international secretariat is still mainly funded by private donations from its national sections. Its total budget was around 11 million pounds in 1990 and around 21 million pounds in 2010 (Amnesty International 2010a).[8] But in spite of the popularity of AI—it won the Nobel Prize in 1977—its growth has remained rather modest when compared with that of publicly funded CSOs. Note that even if AI does not depend on public funding, its agenda and activities have probably also been affected by the use of corporate marketing techniques, which can also lead to organizational changes such as goal displacement.

Small organizations and EU funding

Of course not all CSOs in Europe have grown, whether due to lack of willingness or lack of capacity. Lack of willingness is a more plausible explanation for the 1980s and 1990s, since CSOs applying for EU funding did not necessarily need to meet high professional standards. For the late 1990s, lack of capacity is also important. At this time, EU funding rules and procedures became much more complex, and many CSOs decided not to apply after a cost–benefit analysis. These sporadic CSOs may also have been more picky, less willing to tolerate goal displacement or uninterested in growing their organizations significantly. Many of these medium-sized CSOs started applying for EU funding when it was already too late (when the market was already characterized by seller scarcity) or they applied for funding in more competitive budget lines. This was true more often for development and human rights CSOs than for others. An example is the Spanish CSO, Alternativa Solidaria Plenty. In 1997 this organization obtained an EU grant for the first time, in support of its work with indigenous peoples in Nicaragua. In 1998 it submitted another proposal, but this one was rejected. After this failure, the CSO considered its chances of obtaining EU funding very low, and decided to direct its efforts to alternative public donors.[9] For these sporadic CSOs, the changes that resulted from obtaining EU grants were short-term and limited. This Europeanization process should be considered absorption or accommodation, rather than radical transformation. In the absence of sufficient public funding, sporadic CSOs tend to remain relatively small.

A few CSOs explained that their lack of interest in EU funding was for ideological reasons, rather than due to a cost–benefit analysis. These CSOs placed much more the emphasis on advocacy activities. However, while a few respondents emphasized a lack of willingness, it is difficult to know what would have happened if there were EU or national funds supporting advocacy activities on their topics of interest. A CSO falling within this category might argue as follows:

> The EU promotes racism in certain situations. We are therefore fighting the EU. (...) We cannot trust them. They implement these heinous laws. Programs proposed by governments cannot be used to fight the policies that they themselves implement. They can create new funding opportunities but that is not useful. (...) The EU often funds bogus projects. (...) The only way to benefit from EU funding is at the margins; you could get involved in an EU project, buy a

computer and hire someone to work for a few hours on that project, but then also use these resources to do other things.[10]

2 The EU role in the promotion of New Public Management among CSOs

The EU does not only shape CSOs through its distribution of resources, it also shapes CSOs more directly through its funding requirements and conditions. Through these requirements, the EU promotes specific practices among CSOs. Europeanization is here understood as downloading or as a transfer of practices (Bache 2000; Bomberg and Peterson 2000). The EU requirements examined in this section concern transparency, accountability and efficiency of aid delivery and service provision—they focus on administrative capacity and management. When EU requirements are more prescriptive, as in this section, one would expect less variation among CSOs. However, CSOs have proven very capable of adapting to identical prescriptions in a variety of ways. This section briefly presents the main EU requirements and then looks at the extent to which they have been adopted by CSOs.

2.1 From flexibility to New Public Management

During the first period (the 1980s and early 1990s), EU grants did not include many conditions. The seller-dominated market of the time was not conducive to rigorous funding conditions. As Tim Clark, head of the Civil Society Unit at DG DEVCO affirmed in 2000, 'For the first ten years, there were no formal criteria for NGO co-funding' (Clarke 2000). The Commission was guided by principles such as efficiency, expediency and flexibility. The capacity of CSOs to carry out the work in an appropriate manner was trusted.[11] In the domain of external cooperation, the first general conditions for all kinds of projects were adopted in 1982 (European Parliament 1986).[12] They only included a few general principles, such as ensuring the participation of local communities, an integral approach, and ensuring the viability and continuity of the projects. In its first general conditions for cofunding, adopted in 1988 (European Commission 1988), the Commission imposed a certain number of requirements, such as a clearly specified design for projects, budgetary provisions and ex post evaluation. However, these first requirements were applied with great flexibility. The Commission also wanted to offer a quick cofinancing system and was willing to adapt existing funding opportunities to the needs of the recipients (European Commission 1994b: 1).

The few requirements imposed by the Commission at that time may have contributed to an increase in red tape for the few CSOs that followed reporting conditions to the letter. For the others, the Court of Auditors signaled that there were many gaps in grantees' reports. According to the Court, a few CSOs did not even do analytical accounting, which made any kind of evaluation impossible (Court of Auditors 1991).

During the mid-1990s, the Commission progressively adopted NPM techniques. Following the most widespread definition, NPM tools are characterized by the application of corporate management techniques to the public sector. Understood in this sense, NPM refers to an individualistic type of management developed by utilitarian thinkers during the 19th century (Hood 1998). But for many authors, NPM is a much more all-encompassing concept referring to a variety of innovations in management. The most popular definition places excessive emphasis on efficiency (the efficiency drive model), but other variations of NPM (for example, the downsizing and decentralization model) emphasize other principles. The management tools adopted by the Commission—and presented here—primarily reflect the efficiency drive model, even if some aspects resonate more with other models. NPM tools have been echoed in the Commission's calls for proposals and policy documents, and have thus been transferred to CSOs. During the mid-1990s, several Commission departments, such as DG Employment and DG ECHO, introduced NPM tools for the management of EU funding, such as sound management, a programmatic approach and monitoring, auditing and evaluation.

Sound management has been a top requirement since the publication of the Vade-Mecum on Grant Management in 1998 (European Commission 1998a). It included both binding procedural rules and some optional managerial practices. To justify the promotion of sound management provisions, the Commission argued as follows:

> Managing public funds always carries a special responsibility. Not only must the taxpayer's money be spent in a judicious and economic way, but spending decisions must also obey sound rules that are transparent to the public and to potential beneficiaries.
> (European Commission 1998a: 3)

One of the explicit conditions for obtaining an EU grant is sufficient financial and technical capacity. Since 1998, all potential applicants have had to provide their accounting for the previous financial year and an audit certificate from a registered accountancy firm. The Vade-Mecum includes very specific provisions on the eligibility of costs, in-kind provisions and other related issues.

The programmatic approach, or Project Cycle Management (PCM), is a tool to guide project planning and management. It has been used since the mid-1990s by some Commission services, such as DG Employment and the External Action Services. According to the interpretation by these DGs, PCM includes the Logical Framework Approach (LFA) and a logical framework matrix:

> The LFA should be thought of as an aid to thinking. It allows information to be analyzed and organized in a structured way, so that important questions can be asked, weaknesses identified and decision-makers can make informed decisions based on their improved understanding of the project rationale, its intended objectives and the means by which objectives will be achieved.
> (European Commission 2004a: 6)

The Commission has published a variety of manuals to promote PCM, including sophisticated and detailed instructions, basic templates to be filled in by CSOs and tools such as SWOT (Strengths, Weaknesses, Opportunities and Threats) analysis, quality tests and spider diagrams. NPM principles have not been equally adopted by all Commission services. DG Education and Culture's calls for proposals are considerably less complex, but the amounts of funding given are also less significant.

Last but not the least, during the 1990s the Commission increased its demands for monitoring, auditing and evaluation. During the first years, most evaluations were ex post, which is also reflected in the 1998 Vade-Mecum. During the 1990s, pioneering DGs (DG Employment and External Relations, but also DG Research) introduced more innovative evaluation tools. The Sound and Efficient Management initiative[13] proposed a transversal approach to evaluation. Based on this initiative, Commission services adopted complex evaluation techniques based on criteria designed by the Organization for Economic Cooperation and Development (OECD). On top of the common ex post evaluations, Commission services also arranged ex ante and midterm evaluations. Evaluations generally included a financial audit and emphasized values such as the legality of the projects and their efficiency, effectiveness and economy.

2.2 NPM techniques and CSOs receptiveness: Toward convergence in Europe?

Due to Commission requirements, many CSOs were confronted with NPM techniques, often for the first time. All CSOs applying for EU funding were expected to develop sound management and project planning techniques. Some CSOs have since adopted these management techniques for their overall activities, while others only use them in a superficial way.

A European consensus on NPM techniques

A non-negligible number of CSOs in Europe, including the largest and most popular CSOs, adopted NPM techniques in the late 1990s. Examples of organizations that adopted the project cycle approach include the MPDL (in 1998), MDM-France and MDM-Spain (in 1999), Caritas (in 2001 or perhaps before) and Oxfam (in 2001). These CSOs adopted NPM techniques for all of their activities, not just for the projects supported by the EU or other donors with similar requirements. For example, in reference to the introduction of strategic planning techniques, MDM-Spain affirmed that its new model for all activities of the organization would be based on deductive and strategic thinking and operational planning (MDM-Spain 1999). The extent to which individual organizations are transformed was also reflected in the following quote from MDM-France:

> The requirements (that public donors) impose upon us include a lot of rigor in our accounts, in terms of financial transparency, content of the actions and financial reporting and accountability. Some new words, such as self-assessment of the quality of our missions and financial and qualitative accountability and monitoring, must from now on be an integral part of our vocabulary and projects.
> (MDM-France 1997: 85)

Some CSOs explicitly mentioned in their policy documents that they adopted NPM to meet EU requirements. For example, Caritas Europe, in a discussion paper on its Strategic Organizational Development Approach (SODA), said that the reasons for adopting strategic planning include 'European Commission requirements on managerial and organizational ability of humanitarian aid and development agencies' (Caritas Europe 2002: 4). Caritas also stated that there might not be any direct requirements from European institutions in this respect but that this was one of the criteria for determining the suitability of CSOs for community funding.

The transfer to NPM can be understood as cognitive development (Radaelli 2003), or in other words, as a real transformation of the CSOs' management system. CSOs under analysis have not only introduced NPM into their overall activities, they have also become convinced of its value and effectiveness. As an EU official put it, 'ECHO wants CSOs to be professional. But CSOs also want to be professional in order to offer the best services to people. ECHO moreover wants to respect the integrity of each partner.'[14] This view is also reflected in some CSO policy papers:

> One should keep in mind that the introduction of a systematic approach for improvement of a management system also substantially improves the consistency in performance of the entire organization. It sets up a firm background for planning and decision-making, and thus, should result in more efficiency and effectiveness. If applied properly, such a system allows one to do the 'real field work' better, in a way that is more focused and probably brings more satisfaction to end-users and other stakeholders.
>
> (Caritas Europe 2002: 2–3)

EU NPM requirements are quite specific and there was no resistance from CSOs. Thus, all of the conditions for imposed convergence were met (Andersen 2004). Note that this transformation took place after a learning and socialization process, which will be further discussed in the next section. According to a Commission representative, at first CSOs found it difficult to deal with PCM, but after a time, they agreed that such principles were very useful for their daily work.[15] It could be argued that CSOs are adopting such techniques only to get more funding. But if this were the case, NPM techniques would only have been adopted superficially and would not have been adopted for the overall strategy of the organization, since that is not required by any donor.

The EU has played a significant role in the promotion of NPM among CSOs in Europe. However, its more specific contributions to the shaping of CSOs depend on certain factors, namely, the type of CSOs in question and the country of origin. The EU could only promote NPM effectively among those CSOs with which it had direct and regular funding relationships. Thus, the EU is clearly the most relevant influence for exclusive CSOs. And it has also been crucial for pluralist CSOs such as Caritas since the role of the EU is explicitly mentioned in its reports.

However, there is a lot of evidence that pluralist CSOs are also influenced by other donors. For example, CARE-UK has been following the model of its American counterpart, CARE-US, which published its own manual on PCM according to the requirements of US Agency for International Development (USAID) and Australian Agency for International Development (AUSAID), the development agencies from the United States and Australia, respectively.

The EU's shaping of CSOs also varies from country to country. The EU's role as a catalyst has been particularly relevant in the EU member states that were less familiar with the NPM paradigm. For example, the EU contributed a lot to the diffusion of NPM techniques in France and Spain, where NPM techniques were adopted much later than at the EU level (and in some cases have still not been adopted). As one representative of a French CSO put it, 'European funding allows for the improvement of administrative management, accounting tools and evaluation methods. The conditions at the European level are much more demanding than national requirements.'[16]

By contrast, for many UK-based CSOs, the EU was not the primary reason for the adoption of these techniques, since the United Kingdom integrated NPM long before the EU. Thus, while it contributed to the diffusion of NPM, the EU was joining an already ongoing global trend. The familiarity of UK CSOs with NPM techniques could explain why, as a general rule, UK CSOs were usually much more open than CSOs from other countries to the adoption of NPM techniques. According to a UK CSO representative, the pre-NPM system was easier for CSOs that were already in an inner circle, but it is was far less transparent.[17]

2.3 A widely promoted learning process

NPM techniques and EU rules were not adopted by CSOs in a day; there was a learning/socialization process during the late 1990s and 2000s. This process included training sessions for CSO staff, volunteers and leaders. Large CSOs had the capacity to organize their own internal training sessions; this was the case, for example, with Caritas Europe. The European sections of Caritas created a capacity-building working group in charge of developing fund-raising and quality control skills among its members. This group provided training sessions on strategic planning and project management. Training sessions were also offered by European peak associations and by the Commission itself. For example, EuronAid organized a training session for 18 Oxfam employees in 2001 that emphasized EU management techniques.[18]

Some of the training sessions offered by peak associations were sponsored by the Commission, especially during the late 1990s. At that time, EU-funded sessions reached many small and medium-sized CSOs. One of the most well-known initiatives was the Program for the Support of Co-Financing for externally oriented CSOs (Programme d'Appui au Co-Financement—PACO), in force from 1997 to 1999. Managed by the European development peak association CLONG, the program intended to improve the quality of funding applications and evaluation reports (CLONG 1997a). During this period, there were around 2000 PACO training centers all over Europe. In 1998 alone, PACO experts examined around 1700 project proposals and offered training sessions to staff from about 2320 CSOs hailing from all EU member states (CLONG 1999). PACO's focus was primarily sound financial management, to the expense of other relevant subjects such as the quality of projects (South Research et al. 2000). Similar programs have been implemented by EU-friendly DGs, such as DG Employment and DG ECHO.[19] However, in these cases training sessions were offered only to CSOs that had already obtained EU funding. In the words of an EU official:

> Action programs have important requirements about project cycle management. This is very important because DGs have to report to member states. At the beginning CSOs find it very complicated but at the end they find it very useful or at least this is what they say. The Commission has paid several consultants to provide training for CSOs. The consultants went to visit CSOs and told them what to do.[20]

The Commission is not currently supporting overarching projects like PACO, but, interestingly, such training efforts have not always stopped. In the absence of EU-wide training programs, some national peak associations have set up their own ways to offer training and diffuse information on NPM techniques, sometimes, but not always, with the support of the Commission. One good example is BOND, the British peak association for development CSOs. Since the end of PACO, the British peak association has been offering training activities on PCM, the LFA and planning and evaluation.[21] These training sessions focus on the EU but also cover other donors relevant to UK CSOs, primarily DFID. BOND still offers training sessions on fund-raising and effectiveness, but now it charges for this service.[22] Coordination Sud, the French peak association, also currently offers training sessions on contract management with a specific focus on EuropeAid. These sessions aim to introduce the program and the main EU requirements. They also give specific advice on contract management.[23] Similar training activities have been developed by the German and Italian national peak associations (South Research et al. 2000).

Many other national peak associations do not regularly offer such training sessions and thus CSOs from these countries are expected to be less competitive for EU funding. For example, the Spanish peak association, CONGDE, has offered training sessions to CSOs since 2007 (CONGDE 2012). And according to its activity reports, CONGDE has been offering training on EU funding requirements for only the last one or two years (CONGDE 2013).

Training workshops on fund-raising and PCM have become so popular that they are now also offered by for-profit entities, especially consultancy firms. At the EU level, South Research is a good example. It offers training sessions for CSOs that 'want to integrate project cycle management (PCM) into their activities to meet external (donor) requirements'.[24] This consultancy firm is often hired by the Commission itself to carry out evaluations of Commission budget lines, which increases its reputation. Other examples of consultancy firms offering training sessions on PCM to non-profits are European Consulting Brussels,[25] MDF Training and Consultancy[26] and Inprogress.[27]

2.4 Non-Europeanized CSOs: Old Public Management?

Even if there is a general trend toward the integration of NPM among the largest development and humanitarian CSOs, one would expect non-publically funded CSOs to be less influenced by such techniques. For a more complete understanding of the role of the EU in the diffusion of NPM techniques among CSOs, attention is now turned to sporadic CSOs (that is, those that only occasionally obtain EU funding) and to CSOs that haven't obtained EU grants.

Many CSOs have only adopted EU requirements in a temporary and superficial way. For them, PCM and sophisticated analytical accountability are used in a cosmetic way to ensure the eligibility of their applications. These CSOs follow the Commission's requirements, but only do so formally to get their grants. To this purpose they may have developed a strategy of isolation and symbolic transformation (Lang 2003). In these cases, organizations (CSOs but also administrative bodies) develop two parallel structures: a formal structure to meet donors' requirements and a second informal structure reflecting their daily practices. This strategy is adopted when restrictions are imposed that the CSO is not willing or able to meet. As may be expected, it is hard to find CSOs that admit that they are only superficially meeting EU requirements. However, in sharp contrast to the enthusiasm of the CSOs quoted in the previous section, many medium-sized sporadic CSOs do admit that meeting EU requirements is cumbersome and complex. They dislike the rigidity, the complexity and the contradictions of PCM. In the words of a CSO representative:

> Reality is very complex and the LFA does not always reflect this. When something moves in reality, something else also moves. Everything is interrelated. Other CSOs think that the LFA is very useful, including modifying everything each time some factor changes. But in practice, if you want to do all of this you have to make a lot of effort. Many CSOs are not doing this. They set up the LFA but they never update it.[28]

These CSOs have not adopted NPM into their overall strategies and have not integrated these principles to the same extent as the exclusive and pluralist CSOs mentioned earlier. It is reasonable to assume that for these sporadic CSOs there have been processes of absorption (Radaelli 2003) rather than long-term transformations. It would be interesting to reflect on the sustainability of such symbolic transformations. These ambiguous situations may reflect the early stages of a learning process in which there is tension between the old and new management paradigms. After a transition period, the learning process could be successful, in which case these CSOs will join the European funding consensus. But if the CSOs are not eventually convinced by the new paradigm, they will look instead for alternative sources of funding.

Last but not the least, what has happened to CSOs that have not received EU funding? Have they also adopted the same management techniques? As shown in the previous chapters, most human rights CSOs working within the EU borders do not get EU funding. Some of them also use analytical accountability, mainly to meet national requirements, but they have not adopted NPM techniques to the same extent. Examples include national human rights CSOs such as the Ligue Française des Droits de l'Homme (LDH), the National Council for Civil Liberties and the Liga Española de Derechos Humanos. More often than not, these CSOs explicitly reject the adoption of NPM techniques, citing the vague notion of professionalization. For example, the LDH never introduced NPM techniques, even after a significant transformation process that took place at the beginning of the 2000s and that culminated in the revision of their statutes. According to this French human rights CSO, 'On the eve of the 100th anniversary of the [French] 1901 Law on

Associations, it is good to highlight the vitality of the voluntary sector as a culmination of citizens' commitment and not abandon engagement in favor of ever-growing professionalization' (LDH 2001: 181).

All in all, empirical data support the hypothesis that the introduction of NPM tools among CSOs has largely been due to public donors, and, among them, the EU has played a prominent role. Most CSOs that regularly obtain EU funding have adopted NPM techniques, while CSOs that do not get any funding, or that get it more sporadically, have not developed those techniques to the same extent. But, there are some exceptions to this trend. One example is AI. Even though AI has occasionally obtained public funding (including EU funding) for awareness-raising activities, it could be argued that it is a sporadic CSO in terms of funding sources. Since the late 1990s, AI has adopted a strategic planning approach that aims to increase its effectiveness. AI work is now based on an integrated strategic plan. The last version of this plan, running from 2010 to 2016, sets priorities and goals against which to measure progress and 'provides a basis for systematic evaluation of progress, including transparency in reporting' (Amnesty International 2010b: 2). So, AI has adopted strategic planning even if it does not get much EU funding. In the words of an AI official:

> As the world becomes larger and lines of conflict more complex, research is more complicated. (...) This entails a lot of work and if you still have the same budget, it is not possible to produce information of quality. You need strategic planning and to concentrate your efforts in certain countries. Doing this was difficult internally, because of course it is difficult to say that we are not going to work on a certain country.[29]

It is not surprising that CSOs like AI have adopted NPM techniques. AI presents itself as a highly professionalized CSO. It has regular interactions with the largest CSOs and donors. The adoption of strategic planning and evaluation techniques may also be a way to increase its reputation and credibility among public authorities.

2.5 From NPM to New Civic Management?

The introduction of NPM among CSOs in Europe has repercussions. Management techniques are not simply policy tools designed to reach goals more effectively. They are not axiologically neutral, since they imply specific interpretations of social reality and a specific conception of regulation (Lascoumes and Le Gales 2004). Most prescriptions related to NPM ('the efficiency drive' model) come directly from the corporate world, and thus they might not be a great fit for the voluntary sector. When emphasis is placed on quality and effectiveness, less attention is given to other values such as democracy, participation, philanthropy, selflessness, solidarity, citizenship and responsibilization (Vedelago et al. 1996). The adoption of management tools inspired by the individualist model can displace other models such as the egalitarian (Hood 1998). NPM techniques may result in much more effective CSOs but, paradoxically, this could be at the expense of the core values of the voluntary sector.

Sound management and control of expenses is certainly essential for financial accountability but whether it produces better outcomes is still an open question. It is not certain that principles like transparency and participation are always best served through the application of sound management rules. As a CSO representative put it:

> The paradox is that for a large organization, the best way to avoid transparency is by being transparent. That's because of the complexity.... For example:
>
> —'Could you give me a list [with some specific information]?'
>
> —'Sure, just take this 500-page print-out.'[30]

As this example shows, too much information may not serve the principle of transparency if the level of complexity is such that it becomes impossible for the general public and stakeholders to understand who is funding what and how money is actually being spent. The most relevant information is often buried by confusing digressions on refunds, unliquidated obligations and expenditure adjustments.

NPM techniques such as PCM impose measurable and short-term goals, based on easily identifiable needs that are reducible to indicators. These requirements privilege governments' definitions of effectiveness above that of CSOs (Roberts 2007). Quality and efficiency are at the center of this approach, at the expense of the pertinence of the action. And in some circumstances, the most appropriate action may not be the most efficient. The adjustment of aims to attainable outcomes may in fact lead to actions that are less relevant to the situation at hand. For example, a focus on small-scale objectives places an emphasis on 'helping victims' rather than social change. Analyses of social, economic and political contexts are thus often neglected.

When indicators are used, top priority is given to meeting numerical goals, and the initial objective that the indicators were supposed to serve can be forgotten (Castellanet 2003). Indicators are often criticized for their rigidity and their inability to adapt to the complexity of reality. As may be expected, it was not possible to find examples of such excesses through analysis of policy documents, nor from interviews. However, some excesses have been reported in the press or in policy reports by former humanitarian and development CSO employees. For example, some former employees of a humanitarian CSO said that the organization refused sugar to a person in danger of death because the strategic plan said that this sugar was only meant to be used by expatriates.[31] And in another example, a absenteeism at community planning meetings organized by another CSO was rather shiftily solved by offering money to ensure attendance (Castellanet 2003: 12). In a case like this, the indicator may show quantitative improvement but the real problem, that is, local famers' lack of motivation and engagement, is not really addressed.

The move toward efficiency and quality can also neglect to take into account the views of the target populations and constituencies. The productive mode of reasoning and the focus on expertise assumes a conceptual superiority of offer over demand. Thus, professional or effective action tends to treat target populations as objects and not as actors with specific demands and grievances (Vedelago et al. 1996). CSOs are aware of the dangers of the PMC approach, as reflected in the following statement:

> Quite often a contradiction is felt between doing 'real field work', which of course is the main purpose of charity organizations, and the time load and resources devoted to management issues for building and developing a structured approach. There is a call for the introduction of some standards and at the same time a doubt concerning their bureaucratic nature and consequential risks of limiting flexibility. There is a feeling of dilemma between two quality approaches—a business-like one and another that is based on human rights and includes codes of conduct.
>
> (Caritas Europe 2002: 2)

Even if NPM may in some cases lead to 'professional fundamentalism', on the other side of the spectrum there may also be a 'voluntary fundamentalism' as well (Vedelago et al. 1996). Most organizations occupy a space between these two extremes, and some organizations succeed better than others in ensuring the right balance. Certain organizations have indeed developed innovative ways to deal with these dilemmas, contributing to a 'new civic management' that brings together the principles of NPM and some of the social imperatives of the voluntary sector. For example, many CSOs are now developing social auditing techniques, which aim to account for the many relevant factors that are not reflected in numeric accountability.

Conclusion

Through funding schemes, the EU can promote significant changes among CSOs, even affecting their core values and goals. Public support for CSOs has always raised questions about the potential risks to their autonomy. EU-funded CSOs are often seen as quasi-public service providers, disconnected from the grassroots level. This chapter has shown that the picture is much more nuanced. Even if EU funding schemes and requirements shape CSOs' organizational forms and management techniques, their effects are far from being homogeneous due to the diversity within the voluntary sector. The EU had a huge impact on the growth of many—mainly humanitarian—CSOs through a distribution of resources. However, most of these CSOs have never acted merely as EU service providers. They have developed strategies to diversify their resources, following up on their members concerns. The EU has also promoted the use of sound management and of NPM techniques, thus requiring the professionalization of many CSOs. The EU has successfully promoted the idea that NPM techniques positively impact the quality of service delivery. These management tools are promoted because they are considered to be the most efficient by the most prestigious donors and commentators. Many—if not most—large CSOs have also been convinced by this new paradigm, so shall we conclude that their autonomy is compromised?

It would be difficult to answer this question completely in the affirmative, since the effects of EU funding have been far from homogeneous. Many CSOs have not adopted mainstream management techniques and many others have only adopted them in a superficial manner. One of the major characteristics of the voluntary sector is its intrinsic diversity, and it is very unlikely that a single paradigm will ever prevail.

The success of NPM techniques among CSOs is, however, remarkable, and it is still important to discuss what these changes mean for the core values of the voluntary sector in general. According to many critics, the focus on effectiveness and quality diverts attention from some of the core values of the voluntary sector, such as participation and solidarity. However, many CSOs are well aware of these challenges and are currently developing new ways to adjust NPM techniques to voluntary values, perhaps paving the way for a new form of New Civic Management. The EU could contribute a lot to this new paradigm, if it were convinced that more attention should be given to such values.

6
CSOs and Identity Building: Cheerleaders for European Integration?

Introduction

It's not surprising that the European Union (EU), like many other donors, has promoted New Public Management (NPM) and administrative rules among civil society organizations (CSOs). Much more peculiar is the emphasis placed on the promotion of Europe. The EU has funded CSOs to raise its profile as an international donor and, more interestingly, to diffuse European values and ideas and to increase its legitimacy and reputation. In sharp contrast to member states and to most international organizations, the EU has always had a double mission. As the first referral of the Treaty of Rome says, European Economic Community (EEC) member states were 'determined to lay the foundations of an ever-closer union among the peoples of Europe'. Given this imperative, many EU policies pursue several often incompatible objectives (Majone 2010). On the one hand, EU policies are passed to solve problems and, on the other hand, they are also a means to promote European integration. It is often assumed that EU officials consider CSOs to be vehicles for selling the EU to its citizens or to be cheerleaders for European integration (Cullen 2010). A closer analysis of this presumed function shows that such instrumentalization of CSOs is far from obvious. From the perspective of EU officials, many members of the Parliament and CSO representatives, the EU promotes information and communication activities to raise awareness of EU policies and civic participation and engagement. Is it legitimate to engage CSOs in the promotion of the values of one specific political system? Should CSOs' role be limited to watchdog activities?

This chapter first gives an overview of the mechanisms that the EU is using to promote a European identity and sense of belonging. Focus then turns to how CSOs have interpreted EU requirements and rules, with particular attention on the degrees of Europeanization that this process has entailed. Here it is much easier to attribute such changes directly to the EU, since there are no other international donors or member states promoting a European identity. The ultimate aim of the EU is to reach EU citizens. Thus, the Europeanization process concerns not only the CSOs under analysis, but, much more broadly, European citizens. The data for this analysis came from EU documents—including policy papers, manuals and evaluation reports ordered by the Commission—and from semi-structured interviews.[1] This chapter illustrates its main arguments with examples from CSOs from the different categories presented in Chapter 2 (exclusive, pluralist and sporadic).

1 CSOs' potential contribution to identity building

Supporting CSOs is not a traditional way to build identity or promote nationalism. Most nation-states have customarily turned to other means such as public education, media and military service. The choice of CSOs has certainly been inspired by functionalist and neo-functionalist assumptions (Deutsch 1968; Haas 1968). According to these classical theories of regional integration, interest groups and CSOs are fundamental in the creation of a polity. This section discusses first how the EU has supported visibility actions and the organization of discussions on EU topics. Attention is also paid to a much more indirect, but perhaps more effective way of promoting solidarity and a sense of identity among Europeans, that is, transnational cooperation. The promotion of EU values or EU visibility can be considered an attempt at downloading, at least at first sight. By contrast, one would expect that the promotion of transnational cooperation, which basically consists of intercultural exchanges, is better understood as cross-loading.

1.1 Promoting European values and European integration

Many of the first budget lines set up by the Commission during the 1970s clearly reflect the dual aspects of EU policymaking. For example, since 1979 DG DEVCO has financed awareness-raising and development-related educational activities for European citizens. On top of the issues that have had to be promoted (for example, development cooperation), all awareness-raising activities have had to include a European dimension. According to the first regulation, published in 1998:

> Public awareness and information operations in all Member States, to be implemented under Article 1(2), shall be targeted at clearly defined groups, deal with clearly defined issues, be founded on a balanced analysis and a sound knowledge of the issues and groups targeted, and *involve a European dimension*.
>
> (Council of Ministers 1998: 2) [Emphasis added]

Even if there was a clear interest in promoting a European dimension among CSOs, EU institutions did not at first give many details about the specific content of such a so-called 'European dimension'. During the first years, this was interpreted in a variety of ways, often from the bottom-up. To give a European dimension to their activities, CSOs organized workshops and conferences about EU policies and engaged in intercultural exchanges and transnational networking.

During the early 1990s, in the wake of the Maastricht Treaty and the creation of the EU, there was new interest in relaunching the integration process. Around 1994, the EU established the first initiative aimed specifically at the promotion of European values. Launched by Jacques Delors, the Soul for Europe Initiative aimed to give an ethical and spiritual dimension to the EU. Jacques Delors said, 'If in the next ten years we have not managed to give a soul to Europe, to give it spirituality and meaning, the game will be up.'[2] This budget line only concerned religious communities at first, but it soon evolved into a broader funding scheme directed to all kinds of CSOs that advanced European values.[3]

The CSOs funded were expected to implement activities adhering to the values of the European integration process, including, for example, cultural diversity and European citizenship. In 2004, all budget lines related to the promotion of European values were joined together in the Europe for Citizens program. Its general objectives included developing a sense of European identity, fostering a sense of citizen ownership of the EU and enhancing tolerance and mutual understanding (ECORYS 2013). Its total budget has increased in recent years from 72 million euros for three years (for the period 2004–2006) to 215 million (for the period 2007–2013). In a context of economic crisis and budget cuts, the budget for this program was expected to fall, but cuts have been less harsh than expected.[4] This program has been widely supported not only in the Commission but also in the Parliament, since it has been seen as a very relevant instrument for promoting democratic engagement and civic participation.[5]

1.2 EU visibility and political advertising

While the promotion of discussions on EU topics seems to serve the principle of European integration, EU visibility is much more related to the legitimation of EU action. The principle underlying visibility actions is that the EU would be seen as more legitimate if its citizens were aware of the 'good' policies that are being implemented. Visibility actions, if successful, would also increase positive feelings toward Europe, and toward the process of European integration.

When the Commission considers that its policies are relevant and popular, it includes requirements in its calls for proposals and contracts to ensure their visibility. DG ECHO, created with the specific purpose of increasing the visibility of EU external action, has been a pioneer in this area. Its visibility requirements are specified in the Framework partnership agreement signed between DG ECHO and CSOs:

> The Humanitarian Organization commits to highlight the European Union nature of the humanitarian aid and to promote the understanding of humanitarian values, in particular in the European Union and in third countries where the Union funds major Actions. In information and communication activities, the affected people shall be presented as dignified human beings, not as objects of pity.
> (European Commission 2009b: 8)

The degree of detail in ECHO visibility guidelines is quite impressive. Visibility is mandatory, though there are some exceptions for security reasons. According to DG ECHO, the purpose of the visibility section is to promote the association of humanitarian responses with the EU. DG ECHO states that 'basic visibility goes beyond the displays of logos. It also entails highlighting the European Commission as the donor in media interviews, press releases, etc.' (European Commission 2009a: 7). The Commission provides extensive information about visibility activities in a manual. For each one of these activities, there are specific basic requirements, including regulations on colors and a detailed geometrical description of the EU emblem. Similar requirements are included in other funding programs, such as external action activities (European Commission 2010a) and actions supported by the European Social Fund (European Commission 1996b).

Many member states also include visibility requirements in their funding schemes, while others refuse to advertise their involvement in aid delivery for philosophical or ethical reasons (Evaluation Partnership 2007: 15). According to the latter group, aid should be provided on the basis of need and making beneficiaries aware that their country has provided funding would go against this basic principle.

Since the early 1990s, the EU has been more insistent on the use of political marketing techniques (Dacheux 2004). A communiqué was published covering the conclusions of the Helsinki European Council in December 1999, at which the Commission was invited to revisit EU communications policy (European Commission 2001b). This document advances the principles of political marketing, and is now used by several Commission services, including DG Employment and the external services. This approach, based on effectiveness, has met with extensive criticism. Communicative performance alone is not going to help the EU to solve its legitimacy problem (Dacheux 2004).

1.3 The invention and expansion of the EU transnationality principle

Transnational cooperation, understood as the implementation of EU projects by entities based in different member states, was not an automatic and straightforward evolution. As mentioned above, in development aid, intra-European transnational cooperation was one way to give a so-called European dimension to awareness-raising activities. In the social domain, transnational cooperation is an idea attributed to Philippe Hatt, considered by many the 'father of transnationality' in this area.[6] Following the model of the academic world, he suggested the extension of the principle of transnational cooperation to the domains of employment and vocational training. During the 1980s, the human resources task force within DG Employment was in charge of the promotion of intercultural projects, such as Eurotecnet.

Later, when the Commission was confronted with the subsidiarity principle; transnational (or intercultural) exchanges appeared the most obvious way to justify European action in many domains, including social policy. Domestically oriented DGs were only authorized to provide funding opportunities for European CSOs and for transnational cooperation.[7] Thus, through the principle of transnational cooperation, the Commission was able to justify CSO funding schemes for domestically oriented CSOs at the beginning of the 1990s (European Commission 1996c). The European Commission claimed that transnational cooperation could cause innovation and the transfer of knowledge and experiences. During those first years, the definition of transnational cooperation was unclear. In practice, the concept was developed by the state and non-state agencies and project managers in charge of its implementation (Rouault 2001). Drawing on previous experiences, in the late 1990s the Commission developed its own conception of transnational cooperation. It emphasized the promotion of good practices and the free circulation of ideas (European Commission 2004b). This minimalist conception can still be seen as Europeanization through 'cross-loading'.

The climax of so-called transnational cooperation in social affairs was reached with the Community program EQUAL (2000–2006), which followed the community initiatives ADAPT and EMPLOYMENT (1993–1999). While earlier programs were addressed to nationally based key players, EQUAL aimed to extend the principle of transnational cooperation to social actors at the local level. Because it was a very ambitious program, opinions on it have been polemical. For many, EQUAL was an incontestable success that brought about many policy innovations. For others, EQUAL's transnational dimension was a waste of time and money.[8] One of the most convincing arguments raised against transnational cooperation was that there are easier ways to foster the transfer of good practices (for example, through books or study visits, rather than through intercultural policy implementation). The post-EQUAL situation is extremely disappointing in terms of transnational cooperation. In the period of 2007–2013, transnational cooperation has been no longer compulsory, and has been left to the goodwill of member states. Within this new framework, only eight member states have funded transnational activities; these involved a wide range of actors, including civil society and social inclusion CSOs (EAPN 2009).

Transnational cooperation was not only a means of promoting a European identity; it was also a form of network governance. Even if national CSOs did not necessarily develop a clear European identity, they could still be transformed by the adoption of the principles of network governance. Network governance has brought new forms of interaction based on principles such as interdependence, frequent exchanges, trust, diplomacy and reciprocity (Rhodes 1999). The most frequent criticism regarding network governance is its potential lack of accountability. Networks favor privileged actors with relational resources. Power is concentrated among the most resourceful and these powerful actors would tend not to share their skills and contacts (Fraisse 2002). But, in a more positive light, network governance could also be seen as a new kind of democracy. The legitimacy of actors is no longer based on representation but rather on their capacity to bring forward credible and engaging projects. Representation is thus plural and temporary.

2 The promotion of European values: Civic engagement or instrumentalization?

Even if CSOs have integrated EU topics and values into their agendas, they have not substantially changed pre-existing perceptions of the EU. CSOs have adapted EU requirements to their own priorities, and, more often than not, they have been reticent to assume a cheerleader function.

2.1 How CSOs implemented European values and awareness-raising activities

There has never been a shortage of CSOs willing to promote European values and awareness-raising activities. EU requirements on this topic have always been very broad and thus CSOs have been able to work with those topics that resonated most with their own priorities. For example, development education projects are demand-driven, which means that CSOs can freely select the topic they want to work on. This right of initiative is granted with the explicit purpose of meeting the cooperation priorities of CSOs (Sfez and Scherlock 2008). In contrast, the Europe for Citizens program has some preestablished priorities, but CSOs may still pick and choose among them. Available data show that CSOs have mainly proposed projects targeting the most 'bottom-up priorities', such as intercultural dialogue and active European citizenship. The so-called top-down priorities, such as promoting European integration or the understanding of EU policies, have been much less popular (ECORYS 2013). Even more importantly, most priorities are very broad and open to interpretation. As the representative of the French contact point said:

> Yes, there is a list of priorities and sub-priorities. Small project managers find it very difficult to understand them and to establish distinctions among them. Only experienced project managers familiar with EU jargon can perceive the subtleties between categories and sub-categories. The priorities are also too general; they can hold anything or nothing.

The EU has been promoting activities on European topics and values through different financial instruments designed for different types of CSOs. For example, programs supported by DG DEVCO for awareness-raising activities are currently being used by large and medium-sized CSOs with the capacity to implement large budgets. From 1998 to 2007, the EU financed 690 such projects led by 331 CSOs (Sfez and Sherlock 2008: 38).[9] But the total number of CSOs involved (and potentially Europeanized) is much higher since many of these projects are implemented through consortia.

The CSOs in charge of these types of projects are exclusive or pluralist. For example, Oxfam Spain and Helpage International each obtained a grant for this purpose in 2010, as did Association Peuples Solidaires, Plan International UK, Marie Stops International and Oxfam UK in 2009.[10] DG DEVCO awareness-raising programs are very competitive. The last call for proposals on Development Education in the EU (2011), had a success rate of 14 percent (a total of 504 concept notes were received and only 71 full applications selected).[11] In 2010 the success rate was only 10 percent (33 projects selected out of 336 concept notes).[12] Many CSOs have used these funds, especially during the 1990s, to raise awareness of EU development policies by organizing conferences, workshops and summer schools. However, at present fewer CSOs are assuming this function since emphasis is being placed on transnational cooperation. In the latest version of the program on awareness raising and development education, for the first time the European dimension is not explicitly included as a unique and relevant feature.

In sharp contrast, the Europe for Citizens program has traditionally supported small and medium-sized national CSOs. During the first years of the programming period 2007–2013, DG Communication and Culture annually funded around 100 small projects (less than 60,000 euros each).[13] Europe for Citizens managerial requirements are less strict and more adapted to support small project managers. Forty-three percent of CSOs participating in a beneficiaries' survey had never received EU funding previously (ECORYS 2013). In the words of the person in charge of the French contact point:

> This program is one of the simplest. The budget is calculated automatically and, with some actions, it is even possible to use flat-rate calculations. Receipts only need to be kept in case of an audit. This simplicity permits the participation of small organizations that do not have a professional accountant or program manager specialized in Europe.[14]

The national contact points play a significant role in promoting the involvement of a wide variety of small CSOs, but especially small city councils, in the Europe for Citizens program.[15] They provide technical assistance to potential applicants and engage in a process of sharing good practices among peers. Most awareness-raising projects consist of the organization of events and the distribution of information. Europe for Citizens only offers small grants and thus it has not attracted the interest of the largest CSOs. This program has been used by many sporadic CSOs, including human rights CSOs like the Ligue Française des Droits de l'Homme, which can hardly be expected to access other budget lines.[16] Quite interestingly, at the end of the current programming period, the number of projects funded considerably decreased, while the number of projects submitted continued to increase. The acceptance rate decreased from 46 percent in 2008 (131 projects selected out of 287) to 5.4 percent in 2012 (590 submitted and only 32 granted).[17] Most projects ultimately rejected (around 70 percent) concerned small CSOs (ECORYS 2013). This evolution reflects the EU trend toward funding large projects proposed by a group of organizations from different member states.[18] Through its funding choices, the EU is promoting a partnership principle, expecting benefits in terms of complementarity, cooperation and the sharing of good practices. EU funding schemes are becoming less accessible for isolated and disconnected small CSOs. This is problematic since it could reinforce the gap between connected and disconnected citizens.

Even if awareness-raising and civic education programs are contributing to the integration of an EU dimension among CSOs in Europe, this process does not take place evenly across all member states. This effect is partially reduced by the existence of different funding schemes for use by different types of CSOs. When the EU gives major grants, the money tends to be concentrated in the biggest EU countries. From 1998 to 2007, most projects on development education (up to 43 percent) were managed by CSOs from Italy, the United Kingdom and Germany while other member states did not have projects accepted for several consecutive years (Sfez and Sherlock 2008: 38). Luxembourg and seven new member states only implemented 2 percent of the projects; and Malta and Latvia did not lead any projects, although they participated in some consortia. In sharp contrast, from 2008 to 2013 Europe for Citizens supported projects from a great variety of countries, including Hungary, France, Germany, Austria and Poland. The most underrepresented countries were those in Northern Europe (for example, the United Kingdom, Netherlands, Denmark, Sweden), Southern Europe and the Balkans. The lack of participation of some member states, namely, the United Kingdom, can be explained by national governments' lack of interest in the

Europe for Citizens program. The United Kingdom and Luxembourg, have not supported the creation of national contact points to promote this funding opportunity.[19]

CSOs involved in EU programs are not the only ones potentially affected. The Commission counts on the snowball effect (that is, one discussion of an EU topic leads to other debates on the EU) and the lever effect (the EU never funds any project at 100 percent, and thus the funding dedicated to the promotion of EU values is always superior to the actual amount spent) (Evalua 2004). The results that the EU expected have been confirmed through some evaluations of the Europe for Citizens program, even if the results have to be read with caution. According to a 2009 survey, the portion of participants in awareness-raising activities who wanted to take the role of multipliers (by talking to others about EU activities and events) was 88 percent (ECORYS 2013). A large portion was also very disposed to recommending EU events to others (81 percent). Some even intended to develop ideas or events on their own (45 percent). Even if these figures may be somewhat biased, they reflect the enthusiasm of the participants at these events. The qualitative research (interviews) tends to confirm the positive outcomes of these programs:

> This approach is very interesting. People become aware that Europe is relevant in their daily lives. The projects remain small but that's how we can move forward. Even if there are only around 200 participants, these people are really touched. It's not always about thousands of citizens. At the Commission they would like everyone to be involved and to make everyone understand but it's not so easy. Europe is very recent. We need a lot of pedagogy, even if this is already changing with young people. I'd doubt the effectiveness of a communication campaign, except possibly if it were really very big.[20]

2.2 A bottom-up Europeanizing effect?

Even if there has been clearly a Europeanization effect in the sense that many CSOs have integrated an EU dimension, this effect is not as big as might be expected. The EU does not have the capacity to change European CSOs' views very much. Some CSOs have willingly become cheerleaders, but not necessarily thanks to the EU. Before they could benefit from EU funding, they were already convinced of the benefits of EU policies and the promotion of the EU integration process was already among their objectives. Many CSOs have fully convinced Europeanists among their members. The titles of the projects submitted by Europeanist CSOs clearly reflect such goals, for example, 'Creating Desire for Europe' (in French, *Donner Envie d'Europe*). One would expect that these enthusiastic CSOs are very receptive to feedback from the Commission for the design and implementation of projects. Thus, it is not surprising that some CSOs regularly ask for input or participation from the Commission (Evalua 2004).

However, most CSOs applying for these funds reveal other priorities in the titles of their activities. They do not seem as willing to assume a cheerleading function as the previous group. More interestingly, the Europe for Citizens program does not specify that the funded activities have to be uncritical toward the EU, and this type of funding has already been used to fund activities critical of EU policies (Sanchez Salgado 2007b). As the representative of the French contact point puts it:

> The recipients are mainly pro-European organizations. They are for Europe and for the European construction process but not necessarily for the kind of Europe that we have right now. They want a stronger Europe but not necessarily following the current policy lines. I have never seen organizations that were anti-European applying for this program.[21]

Commission officials should in principle refuse funding to CSOs opposed to the goals of the EU. However, the Commission lacks the administrative capacity to perform this filtering effectively. As a general rule, the Commission does not systematically monitor the content of actions, except in final evaluation reports:

> The operational monitoring from the Commission is very weak, especially due to lack of time. The Commission is seldom present at the activities (especially if they take place away from Brussels) and not much attention is given to the materials produced by the organizations within the framework of the projects. Besides, there is no control over the content, since the Commission only takes into account declarations coming from CSOs themselves.
>
> (Evalua 2004: 8)

The lack of monitoring by the Commission is widely known by concerned CSOs. As a representative of a CSO funded by Citizens for Europe said, 'The European Commission checks how funds are spent but they do not check the content of the actions. (...) For other programs, such as EQUAL or the European Social Fund (ESF), there is closer supervision.

They look more closely at the evaluations.'²² CSOs can pretend on paper that they support the European integration process but this does not necessarily affect their activities. When applying for EU funding, CSOs also often use the type of language that the Commission wants to hear:

> It's about exchanging good practices, about engaging citizens in the European policy process, about voting, sharing and discovering the other in this European common space. It's also about showing what Europe does for us (...) Roughly speaking, it seems that everyone understood that they had to write in their applications what the Commission wanted to hear.[23]

The most paradoxical example is that of the French association Association for the Taxation of Financial Transactions for the Aid of Citizens (ATTAC), which was funded by budget line A-3024 in 2003 (the predecessor of Europe for Citizens) (Evalua 2004: 36). This alter-globalization CSO was widely known for its positions against the EU, particularly during the French referendum in 2005.

This Europeanization process can be understood as a process of absorption or accommodation. The EU does not necessarily succeed in creating a feeling of Europeanism among funded CSOs. The Commission cannot ensure that CSOs that are more critical about the EU will change their overall attitudes. EU funds only promote a real transformation among those CSOs with no previous opinions on the EU. And even in those cases, it is not possible to know beforehand if they will develop a positive attitude toward Europe.

But in any case, critical CSOs can still contribute to the building of a political community. The development of positive attitudes toward the EU is not a necessary condition for this. What really matters is that the EU be considered a legitimate level for policymaking. The most desirable objective for a would-be political system is to be able to accommodate internal conflict without collapsing (Cram 2009a).

Previous research has concluded that European CSOs were unable to contribute to the Europeanization of EU citizens, since they did not undertake substantial efforts to educate their supporters (Warleigh 2001). However, this research focused on CSOs obtaining EU funding for service delivery. Funding schemes that are specifically aimed at involving citizens have not been taken into account up until now. Funding schemes specifically addressed to citizens have had more impact than average project funding. According to a 2009 survey, 93 percent of the 675,000 citizens participating in Europe for Citizens in 2007 felt more European or more solidarity and/or tolerance after the program (ECORYS 2013). According to this same survey, only 56 percent of the participants felt that the activity fostered a sense of ownership of the EU, while all other objectives that participants were asked about had positive scores of more than 70 percent. Even if these figures have to be taken with caution, it is undeniable that CSOs promote knowledge on European topics and values among their supporters if the EU explicitly finances such activity.

3 Promoting EU visibility through CSOs: Mixed results

The promotion of EU visibility through CSOs is an interesting case of interactive Europeanization where it is difficult to determine who is using whom. On the one hand, the EU tries to use CSOs to gain visibility for the most popular European public policies. On the other hand, CSOs do not automatically follow European prescriptions. When CSOs perceive that EU visibility could undermine their own visibility, they tend to avoid this function. Visibility requirements are only successfully implemented when doing so enhances the position of national CSOs. Rather than assuming a cheerleader function, CSOs tend to avoid EU requirements or to engage in 'usages of Europe' (Woll and Jacquot 2009).

Among the CSOs studied, humanitarian and development CSOs are the least enthusiastic about the promotion of EU visibility. One would expect humanitarian CSOs, the most dependent on EU funding, to be the most willing to follow EU requirements. However, as they themselves acknowledge, they don't emphasize EU visibility. Even exclusive CSOs seldom use their websites to promote EU visibility. To meet EU requirements, CSOs tend to focus on promotional material to the detriment of more effective visibility strategies, such as EU promotion in the media or on their websites. According to a survey ordered by DG ECHO, 89 percent of the consulted CSOs systematically used ECHO materials, namely, promotional items such as posters, stickers, supplies and display panels (Evaluation Partnership 2007). Quite interestingly, ECHO visibility is much less promoted in the media and websites of the consulted organizations (only around 30 percent of the respondents used these tools). According to the great majority of partners participating in this survey, their efforts are relatively effective. This self-assessment is to be taken with great caution, especially since ECHO partners have no structured means to measure their impact in terms of visibility.

Humanitarian and development CSOs often perceive the EU's visibility strategy as a nuisance to their own visibility strategy. ECHO partners also say that visibility requirements divert attention from their main goal, which is to provide humanitarian aid. However, using their own logos does not seem to cause problems, in their view. CSOs also suggest that ECHO should take responsibility for its own communication. The EU flag is seen as a political symbol that could endanger their reputations as apolitical CSOs.

Given the serious gaps in the implementation of EU visibility requirements, Commission services give very precise instructions on how to define and present the EU brand. However, CSOs continue to argue that the EU has not developed a particularly professional communication strategy, since it is not very clear what exactly the EU is trying to convey (Evaluation Partnership 2007). CSOs—especially those that have a very professional approach to communication—feel that the EU lacks clarity in the definition of its goals. Quite interestingly, the EU is also criticized for promoting a standardized approach, which is considered inappropriate for communicating with different audiences in different situations. According to some interviewees, it is also difficult to convey specific information about the functioning of the EU, since most of the beneficiaries do not really understand the complexities of multilevel governance. Certain CSOs also say that the EU logo does not convey any specific meaning and that many beneficiaries do not understand it. However, it is hard to believe that aid beneficiaries (especially within Europe) are not able to identify the EU flag.

These CSOs clearly express a lack of enthusiasm about the promotion of EU visibility. Even if CSOs' opinions are not the most reliable indicator of real effectiveness for the Commission's visibility strategy, one would expect that CSOs that do not want to act as cheerleaders are not going to perform this function very well. Many factors can be used to justify the non-application of visibility requirements by some CSOs. One of the most serious limitations is the context of multiple donors, which leads to a dilution of visibility (Evaluation Partnership 2007). EU partners are usually supported by a variety of donors, which also have their own visibility requirements. CSOs tend to give equal visibility to all of their donors, including those that only made very small contributions or that do not have specific visibility requirements. Given the multiplication of logos, the message conveyed is confusing and unclear.

According to our interviews, EU officials often insist on the importance of visibility measures, but they are not always in a powerful position. For example, on occasion EU officials would like to dedicate funding to a specific country or region, and only a few large and well-resourced CSOs are actually able to assume this task. In these cases, CSOs have more leeway to impose their own conditions on the partnership agreement and in many cases, they ask for exceptions concerning visibility obligations. One would expect that pluralist CSOs have much more power than exclusive CSOs when negotiating with the Commission. More importantly, as is the case with awareness-raising activities, the Commission lacks the necessary monitoring capacity to ensure the implementation of visibility requirements. The DG ECHO communication unit had only eight staff members in 2007, which made it very difficult to supervise about 700 contracts in 85 countries on a yearly basis (Evaluation Partnership 2007). Only those Commission services dealing with a small number of CSOs can actually monitor visibility requirements on a regular basis. A DG Employment official said, 'DG Employment regularly checks whether CSOs put their logo on their materials and websites. Sometimes they do not do that, so we have to remind them that it is important.'[24]

Not all CSOs are reluctant to implement visibility requirements. Sometimes EU visibility can serve CSOs, which engage in a logic of positioning or of justification (Woll and Jacquot 2009: 117). CSOs can use EU visibility to enhance their own. The EU dimension can bring support from the general public (the logic of justification) or can improve their position in the policy process (the logic of positioning). For many national CSOs, participation in a European project brings legitimacy and credibility. As a Catalan CSO representative said, 'The ESF has a lot of visibility. It brings with it a lot of recognition, credibility and prestige.'[25] European projects are more attractive than national and local projects, as they have that extra dimension. CSOs that are involved in European projects are also presumed to have more expertise. A European or transnational dimension can also increase visibility in the media and among beneficiaries due to the presence of foreigners. The EU trademark often improves CSOs' reputations and makes them feel proud (Evalua 2004). In these cases, CSOs are rather willing to use the EU logo and flag. They also highlight the EU dimension in their press releases and other communication activities.

When the EU is perceived in a positive way, EU visibility can encourage 'usages of Europe', contributing to the Europeanization of CSOs and to the achievement of EU aims in terms of visibility. Thus, the best way to promote EU visibility is not to focus on CSOs' communication strategies, but, rather, on developing EU attractiveness. This Europeanization process is better understood as absorption or accommodation, since the EU doesn't seem to be able to have a very significant impact on the beliefs or interests of CSOs. The EU is much more popular in some countries and policy areas than others. For humanitarian and development CSOs, the EU's involvement is less valuable because their projects and partners already have an international dimension. The Spanish and French CSOs studied were more keen to promote EU visibility. The cultural status of EU foreignness is more positive in these countries than in the United Kingdom.

4 Transnational cooperation: Europeanization as cross-loading

Through the promotion of transnational cooperation, the EU has launched a Europeanization process that is mainly characterized by cross-loading. In the absence of a clear EU direction, the outcome of the Europeanization process is the result of interactions among CSOs and thus the diversity of outcomes is remarkable. First, this section shows that transnational activities have become very relevant in Europe because of EU support. Then, attention turns to the effects of such practices on specific CSOs. Interestingly, transnational cooperation tends to bring about more changes in national CSOs than the Europeanization mechanisms just presented. While EU logos and awareness-raising activities do not usually contribute to substantial organizational changes or identity building, transnational cooperation often leads to identifiable and durable changes.

4.1 Transnational cooperation and the transformation of CSOs

In spite of the difficulty, a lot of European CSOs have engaged in transnational cooperation due to EU incentives. As previously mentioned, each DG has promoted transnational cooperation differently, and thus the extent to which CSOs have engaged in it varies greatly across policy areas.

As previously explained, awareness-raising activities often have a transnational component. For example, out of the 690 awareness-raising activities supported by DG DEVCO between 1998 and 2007, 97 were implemented by consortia of CSOs from different countries. The number of consortia in this policy area has considerably increased since 2000 (Sfez and Sherlock 2008). Extra-European transnational cooperation is already common currency among humanitarian and development CSOs. Even if EU funds have helped them develop their contacts, the transformations have not been as important as it was for domestically oriented CSOs.

Transnational cooperation has been widely promoted among domestically oriented CSOs, especially in the social field. The Community initiatives ADAPT and EMPLOYMENT (1995–1997) funded a total of 10,162 projects. Out of these, 1355 were led by voluntary organizations (13.33 percent).[26] The Community Initiative EQUAL (2000–2006) supported around 3357 partnerships involving around 36,000 partners. Non-profit organizations implemented 36 percent of the projects, while only 31 percent were implemented by public authorities.[27]

Transnational cooperation has sometimes been implemented in a very superficial way. Consortia and transnational networks can be just formed to meet EU requirements for funding rather than to carry out effective projects. In these cases, most actions are implemented at the national level and the coordination between partners is minimal. According to a survey ordered by DG DEVCO, a quarter of the consortia under analysis did not work properly or were considered risky. Their members did not know each other very well and did not seem to have collaborated much in the formulation of proposals (Sfez and Scherlock 2008: 60). When the transnational dimension is only implemented in this superficial way, it consists mainly in the exchange of information and materials, and, more often than not, competition and comparison between partners prevail. A project manager who tried to minimize the transnational dimension said this:

> We were very specific regarding the transnational agreement. We detailed what we wanted to do and what we did not want to do. We did not want to implement useless projects. No more than one meeting per year! Our view on transnational cooperation was very modest but we did what we said we would.[28]

A self-interested or modest implementation of a project seems also to be related to institutional factors such as administrative constraints. Many project managers were so absorbed in fulfilling administrative requirements that they did not have enough time to develop the transnational dimension (Sanchez Salgado 2008). When projects are only implemented superficially, the Europeanization of CSOs is minimal and does not survive the project. Thus, the transnational dimension is only absorbed or accommodated by CSOs, and there is no real transformation.

In spite of some superficial partnerships, the few figures available suggest that in most cases, transnational partnerships are efficient. According to the above-mentioned survey, three-quarters of consortia worked properly. The more successful partnerships were implemented by CSOs with common thematic approaches or with complementary know-how. CSOs in successful partnerships were also used to working together and had trusting relationships. They held common objectives and implemented coordinated actions (Sfez and Scherlock 2008: 61). CSO representatives interviewed also highlighted the importance of good relationships among transnational partners as one of the main factors for success. Other relevant factors are openness and an authentic engagement with the project (Sanchez Salgado 2008). CSOs engaging effectively in transnational cooperation experience many more identifiable changes, including in their perception of the other and in their feelings about Europe. Changes also include regular use of foreign languages and the creation of multilingual websites, materials and products. After having engaged regularly in transnational cooperation, CSOs also become integrated in European networks and communities of practice (Sanchez Salgado 2011).

4.2 Promoting a European identity?

Even if the EU may have promoted transnational cooperation among many CSOs, whether it has contributed to the diffusion of a European identity is still an open question. Some think that cultural exchanges promote tolerance, solidarity among European citizens, intercultural understanding and even common values and a common identity. These claims are inspired by the humanist tradition. Authors such as Kant or Montesquieu (and other authors within the tradition of political and economic liberalism) have argued that intercultural contact contributes to prosperity and peace. More recently, Deutsch (1968) wrote that mobility is a necessary condition for the success of regional integration and the emergence of a common bond among the peoples of different countries.

Inspired by these traditions, a few studies have tried to measure the effects of mobility and transnational exchanges on identity building, using the so-called contact hypothesis. They tend to conclude that mobility brings positive effects, such as knowledge of foreign languages and of other countries (Sigalas 2010). However, the conclusions regarding a common identity are much more mixed (Budke 2008; King and Ruiz-Gelices 2003; Sigalas 2010). Studies ordered by the EU, carried out by consultancies and based on self-assessment, are indiscriminately optimistic about the positive effects of intercultural contact. As an example, a study ordered by the Commission concluded, 'Students also reported a significant positive impact on their understanding of people from other cultural or ethnic backgrounds (another key goal of the EU)' (Souto Otero and McCoshan 2006: 11). Just under 75 percent of students reported improvements to a large extent in this area, and a further 20 percent of students reported changes to some extent.

Academic studies are far less optimistic. Even if Erasmus students engaged in a mobility experience indeed tend to see themselves as more 'primarily European' than non-Erasmus students, there is still not much evidence that this outcome has been produced by the study abroad experience itself (Sigalas 2010). Thus, the connection between mobility and the development of a European identity remains as unclear as the link between mobility and attitudinal change in a positive direction (Stangor et al. 1996). The current mixed results on the effects of mobility are often explained by different conceptions of European identity and a lack of attention to intervening factors (Sanchez Salgado 2011).

The empirical data can be interpreted in many different ways depending on one's definition of identity. There is not much evidence that the EU is contributing to the development of a traditional identity considered in essentialist terms. However, scholars adopting a process-based definition of identity are much more optimistic about the potential transformative effects of the EU (Cram 2009a). Intercultural exchange can have positive, negative or neutral outcomes, depending on factors like the type and content of the mobility programs, the quality and quantity of contact, the existence of negative contact and intercultural training programs (Stangor et al. 1996). Some of these factors cannot be easily altered, such as individual personality traits or the occasional negative contact, but a few of them are *institutional*, and thus could be surely improved to ensure better policy outcomes.

As far as CSOs and equivalent actors are concerned, the only studies on this topic conclude that mobility encourages the emergence of a diverse range of different identities (Sanchez Salgado 2008). Since the EU is promoting mobility through many different programs and policy tools, and since all of these programs are perceived and implemented differently within member states, this outcome is not surprising.

Transnational cooperation in the domain of the fight against unemployment has not led to a significant change in attitudes among CSO staff when the partnerships were purely superficial. The individuals involved in such projects have continued to hold stereotypes of the European other. However, effective implementations of transnational projects have led to changes in attitudes, though not always to the development of a common European identity or supranational identity (Sanchez Salgado 2008). The multiplication in exchanges has led in some cases to a feeling of familiarity and solidarity among Europeans. What was considered to be strange and foreign has become familiar and close. This closeness can be considered the first step toward the development of a 'we' feeling and is essential for the development of a successful political community of the traditional type. However, the multiplication of exchanges can also lead to a postnational identity. When this happens, individuals detach themselves from their own national identity without becoming attached to an alternative European identity.

Conclusion

The EU has tried to take advantage of CSOs' potential to increase its legitimacy and promote European values and the European integration process. To this purpose, it has used different policy tools. Certain policy tools, such as the support of awareness-raising activities with an EU dimension or EU visibility, can be more easily perceived by CSOs and observers as top-down instrumentalization. Even if this was the real intention of the EU, its goals are very vague and the Commission lacks the sufficient monitoring capacity to ensure a top-down Europeanization process. CSOs have had a lot of leeway to use EU funding in ways that most fit their priorities. The Europeanization process is much more interactive than one would have expected. Most CSOs became more familiar with EU issues, but many of them did not become positive toward EU policies. They developed quite critical attitudes toward the EU, which could be interpreted as 'retrenchment' (Radaelli 2003).

The promotion of European integration and sense of identity through transnational cooperation seems to be more effective. Transnational exchanges can indeed bring changes in the organizational structure of CSOs and attitudinal changes among staff and volunteers participating in transnational activities. Quite interestingly, transnational cooperation leads to a diverse range of different identities. Thus, the development of a common single European identity seems unlikely.

Part III
Europeanizing Civil Society through Participation

7
The Europeanization of CSOs' Participation: Beyond the Brussels Consensus

Introduction

This chapter builds on previous literature on the European Union's (EU's) impact on civil society organizations' (CSOs') strategies and advocacy activities. The existing research is valuable, but previous studies have focused on one specific level of governance, giving a rather limited picture. For a more complete accounting, it is necessary to bring together three different strands of literature on the EU's structuring of CSOs: studies focusing on EU-based CSOs, studies focusing on the participation of national CSOs in European policy initiatives and studies dealing with the Europeanization of protest.

This chapter focuses first on EU-based CSOs, also often referred to as Eurogroups or European networks. A Eurogroup has been defined as 'an actor in its own right, an instrument for its members or a forum in which its members build their opinions' (Eising 2009: 65). When analysis is limited to EU-based CSOs, the EU participatory regime appears to be restricted to an elite of large organizations. The impression given is not necessarily incorrect, but it can be misleading. EU access opportunities go far beyond the Brussels complex. National CSOs also participate in the EU policy process at the national level and through European peak associations. The last section of this chapter shows that the EU has also contributed to the shaping of countermovements, or, in other words, to the shaping of protest against itself. To include both social movements and CSOs acting as interest groups in the same analysis allows for a more complete overview of the role of European institutions. This chapter refers to previous research when it exists, and uses original data to illustrate a few aspects that are currently understudied. Data are drawn from EU policy papers, CSOs' documents and semi-structured interviews. To have a clearer view of the activities of CSOs engaging in contentious action, data have also been collected from newspapers reporting on protest events, such as the European Social Forum (ESF).

1 Revisiting portrayals of the CSOs Brussels Consensus

The EU participatory regime rewards—informally—certain types of behavior and thus contributes to the shaping of CSOs. Brussels-based CSOs tend to use conventional or insider strategies, based primarily on the provision of expertise. EU-based CSOs avoid confrontation and try to establish long-term relationships based on mutual trust with members of the Parliament and Commission staff. This has been confirmed to hold true for many policy sectors such as migrant rights (Geddes 2000), economic interest groups (Saurugger 2003), social CSOs (Wolff 2013) and environmental associations (Marks and McAdam 1999). The classic repertoire of insider interventions is also fully exploited at the national level (Kriesi et al. 2007; Mosley 2012). However, some authors argue that at the EU level this trend is much more pronounced. EU-based CSOs tend to imitate professional international CSOs (Giraudon 2000) or to adopt less conflictual strategies:

> Groups do not act in Brussels as they do in their national contexts. Instead of demonstrating their grievances before the mass media, they lobby Commission officials, engage consultants to write impact reports, coordinate the policy papers among themselves, instruct lawyers to pursue cases before the European Court of Justice, and only on occasion, organize public protest outside the European Parliament Building in Strasbourg.
> (Marks and McAdam 1999: 102)

The absence of contentious action at the EU level has also been related to the absence of a sense of belonging to Europe, the absence of a public space and the fact that protest is usually territorially rooted (Marks and McAdam 1999). This section gives a detailed account of the EU preferences on action repertoires and the extent to which these preferences have affected CSOs' participatory behavior.

1.1 How the European Commission promotes a Brussels Consensus

The Commission has never published an official position about the best way to engage in EU dialogues, but its preference for non-conflictual strategies and the provision of expertise is clear in many of its policy papers and statements. The ideal mode of participatory governance according to the Commission would be 'working together' to achieve EU policy objectives (Wolff 2013). CSOs are often seen as partners that should have access to the policy process, but at the same time, they should work hand in hand with the Commission to achieve EU aims. This implies that a consensus around goals is necessary for change to happen.

CSOs not willing or able to 'work together', or that opt for more confrontational strategies, fit much less into this framework. Grassroots campaigns are a relatively new phenomenon in Europe and their public and aggressive tone is seen as an unwelcome departure from the European traditions of governance (Billet 2007). For example, in its green paper on transparency the Commission is not very supportive of mass campaigns, a typical grassroots lobbying technique. According to the Commission, 'Modern communication technologies (Internet and e-mail) make it easy to organize mass campaigns for or against a given cause, without the EU institutions being able to verify to what extent these campaigns reflect the genuine concerns of EU citizens' (European Commission 2006: 6). In this same document, mass campaigns are presented as lobbying practices that are 'considered to go beyond legitimate representation of interests' (European Commission 2006: 5). The rejection of grassroots lobbying is even more evident in the French version of this document, which uses the expression 'irregular lobbying methods' (*méthodes de lobbying irrégulières*).

Another striking example is the coolness with which the Commission has accommodated European Citizens' Initiatives (ECIs). The Commission initially proposed very strict conditions for ECIs, such as high admissibility thresholds (300,000 signatures) and the presence of signatories from at least one-third of member states.[1] As ex-Commissioner Meglena Kuneva put it, politicians are very optimistic about democracy tools in public, but they express doubts in private. According to the *EU Observer*, 'Some claim the Commission is not overly enamored of the idea of getting up close and personal with citizens' wishes.'[2] The Commission and some members of the Parliament have been concerned by the possible misuse of ECIs by Euro skeptics. The Commission also argued that a low threshold would be conducive to media headlines that would harm its reputation, such as 'Brussels gives green light to abortion'.[3]

The EU doesn't just reject conflictual strategies; there are many features of the current system that actively promote professionalized advocacy based on the provision of expertise. This is seen by interest group professionals (including professional CSOs) as the most effective way to influence the European policy process (BOND 2011; Venables 2007). The vast majority of the Commission's consultations are meant to acquire information from stakeholders (Quittkat 2011). Indeed, online consultations concern highly specialized topics that are not easily related to the broader political discussions that attract EU citizens. However, the Commission's conception of expertise is wider than what one would expect. The evidence used for EU decision-making takes into account stakeholders' opinions, needs and expectations (Wolff 2013).

The promotion of an action repertoire based on expertise is also encouraged by high sectoralization, specialization and the technical character of most EU regulations (Richardson 1993). These features have shaped CSOs' possibilities while exacerbating internal tensions and undermining coordination efforts (Cullen 2010). Sectoralization has helped marginalize certain organizations, thus creating tensions across the CSO sector. Sectoralization also militates against CSOs' cross-issue mobilization since it encourages competitiveness and exclusivity. Focusing on expertise and sectoralization can also contribute to the depolitization of the policy process. This is because the absence of political conflict hinders citizens' participation (Kohler-Koch 2001). Average citizens, non-specialized CSOs and grassroots groups do not dispose of the necessary analytical skills to identify the underlying political options implied by technical and specialized regulations (De Schutter 2002). However, a few scholars also argue that politization is not the best solution for the EU and point to its risks (Bartolini 2006; Dehousse 2005). Depolitization (here understood as the absence of ideological battles) encourages a more rational and civilized policymaking. Interest groups and CSOs in such a system feel compelled to provide complex arguments instead of reductionist catchwords and simplistic slogans (Debouzy 2004).

1.2 The EU's shaping of EU-based CSOs

In the absence of specific guidelines for consultation and representation of interests, the EU's shaping of CSOs takes place through emulation and a learning process. The evidence presented below shows that under favorable conditions the EU has affected the action repertoires and goals of CSOs. This process can be interpreted both as adaptation and as transformation.

One example of how CSOs adapt their actions to EU norms comes out of the consultations launched by the Commission. Even in the absence of specific guidelines on the content and format of contributions, there is a clear tendency toward homogenization (Michel 2005). Frequent players in Brussels tend to write their contributions according to the same model: short papers that include a summary of key points and use the same Euro jargon. These contributions are always constructive and focus on the provision of expertise, including examples and figures. By contrast, CSOs participating in consultations for the first time tend to not follow this model. They submit long papers that lack distinctive marks. For all CSOs, emulation is facilitated by the fact that most contributions are posted online. There is a tendency to copy the writing style and physical format of the contributions from the CSOs with the best reputations among EU policymakers. This process is facilitated by manuals written and diffused by CSOs themselves. As one CSO's manual stated, 'The provision of objective, reliable and well-researched evidence from across the Union is the key to successful lobbying and it will distinguish your lobby from others who just provide wish lists. EU legislators are relatively open-minded and can be persuaded by arguments well-supported by the facts' (Venables 2007: 14).

The shaping of CSOs can also come out of their participation in institutionalized dialogues. Commission dialogues do not always meet the conditions that should be present for the launching of a learning process (Checkel 2001). One would expect that many institutionalized dialogues do not have significant effects since they only involve superficial contact and exchanges of information. This is typical of dialogues that include a wide variety of actors with different policy preferences (CSOs, law firms and business groups). In such configurations, actors do not change their preferences or mind-sets. One example is the institutionalized dialogue on the liberalization of services initiated by DG Trade (Michalowitz 2005). According to interviews, in the development policy field dialogues such as the Palermo process did not generate much trust and mutual learning. This outcome can also be explained by the deterioration in relationships between DG DEVCO and CSOs at the end of the 1990s, which was related to the CLONG funding crisis (Chapter 4). Current opinion is also quite mixed on the Commission's most recent institutionalized dialogue in this area, the Policy Forum on Development. Even though a few CSOs' recommendations have been adopted, overall CSOs remain unsatisfied.[4] Development CSOs often feel used by Commission services and that there is a lack of real listening from both sides.[5] The EU peak association in this area shares this mixed view: 'CONCORD still struggles to have a meaningful dialogue with the Commission, however, the willingness to meet and discuss issues is improving and CONCORD has established good working relationships with a number of units particularly in DG DEVCO' (CONCORD 2013: 36).

Many institutionalized dialogues better meet the conditions to facilitate learning processes. In these, participants are engaged in accomplishing the same objectives and share common ideas. They work on the same topics and, more often than not, share the same professional backgrounds (Giraudon 2000). The absence of business interests reinforces group cohesion. One example is the ongoing dialogue in the framework of the FPA Watch Group between DG ECHO and VOICE, the European peak association for humanitarian CSOs. This dialogue has helped to create trust and understanding between ECHO and CSOs (VOICE 2004: 13). As an EU official points out:

> ECHO depends on CSOs a lot for its work. ECHO is more dependent on CSOs than the Commission's other services, such as DG DEVCO and DG RELEX. ECHO works very informally with CSOs. Other departments have longer procedures and see CSOs as overly demanding. But with ECHO, there is a real partnership or ... a mutual dependency.[6]

Another example of close dialogue has occurred between DG Employment and social CSOs. Especially since the creation of the Social Platform in the mid-1990s, there have been frequent interactions that have led to a learning process. As an EU official at DG Employment put it, 'We agree on a lot of things because we are working on the same topics and we have the same objectives. There is much more confrontation with other DGs.'[7]

Interviewed CSOs share this point of view. 'We work closely with the employment unit and the social policy unit,' said a CSO representative. 'It's more about cooperation. There are two staff members at DG Employment who previously worked for EAPN, which facilitates contact. But to be influential is much more difficult.'[8]

At present, a partnership is organized around the European Platform against Poverty and Social Exclusion (EPAP). This initiative largely constitutes an exercise in rebranding consultation procedures that already existed. However, for the first time the dialogue on poverty and inclusion is reaching some Commission services beyond DG Employment.[9] Within the framework of this initiative, DG Employment organizes an annual convention to generate dialogue between policymakers and key stakeholders. Dialogue on the fight against poverty and exclusion brings together the presidents of the Commission, the European Parliament and the European Council, as well as key commissioners and key representatives of social CSOs. On a more regular basis, the Commission has also launched an EU stakeholders' dialogue. The composition of these close partnerships is rather homogeneous (EU-level CSOs and social partners, think tanks and foundations), which makes a socialization process much more likely.[10]

1.3 EU-based CSOs: Advocacy groups or consensus hunters?

There is a lot of evidence supporting the hypothesis that the EU is promoting a specific repertoire of action among CSOs. Most CSOs engaging in direct dialogue with EU institutions, particularly with the Commission, focus on the provision of expertise. However, even if European peak associations do not engage in contentious activities, this does not necessarily mean that they are tame or that they are not very critical of the Commission (Armstrong 2010; Cram 2011; Sanchez Salgado 2014a). EU-based CSOs also occasionally engage in conflictual strategies, including seeking media attention and petitions.

As may be expected, the groups that have more clearly adopted the action repertoires promoted by EU institutions are EU-supported CSOs, such as the Social Platform, Confederation for Relief and Development (CONCORD) and VOICE. In the view of EU officials, these CSOs belong to the innermost circle of EU-based CSOs (Wolff 2013). Most resources of EU-based CSOs (up to 80 percent) come from EU institutions and can only be employed for fact-finding reports and awareness-raising activities. For example, in 2010, CSOs funded by the Commission under Community Programme for Employment and Social Solidarity (PROGRESS) carried out 462 information and communication events for a total of 27,036 participants (European Commission 2011). In the absence of sufficient resources, the communication departments of most EU-supported CSOs focus on EU-supported activities or on low-cost media-related activities.

Even if there is a clear tendency at the EU level to favor consensual strategies based on the provision of expertise, this is not the only action repertoire used by EU-based CSOs. CSOs are becoming increasingly aware that their success depends on the management of public attention. In a context of audience democracy, political representatives face more pressure to respond to public opinion, even in Brussels (Kriesi et al. 2007). Many of the most striking CSO successes in Brussels have been related to advocacy campaigns that were widely relayed in the media and supported by public opinion. Some examples are the Directive for Services of General Interest or the rejection of the Anti-Counterfeiting Trade Agreement (ACTA) treaty by the European Parliament.

In the absence of full-fledged media strategies or powerful and popular brands, it is understandable that EU-supported peak associations are not very present in the EU media. For example, from 2001 to 2013, CONCORD has only been quoted eight times by the *EU Observer*.[11] In all of these occasions, CONCORD is presented as an expert on development issues.[12] During the same period, the Social Platform was only quoted in 11 articles in the *EU Observer*. Other well-known EU-supported CSOs such as EAPN (quoted five times) and the European Women's Lobby (EWL; quoted nine times) were not very well covered.[13] Given the lack of media coverage and their focus on low-cost media-related activities, EU-funded social CSOs tend not to prioritize demonstrations or symbolic actions. However, they regularly support these activities when they are organized by their members and by other Brussels-based organizations, namely, the European Trade Union Confederation (ETUC).[14] For example, the Social Platform participated in a march across Brussels against the Service Directive in 2005.[15] In December 2001, the Social Platform also participated in a symbolic action organized by the Union of European Federalists calling for an open mandate for the Convention on the Future of Europe.[16]

CSOs such as Oxfam, Amnesty International (AI) and Greenpeace have popular brands and professional media strategies. They are much more proactive in developing contacts with the most important European newspapers.[17] It is not surprising that these pluralist CSOs are far more visible in the media. For example, from 2001 to 2013 Greenpeace has been quoted in the *EU Observer* 230 times, and AI has been quoted 200 times. In addition to this, Greenpeace has engaged in more aggressive repertoires of action and even in public disobedience. For example, in December 2009, a group of 11 Greenpeace activists inserted themselves into the convoy of vehicles heading to the European Council, for the purpose of making an announcement in front of the television crews that routinely await the arrival of the heads of national governments.[18] And in August 2011, 170 Greenpeace activists blocked access to the European Business Summit in Brussels to single out as laggards a number of companies that were not respecting the target for a 30 percent reduction in CO_2 emissions for Europe by 2020.[19] Greenpeace's symbolic actions have been tools to raise the visibility of issues that would otherwise be overlooked by the media and given less attention by European policymakers. While doing so in much less aggressive terms, other pluralist EU-based CSOs have also occasionally engaged in symbolic activities aimed at attracting the attention of policymakers and the media in creative ways.

Even if EU-based CSOs engage in symbolic/contentious action at the EU level, they generally don't employ mass lobbying or other activities that require the participation of EU citizens. As explained before, these action repertoires have always been regarded with mistrust by the Commission. EU-supported CSOs are federations of associations that have no direct contact with citizens. As a general rule, it is rather difficult for them to engage directly in grassroots strategies such as demonstrations, petitions and protests. The EU offices of pluralist CSOs such as Greenpeace, AI and Oxfam also dedicate most of their efforts to lobbying EU institutions, while contact with citizens is handled by their national sections. The EU units of AI and Greenpeace do not use their websites for online petitions, creative competitions or twitter protests (Hanke 2012). This is in sharp contrast with their national sections, which heavily use the Internet and the social media to engage citizens in their activities. More interestingly, the EU section of AI does not use the organization's most popular action tool: engaging citizens to appeal directly to leaders for action on specific issues.[20] In the words of an EU-level AI policy officer:

> The EU office is a pure lobbying office. We have no members. Sometimes we propose that national Amnesties write to their MEPs but we do not send junk mail. We do not write pre-formulated letters. It is not a good method as the recipients would have negative opinions of us. At the national level they do more activities at the grassroots level, such as demonstrations, etc. We don't do lawsuits either. National organizations do that at the national level. We only focus on EU-level legislation in-the-making. Filing a lawsuit would be very time-consuming and there are just four of us in the office. It would also be very hard to identify suits that would be worthy, since our goal is to change existing law and not simply to file suits at random.[21]

Many EU units of CSOs including AI and Greenpeace do not consider it their role to engage citizens in their activities since they have been specifically created by the national sections to lobby EU institutions (Hanke 2012). This tends to confirm the argument that there is a distribution of tasks between national CSOs and EU units of CSOs in a multilevel system. It is difficult to get these different offices working together toward a cause, but one would expect that when they do, it is extremely effective.

Quite interestingly, EU-based CSOs' disregard for citizen engagement has changed somewhat with the establishment of the European Citizens' Initiatives (ECIs) (Greenwood 2012). Since the official establishment of the ECIs, this option could no longer be considered illegitimate or irregular. EU-based CSOs—even when they are strongly supported by the Commission—are now quite willing to become more involved with ECIs. For example, the European Disability Forum (EDF) launched a very successful petition for an all-encompassing legislative instrument for the rights of peoples with disabilities. And the Social Platform, EAPN and other EU-based CSOs were amongst the supporters of the successful ECI Water is a Human Right.[22] Pluralist EU-based CSOs such as Greenpeace and Friends of the Earth also initiated EU petitions. Quite interestingly, when these CSOs engage in ECIs, it is often not the EU office that is in charge (Greenwood 2012).

2 The Europeanization of CSOs beyond the Brussels complex

The EU's shaping of CSOs does not only concern the Brussels CSO community. First, national CSOs also get involved in EU-promoted participatory procedures at the national level. Second, national CSOs participate in EU-based peak associations. Participation in peak associations is often considered insufficient by scholars and observers but the fact that there are several types of European peak associations promoting different types of participation among their members has rarely been addressed. The first type of European peak association, the EU-supported, gathers together national peak associations and represents highly generalized interests. These EU peak associations coexist with highly specialized EU-based CSOs composed of individual organizations (Grande 2003). One would expect that national CSOs' participation in EU-based CSOs has contributed to the indirect transformation of their repertoires of action and that the degree of change depends on the type of EU peak association.

2.1 Europeanization through national dialogue processes: The prevalence of diversity

In the traditional community method, the EU has tended to focus on Brussels-based consultation procedures. EU-based peak associations are expected to channel national CSOs' points of view; this will be discussed in the next section. But when it comes to new forms of governance or when competencies are shared with member states, the EU has also been concerned with the promotion of participation at the national level. To illustrate the effects of EU efforts, this section discusses the promotion of participation within the framework of the Open Method of Coordination on Social Inclusion as well as within the framework of the European Social Fund (ESF).

The EU has been promoting consultations and partnerships in the social field at the domestic level since the establishment of policy coordination instruments in the early 2000s. The Open Method of Coordination on Social Inclusion is seen as the most successful of these instruments in terms of CSO inclusion (Zeitlin 2010). The Europe 2020 strategy also emphasizes the need for cooperation with stakeholders and explicitly mentions 'representatives of civil society' (European Commission 2010b: 29). A permanent dialogue between key stakeholders and public authorities is expected to contribute to the elaboration and implementation of the National Reform Programmes. As per these obligations for dialogue, the Commission is currently promoting the participation of EU-level CSOs through the flagship program Platform against Poverty and Social Exclusion (European Commission 2010b). The Commission also intends to promote key stakeholders' participation in the member states. To do this, it has planned to elaborate voluntary guidelines on stakeholders' involvement in the definition and implementation of actions and programs to address poverty and social exclusion (European Commission 2010b: 17).

For a long time, partnership with stakeholders has also been one of the key principles for the implementation of structural funds. Article 5 of the new draft of the Common Provisions Regulation said that member states would organize partnerships with 'bodies representing civil society, including environmental partners, nongovernmental organizations, and bodies responsible for promoting equality and non-discrimination' (European Commission 2013: 26). Member states have a clear obligation to organize partnerships with CSOs, but the procedures to engage with stakeholders are left to national authorities. To ensure appropriate implementation, the Commission recently published a Code of Conduct on the principles that should guide EU member states when they organize participation with key stakeholders. This Code of Conduct (a Commission-delegated regulation) is binding and entirely and directly applicable in all member states (European Commission 2014). The Code of Conduct includes detailed guidelines on how to involve partners in the different stages of the programming and implementation process. For example, member states should set rules to ensure transparent and effective involvement of relevant partners. Key stakeholders should also be invited to participate in monitoring committees and in the definition of calls for proposals.

In the above cases, Europeanization takes a peculiar form. Since the EU does not offer opportunities and incentives directly, but rather through member states, the form and the quality of the procedures varies widely across countries and policy areas. Before the Commission published the above-mentioned working paper on best practices, it had never been very precise about the procedures for member states to effectively involve stakeholders. Some countries have been much more willing than others to organize effective consultation procedures. The success and lifespan of partnerships with stakeholders also tends to depend on context, for instance, the economic situation and changes to local or national governments. Effectiveness also depends on the capacity of national CSOs to contribute substantively to the process, which raises the question of capacity building (European Commission 2012b).

Quite a few studies have illustrated the different impacts of EU obligations when national CSOs participate in EU-initiated processes; these studies focus on the Open Method of Coordination on Social Inclusion (Brandsen et al. 2005; Johansson 2007; Kröger 2007) and the Convention on the Future of Europe (Lucarelli and Radaelli 2004). To my knowledge, there has not been any equivalent research on the implementation of the principle of partnership with CSOs within the framework of the structural funds. Existing studies offer a clear overview of the variety of strategies adopted by member states, which have led to highly differentiated Europeanization processes. Many member states use existing channels of participation to accommodate EU obligations. In these cases, Europeanization is weaker since European issues are just included in ongoing consultation processes. On many occasions, EU requirements lead to the establishment of new participation procedures in a few member states. These new participatory procedures substantially change the types of relationships between CSOs and public authorities, which has consequences for CSOs' advocacy activities. Even if the EU has promoted dialogue with CSOs in many member states, there are still some states that have not effectively included CSOs, and thus one would expect little or no Europeanization.

Since the introduction of the Europe 2020 strategy, the high degree of variation between member states has persisted. Though a few member states have improved participation by stakeholders at the national level, a general downward trend has been seen both by EU representatives and by CSOs. This trend may be related to the economic crisis, which has led to smaller budgets in the social area (EAPN 2012: 27). The downward trend in participation may also be related to the elimination of national reports on social inclusion. CSOs in the social area had been pretty satisfied with their participation in the elaboration and implementation of such reports (EAPN 2010).

By contrast, participation in current National Reform Programmes has been hermetic for social CSOs. According to EAPN, all of its members—with the exception of the United Kingdom—have dedicated a substantial amount of time to follow-up and have engaged in the advocacy activities on the National Reform Programmes, but no single group reported having had any influence. In most cases, CSOs did not receive drafts of plans before they were sent to the Commission and the officers in charge of the drafts were not available to national CSOs (EAPN 2013). Spain exemplifies this downward trend. In 2011 EAPN-Spain was very satisfied with the consultation process. CSOs claimed to have influenced the 2011 National Reform Programme. However, in 2012, the new conservative government unilaterally stopped most efforts at cooperation with CSOs active in the areas of poverty and social inclusion; only some large CSOs have since been consulted on an ad hoc basis.[23] There was a slight improvement in 2013; the Spanish government accepted comments from social CSOs, which were still not allowed to consult the draft plan (EAPN 2013).

The downward trend has also been evident in the United Kingdom, where there have been no stakeholder meetings for the elaboration of the National Reform Programmes (EAPN 2013). The process seems to have taken place in an 'extremely narrow environment that did not support the inclusion of a broad range of actors (Caritas Europe 2011: 46)'. This is in sharp contrast with the situation a few years prior, when a Social Policy Task Force was explicitly created to monitor the evolutions of the national plans on social inclusion (Brandsen et al. 2005). This task force was a civil society dialogue partner in the National Reform Programmes beginning in 2001 (EAPN 2010). It included representatives from CSOs and people living in poverty, and CSOs found it a very good first step toward the instauration of dialogue with public authorities.[24]

In France the downward trend is not so visible. There have been participation processes at several levels for the elaboration of National Reform Programmes but they do not deliver on effective participation (EAPN 2013). In the last round, the French government annexed the comments of social CSOs to the submission of the National Reform Programme, but the plan itself did not reflect them.

The programming and implementation of structural funds has tended to include some CSOs, in line with the partnership principle included in the EU regulation. However, in most member states this principle has been interpreted very narrowly, and only a few large CSOs have been effectively consulted (EAPN 2009). Spain clearly represents this general trend. The participation of social CSOs in the definition of the programming documents was ensured in the programming period 2000–2006, but was limited to five large CSOs acting as intermediary bodies, which were also full members of the monitoring committee (Fundación Vives 2006). In sharp contrast, France and the United Kingdom (along with Ireland) have developed partnerships with a wider range of CSOs.

All in all, the EU promotion of participation between national governments and stakeholders has been a very volatile phenomenon within the framework of the Lisbon Strategy and Europe 2020. In the absence of clear obligations and monitoring mechanisms, the degree of involvement of national CSOs in consultation processes depends very much on the goodwill of the member states and on economic and social contexts. Interestingly, even if some governments are reluctant to consult CSOs, EU incentives have generated expectations among national CSOs. Many CSOs now push for the establishment of consultation procedures and to have their views reflected in the National Reform Programmes (EAPN 2013). EU-based peak organizations can play a significant role in supporting the involvement of national CSOs by giving them visibility at the EU level. Their reports 'shame' those member states that are not properly implementing their obligations regarding the involvement of stakeholders in the Europe 2020 process. Even if member states neglect CSO input, the Commission often takes national CSOs' comments directly into account in its recommendations.[25] However, if the current downward trend persists, there is a risk that national social CSOs will become less engaged in this process (EAPN 2013). Or, the shaming strategy and the boomerang effect may have some positive results in the long run, as has often been the case at the global level (Keck and Sikkink 1998).

The procedures organized within the framework of the ESF grant the participation of at least a few CSOs. As requested by the EU, CSOs are consulted on the elaboration of the programs and involved in the monitoring committees. This greater success seems to be related to more detailed requirements in terms of participation, and to the potential risk of not obtaining funding. The participation of CSOs in the structural funds may improve after the adoption of the 2013 ESF regulation (European Parliament and Council 2013). This regulation states that at least 20 percent of the total ESF resources has to be dedicated to the promotion of social inclusion and combating poverty and discrimination. Regarding the Europe 2020 process, one would expect that the involvement of national CSOs would also improve if detailed guidelines were published and if CSOs' involvement in Europe 2020 was a condition for the receipt of ESF funding.[26]

2.2 More Europeanized CSOs have less impact?

EU-supported groups focus on general causes or on giving voice to groups facing exclusion or discrimination, such as people with disabilities, women and poor people (Sanchez Salgado 2014a). EU peak associations obtaining funds for their advocacy activities have to fulfill certain criteria in terms of governance. For example, EU-supported groups should ensure formal representation of their members (European Commission 2010c: 13) and represent citizens from across the entire EU (Greenwood 2007; Wolff 2013). The emphasis on geographic representation has led to the establishment of large European peak associations, composed of national platforms and international CSOs. For example, CONCORD, the Social platform and EAPN bring together thousands of members from across Europe. EU-funded peak associations often obtain specific EU support to develop contacts and to promote membership.

The representation of members is usually ensured through national or sectoral platforms, which means there is a very long chain of representation. A large number of members complicates the organization of direct representation, reflecting the tension between the logic of influence and the logic of membership (Schmitter and Streeck 1981). Efficient performance in Brussels often hinders effective communication between EU offices and the grassroots level (Buth and Kohler-Koch 2013). The thousands of members in these large umbrella associations cannot possibly have a general assembly for making decisions on a regular basis.

To ensure representation, EU peak associations have often promoted the structuration of participation in member states. The EU participatory mode, based on the aggregating efforts of umbrella organizations, has thus been transferred to the member states.[27] The Commission has also supported the creation of national peak associations. For example, many development national peak associations have been created on the model of CLONG (the first EU development peak association). In France, the national peak association Intercollectiv d'ONG was officially set up in 1983 to represent French development and humanitarian CSOs before CLONG. The British Overseas NGOs for Development (BOND) was also set up during the 1990s following the model of CLONG (Smillie 1994). The Spanish peak association in this policy area, created during the

1980s, followed the model of CLONG and its other European counterparts. CONCORD, the successor of CLONG, clearly states that it 'aims at supporting its members to strengthen themselves, so that the national platform in every Member State can act as the primary influencer of its national government and politicians on EU sustainable development policy and practice; and that networks are as effective as possible in influencing EU institutions' (CONCORD 2013: 40). The diffusion of the EU participatory mode is also typical in the social arena. Many national platforms have been created after the models of the EWL and EAPN (Johansson 2012). In the words of a CSO representative:

> The process of formation of national EAPNs has been facilitated by EAPN and, indirectly, by the Commission. The Commission gave us a grant of 1 million euros to help with the creation of national sections. EAPN helped create these national EAPNs and provided them with services like information about the EU level, help with creating partnerships, etc.[28]

These efforts have sometimes been very critically regarded by CSOs that feared the exclusion of relevant topics and the neglect of minority interests (Buth and Kohler-Koch 2013).

The impact of Europe is thus mediated by European, national and sometimes local platforms. The formalized structure of multilevel representation prevents the EU from directly shaping domestic CSOs. A complete analysis of patterns of representation in EU peak associations needs to operate at different levels (Johansson 2012). In the countries studied, there are significant differences in the way members are represented. The French and British members of CONCORD have established EU policy working groups in charge of bringing issues to the EU peak association. However, the Spanish platform does not currently have a working group exclusively dedicated to EU topics where national CSOs can coordinate their positions (CONGDE 2012). National platforms tend to be more representative when they are composed of members that are already working on EU issues, but such is not always necessarily the case.[29] On many occasions, European peak associations have made substantial efforts to involve members or even wider constituencies in the policy process. This has been seen a lot in the social area, where CSOs like EWL, EAPN and European Federation of National Organizations Working with the Homeless (FEANTSA) have taken action in this direction (Johansson and Lee 2012). In the external action policy area, CONCORD initiated in the last few years a process to create more transparency around its board responsibilities and working practices. According to its members, there is now a good balance between leadership and consultation (CONCORD 2013).

Another obstacle to addressing member issues is the lack of consensus within the CSO community (South Research et al. 2000). EU peak associations with a large and diverse membership are much more legitimate than other types of CSOs, but they are also less effective (Heinelt and Niederhafner 2008). In such associations, the secretariat normally acquires increased autonomy. Since it is difficult to reach agreements between diverse members, the positions eventually adopted are vague and tend to get watered down to the minimum common denominator. Whenever peak associations take positions that privilege particular organizational agendas or ideologies, problems arise (Cullen 2010). Large EU-based peak associations also encounter many obstacles when consulting a large number of members:

> Brussels activists would like to consult their members, but consultation is often difficult, time-consuming and inconclusive. They are consequently obliged to decide for themselves on issues of strategy, for instance, or on how to advise the Commission on the channeling of funding to national projects. This may lead to accusations that they are insensitive to local views, bureaucratized, or that they cater to vested interests.
>
> (Ruzza 2004: 103)

From another perspective, the lack of participation in EU-based peak associations does not deserve such an elaborate explanation (Olson 1965). Not participating can be seen as the most rational strategy for individual members. When a peak association is very large, individual members have very little opportunity to make their voices heard. Since it is not very likely that their voices will have impact, CSOs tend to not spend their time and resources taking positions on European topics, which as general rule are complex and technical. When interviewed, CSOs affirm that they do not participate as much as they would like in the national platforms' working groups for lack of time. Small CSOs tend to conclude that large CSOs should assume the burden of advocacy activities and participation, in what is referred to as the exploitation of the large by the small (Olson 1965). This scenario fits quite well with the reality of advocacy activities at the EU level presented in Chapter 2. Only large and resourceful CSOs have established direct contact with EU institutions. Small and medium-sized CSOs are more active at the local and national levels. They often complain of EU-based peak associations' lack of responsiveness and they tend not to be satisfied with their performance. However, when the legitimacy of EU peak associations is challenged and their survival is at stake, these same small and medium-sized CSOs tend to give their support. The examples of the legitimacy crises of CLONG (see Chapter 4) and VOICE illustrate this claim. The legitimacy of the humanitarian peak association VOICE was challenged in the early 2000s by a few European officers. Following these claims, VOICE, which represents around 100 members, gathered around 100 signatures from humanitarian CSOs supporting its work (VOICE 2004). Likewise, when the legitimacy of CLONG was challenged by the Commission, this peak association was also able to mobilize the support of a significant number of national CSOs.

2.3 Less Europeanized CSOs have more impact?

Pluralist CSOs often obtain grants from the Commission, but those grants are not directed to cover operating costs. Thus, these CSOs are not compelled to follow the strict Commission requirements in terms of formal representation and geographical coverage. Pluralist EU-based CSOs are usually the most prestigious and popular in their policy areas. They tend to be much more selective in accepting members and are often regional declinations of international CSOs.[30] In the social area, EU-based CSOs exclusively supported by member contributions or other private means represent relatively wealthy citizens or are linked to some specific interest. They are composed of professionals, such as nurses, landowners and shipowners, or they are related to the state or the church (Sanchez Salgado 2014a).[31] Without the support of the EU, only these large organizations would be represented, at the expense of the many medium-sized and small CSOs operating in Europe.

Since these large CSOs are composed of only a few members, coordination at the EU level is simple. Their position statements are not simply based on the coordination of a minimalist position. A small membership also allows for cooperation. Groups with fewer members have more capacity to produce detailed positions but even if they are more effective, they are far less legitimate (Heinelt and Niederhafner 2008). Pluralist EU-based CSOs, such as Oxfam or AI, usually expect every national unit to have one contact person on European affairs. These designated EU contacts, normally lobbyists, meet twice per year with the EU office to decide on EU issues. Some sections, such as AI-UK, have even more staff devoted to EU issues.[32] AI sections elect an administrative council to supervise the implementation of their guidelines (Amnesty International 1998; CLONG 1996; Gray and Statham 2005). As may be expected, the degree of Europeanization of national CSOs also depends on willingness and organizational capacity. In these pluralist CSOs, the chain of representation is much shorter and national members are better informed. Thus, bottom-up dynamics are much more likely. However, even in cases where national sections are very active on EU issues, most initiatives are still taken by the EU office or the international headquarters.[33]

In this configuration, one of the most relevant issues is a potential loss of autonomy for national associations (Coen and Dannreuther 2003). Within EU-based pluralist CSOs, national CSOs can more easily go beyond EU coordination. They may engage in common actions that could weaken the autonomy of individual sections to the benefit of the group. One of the most original initiatives came out of Caritas Europe. In the late 1990s, this association created a solidarity fund to support national sections from Central and Eastern Europe. The ultimate aim of this initiative, which only involved European members, was to reinforce cohesion among European national sections (CLONG 1997b). In another example, in the beginning of the 2000s, AI initiated a strategy of 'European mainstreaming', intended to ensure that EU issues would be more broadly considered by different departments at the national sections. Another interesting example concerns the humanitarian CSO MDM-France. In the late 1990s, MDM set up a policy of transfer of competencies among its sections. Certain dimensions of humanitarian projects were exported from one section to another. This close coordination is not rare among international humanitarian CSOs (Smillie 2000). Some representatives of MDM have been considering the creation of MDM-Europe, which would distribute tasks among different sections.

However, even within these smaller and more cohesive EU-based CSOs, there are still many obstacles to effective European common action, especially when national sections have to agree on political issues or on advocacy campaigns. It is quite difficult to agree on topics at the EU level as different national traditions affect perceptions of EU issues.[34] The problems that national sections encounter in reaching agreements on EU topics are reflected in this quote:

> The international functioning within Europe, especially when it refers to common positions, is still problematic. It is always very

difficult to organize an advocacy campaign at the EU level. Is this related to different timing, sensibilities, options, priorities and/or personalities? A little bit of all of this, without any doubt. On top of that, the question of financial independency of CSOs regarding the main donors, especially the EEC, is still dividing us, given its consequences for our growth.

(MDM-France 1994: 13)

Another factor that significantly hampers cooperation on European issues is potential competition between the international and European levels, which is especially relevant for externally oriented CSOs. This reflects the tension between the dynamics of Europeanization and globalization (Anderson 2003; Schmidt 2004; Verdier and Breen 2001). There is an ongoing discussion in many associations about whether or not European issues should be subordinated to global issues. The EU dimension is more significant for EU-based CSOs with autonomous European offices, such as Caritas, Oxfam, the FIDH-AE and AI. The degree of autonomy of these European offices varies. Some are just Brussels lobbying offices, but others have exclusive competence for EU internal politics.

Many CSOs that do not have EU offices have, nonetheless, transferred their international secretariats to Brussels. That is the case, for example, of International Workers Aid. Created in 1951, the secretariat of this association, now called SOLIDAR, was transferred to Brussels in 1995.[35] The Europeanization of these international CSOs has followed a period in which more competencies and power were transferred to the EU. This Europeanization process was not linear and definitive. Some of the CSOs analyzed transferred their international secretariats from Brussels to Geneva during the 2000s. For example, at the end of the 1980s, MSF signed the Toulouse Convention according to which 'the European structuration of movement is a major issue for our future; we should learn to state our problems in European terms, including the development of MSF and its satellites, training sessions and diplomatic problems in the field (MSF-France 1989: 20)'. Following the convention, MSF created five new positions in charge of European affairs at its international secretariat in Brussels. But during the 1990s, MSF interest in EU issues decreased and in 2004, its international secretariat was moved to Geneva. A similar evolution took place with Action Aid. The European members of this 'big family' created an Alliance (Action Aid Alliance) to be based in Brussels in 1999. At that time, EU issues were clearly prioritized. In 2004, this big family established its international secretariat in Johannesburg and the Alliance was then off of the agenda.[36]

3 The Europeanization of advocacy activities from below

The EU has actively promoted CSOs' participation in Brussels and in the member states. Even if the Europeanization of CSOs through access opportunities has mainly been EU-driven, there are many instances in which CSOs decided to go European without EU intervention. One would expect that CSOs that are not in contact with EU institutions or peak associations have followed a different path toward Europeanization. Europeanization is not only a process characterized by downloading or cross-loading but also by counterloading. Counterloading occurs when CSOs take EU preferences as an example of what not to do. Thus the EU still indirectly affects the goals and action repertoires of these CSOs. Through the promotion of a consensus, the EU shapes the boundaries of the acceptable and therefore the behavior of actors that do not want to be part of that consensus.

3.1 Beyond the Brussels Consensus: A bottom-up Europeanization of CSOs

National CSOs have often engaged in a weaker strategy of Europeanization: internalization (Chapter 2). Even though the EU shapes these CSOs agendas, it does not affect their repertoires of action and targets. Interestingly, even if Europeanization is weak, there is still a lot of room for different types of impact. Some CSOs have simply added European issues to their daily work in a pragmatic way, while others have engaged in a process of cognitive development. This differential impact will be illustrated with human rights CSOs. Chapter 2 showed that these CSOs have not engaged in more ambitious Europeanization strategies, and thus they are the most appropriate group for studying Europeanization through internalization.

The British CSO Liberty is a good example[37] of an organization that can easily accommodate EU issues in its daily activities without changing its action repertoires or its overall strategy. Liberty occasionally includes European issues among its range of topics, but only when they confer new rights upon UK citizens. When Liberty works on EU topics, like the European Charter on Human Rights, it writes policy papers and statements addressed to Westminster and Downing Street.[38] The main reason for not engaging directly in action at the EU level is a lack of economic resources and expertise.[39] For example, even though Liberty launches legal procedures in the United Kingdom and before the European Court of Human Rights in Strasbourg, it doesn't do much litigation before the Court of Justice of the EU, because it does not have the required legal expertise. As a CSO representative said, 'This work is very different from what we are used to. It's very difficult to deal with these issues while based in the UK. Our priority is to deal with issues in the UK.'[40] Resources, understood in a broad sense (including expertise), are one of the main limitations for the Europeanization of CSOs. This is much more obvious in Spain, where human rights CSOs address EU topics in a superficial manner.

The inclusion or exclusion of EU issues in the agendas of CSOs is not always so based on practical considerations. For a few CSOs, there has truly been cognitive development. For example, the French Human Rights League hardly gave any attention to EU issues during the 1970s and 1980s. European issues were ignored or met with skepticism. As this CSO stated at the time, 'Our priority is to fight in France and for France' (LDH 1977: 1). Europe was at first perceived a threat to the French tradition of human rights protection. 'When the head of state proposes a common judicial space to her European partners, a space wherein extradition would be automatic, the Ligue Française des Droits de l'Homme (LDH) leads the fight to respect the French tradition of offering a right to asylum' (LDH 1977: 1). After the signature of the Single European Act, the LDH underwent a true evolution. There was increased interest in European issues and in the establishment of exchanges with other European human rights CSOs. A European policy group was created at the beginning of the 1990s within this CSO and the 63rd Congress of the LDH was given the theme 'Be citizen in Europe' (LDH 1992). In 1999 the LDH president continued to insist on the need to act as European citizens (LDH 1999). Due to this cognitive development, the LDH was much more prone to engage in transnational cooperation. An internalization strategy has now evolved into a more ambitious Europeanization strategy. But, though LDH has undergone some changes, they have been limited. While it has attempted externalization and transnationalization strategies, it has not been very successful so far due to a lack of resources and differences with its partners.[41] The next section more specifically discusses the challenges of transnational cooperation among CSOs beyond the Brussels Consensus.

3.2 Transnational cooperation beyond the Brussels Consensus

A few CSOs have engaged in a bottom-up process of transnationalization. More often than not, transnationalization beyond Brussels has taken the form of contentious collective action (Della Porta and Caiani 2009). Examples of the first European protests include the European March against Unemployment, which gathered around 50,000 people from all over Europe to call for policy measures against poverty, social exclusion and unemployment; and the countersummits held before the openings of the European Summits in Nice, Barcelona, Seville and Copenhagen (Peugeot 1997). During the early 2000s, the movement of countersummits developed into a different form of protest: the European Social Forum (Della Porta and Caiani 2009: 4). The groups engaging in contentious actions have been very different from the groups active in Brussels:

> There are groups in Europe constituted of radical anti-globalisation activists that achieve only very limited acceptance and policy success but are still able to maintain a public presence through their media visibility. But they are unlikely to be represented in Brussels because they would be screened out due to a lack of Commission funding, lack of access and their ideological refusal to engage with mainstream policy actors.
>
> (Ruzza 2004: 138)

One would expect that the EU has not affected social movements engaging independently in European collective action in the same way that it has influenced groups at the Brussels complex. Protest groups would rather use the action repertoires they are familiar with and deal with the topics that are most relevant to their members and supporters. But, a few groups that are relatively new to political discussions also invest in the European public space, since they consider it better adapted to their claims and less invested in by traditional social partners embedded at the national level (Féron 2005).

These assumptions, while interesting, do not give enough attention to one of the most relevant factors that determines these groups' actions: popularity and media visibility. Media visibility is essential to attract new members and sympathizers and to influence the policy process when direct access is restricted. Gaining media visibility is not an easy task. Social movements' leaders often need to adapt to media expectations and thus they do not always represent their members or supporters. The trade-off between influence and participation is also relevant for groups outside of the Brussels complex.

Interestingly, social movements Europeanized from below have also adapted to the EU agenda, or, more specifically, to those EU topics that have gained more media visibility. Their demands are adjusted to the salience of topics at different levels of governance, thus supporting the hypothesis that each level of governance shapes its own protests.

An analysis of activities organized during the European Social Forum in Malmö[42] supports this idea. Most European Social Forum activities targeting EU institutions deal with questions of the 'democratic deficit', external trade and external relations. Activities about member states deal with topics that have gained visibility at the national level, such as privatizations, racism and xenophobia.

The de facto exclusion of countermovements from the Brussels Consensus and the EU policing of transnational protest have also shaped the action repertoires of these groups, for example, by radicalizing their activities. CSOs face a choice between approaches involving consensus or protest. European political leaders and technocrats define what demands are acceptable and open to negotiation. A consensus on goals is then established and stakeholders are invited to work together. The Brussels Consensus is difficult to define but it definitely includes an acceptance of capitalism and market freedom. CSOs that endorse this gain access and possibly influence in European institutional dialogues. Even if agreement on goals is required, there is still a lot of room for disagreement on priorities, the most effective means to achieve these goals and the timing.

Those groups not willing (or able) to engage in the Brussels Consensus are still affected by the EU. They construct their identities through opposition to the identity of their opponents, and thus adopt the Brussels Consensus as a 'countermodel'. The emergence of a participatory regime at the EU level based on expertise, professionalization and sectionalization has possibly contributed to the emergence of its counterpart: an arena where symbolic protest and more or less populist arguments predominate (Eder 2001). Engaging in contentious actions is not just instrumental, as was the case with Greenpeace's symbolic activities in Brussels. Beyond the instrumental dimension, which aims to get media attention in order to set things on the agenda, contentious and radical action repertoires also aim to strengthen motivations among protestors by developing feelings of solidarity and belonging (Della Porta and Caiani 2009). Events such as the ESF produce what has been referred to as 'high-power social drama'. They give participants the impression that they are engaged in an amazing experience or are part of a huge global movement.

For example, in sharp contrast with Brussels Consensus hunters, the main action repertoire of the European March Against Unemployment is direct action, for instance, marches, occupations, demonstrations and other symbolic events (Chabanet 2002). Many of these techniques have been inspired by the action repertoires of national CSOs, such as the French Agir Contre le Chômage. The European Marches organize actions in different cities on their way to Brussels. For example, while in Île de France, the European Marches occupied the royal room at the Castle of Versailles. There are opportunities to discuss employment-related issues at the EU level, either directly with DG Employment or through the intermediary of European associations such as the Social Platform. However, CSOs of the 'Other Europe' prefer not to cooperate with EU-based peak associations because they consider them in the service of the interests of EU institutions and part of the official European establishment. Engaging in direct dialogue with EU institutions or with EU-based associations is against their principles and identity, and would not be accepted by the supporters of these movements (Dahan 2004).

The policing of transnational protest has also played an important role. The assimilation of troublemakers to activist organizations contributes to the radicalization of some movements (Della Porta et al. 2006). After a few years in which successive police provocations exacerbated EU protests, more subtle techniques, such as information gathering and the restriction of freedom of movement, have pacified Euro summits.

The refusal to participate in the groups and associations of the Brussels Consensus is reflected in the existing gap between EU-based CSOs and CSOs that do not have regular contact with the EU. CSOs not regularly involved in EU policymaking gather in alternative spaces such as the European Social Forum. An analysis of the groups and coalitions participating in EU activities within the European Social Forum shows that most have not established any contact with the EU or with EU-based CSOs (Table 7.1).

There are also many differences in terms of organizational capacity, cognitive frames and strategies. While EU-based CSOs follow the example of highly professionalized international CSOs, national CSOs reacting to the Brussels Consensus take highly professionalized CSOs as a countermodel. Contrary to European peak associations, the movements of the Other Europe are weak federations and temporary devices. They do not have permanent staff and, consequently, most of them are only active for specific events, such as EU summits or the European Social Forum. The groups of the Other Europe have been created to focus on unconventional action repertoires. They are not so concerned with fund-raising since protest activities require less resources than actions like lobbying or litigation (Vanhala 2009). The CSOs with a strong presence in Europe mentioned earlier in this chapter, such as CONCORD

Table 7.1 EU networks engaged with Brussels (day one)[43]

Not active in Brussels	Some contacts with Brussels
European Attac Network	Women in Development
Seattle to Brussels Network	Europe—WIDE
European Network for Public Services	Association Européenne pour les Droits de l'Homme—AEDH
Euro marches	Friends of the Earth Europe
Charter for Another Europe Network	European Farmers Coordination—EFC
European Coordination via Campesina	
Stop EPA	
EPA 2007, 2008	
Alter-EU	
Enlazando Alternativas (Europe, Latin America, Caribbean)	
Asia–Europe People's Forum	
European Federation of Journalists	
Big Ask Campaign	
Labour and Globalisation	

Source: Author's analysis of activities at the ESF in Malmö.

and Greenpeace, do not participate in the European Social Forum and similar protest arenas. Spaces such as the ESF have strong left-wing profiles and a significant number of activists are even from the extreme left (Della Porta and Caiani 2009). Thus, it is not surprising that organizations such as Oxfam or AI, which have also liberal and conservative contributors and supporters, are not inclined to participate very visibly in these protest events.

European social movements and their national members are not isolated from politics. The leaders of these social movements are in contact with members of the European Parliament and national politicians sympathetic to the alter-globalization movement. Their contacts are especially from the left and extreme left, and they also participate in alter-EU activities.[44] Less sympathetic political elites also interact with alter-globalization groups, but not in a relationship of mutual trust and cooperation. They just feel obliged to listen to these groups to try to reduce the so-called democratic deficit. However, for the social movements of the Other Europe, whether or not to cooperate with EU policy makers is a difficult choice. Organizations that cooperate with European institutions (such as many trade unions) are considered 'traitors' in spaces such as the European Social Forum. As a general rule, alter-globalization movements do not trust political leaders because these leaders try to discourage them from engaging in contentious politics (Féron 2005).

Conclusion

The EU has been often depicted as a system dominated by an elite of Brussels-based CSOs. This picture prevails when one focuses on what happens in the Brussels complex. However, when the EU is conceived as a multilevel system, where CSOs can exploit multiple opportunities at multiple levels, the picture is much more complex and nuanced. This focus on a well-delineated empirical issue—the study of the EU's effects on CSOs—has brought together studies focusing on distinct forms of CSO participation at different levels.

As highlighted in many studies, the EU has been promoting action repertoires that are based in the provision of expertise and non-contentious action. The Brussels Consensus has given the impression that Brussels is just talking to Brussels. This has raised many critical questions regarding the democratic potential of CSOs and the representativeness of EU peak associations. When the EU is conceived of as a multilevel system, CSOs' participation can be seen as a complex and heterogeneous process, where the quality of participation varies across sectors and member states. Inequalities and difficulties exist, but there are also examples in which CSOs have been effective at getting their topics into the policy agenda.

EU structuring effects would be very weak if they only affected EU-based CSOs. This chapter has shown that the EU also reaches national CSOs through EU-instigated national policy processes and through EU peak associations. The inclusion of national CSOs is far from being effective. It depends on the capacity and willingness of member states and peak associations. However, EU guidelines have changed mentalities and created expectations among CSOs that may bear some fruit in the future. Participation in EU-supported peak associations is particularly problematic, since there is a trade-off between inclusiveness and representativeness. When the number of members is too high and too diverse, it is very difficult to organize representation. The Europeanizing effects are also less significant. Pluralist EU-based CSOs share more core values, their members are closer and they perform similar activities; this leads to stronger forms of Europeanization.

The EU empowerment of national CSOs can contribute to their effective participation in EU-based peak associations.

EU influence goes far beyond the Brussels Consensus and far beyond the promotion of participation at the domestic level. Many CSOs without direct relationships to Brussels are also discussing EU topics and participating in EU politics in their own ways, following their own preferred action repertoires. The EU has also contributed indirectly to the Europeanization of these groups, even if this form of Europeanization is more sporadic and weaker. When the EU is perceived as the enemy, it has served as a countermodel in CSOs' identity-building processes. Social movements and protest groups are often considered the ideal type of CSOs to represent the interests of organized citizens. However, a closer look at the internal dynamics of these groups shows that they also face many challenges regarding their autonomy and representation.

Conclusion: The Political Construction of European Civil Society: Legitimate and Democratic?

Introduction

Contemporary research on public policy and governance has to keep pace with society. Europeanization studies need to be placed in a broader social context, since Europe affects politics and society differently. Existing analytical tools have to be adapted to the study of social actors. Bringing Europeanization studies closer to society not only increases understanding of the European Union's (EU's) shaping of civil society organizations (CSOs), it also improves understanding of the concept of Europeanization. It challenges current assumptions and calls attention to neglected areas of study.

This book also offers new insights for the major debates on the relationships between governments and the voluntary sector, thus contributing to the normalization of EU studies. The relationships between CSOs and governments are one of the most salient topics in looking to the future of the voluntary sector (Roberts 2007). How does state action affect the special characteristics and autonomy of this sector? Is state intervention contributing to the healthy development of CSOs, or is it turning them away from their key values and missions? Are the advantages of state action worth the risks? Are sound accountability and New Public Management (NPM) the best way to ensure effectiveness in the provision of public services? Should state agencies support the advocacy activities of CSOs? Are CSOs an effective and reliable way to promote a European identity? So much is expected of CSOs that, without clarifying their role, little can be said about how they perform so many potentially conflicting functions (Ruzza 2007). Most of the arguments on these issues are not sufficiently supported by empirical evidence. This contribution will hopefully lead to a more fact-based discussion.

1 Integrating a sociological dimension in Europeanization studies

A sociological approach reveals many of the blind spots in Europeanization studies. When the sociological dimension is missing, research findings run the risk of not being sufficiently nuanced. For example, top-down Europeanization studies tend to single out one type of EU pressure, which is not necessarily the most relevant for the topic under study. The interaction between institutional constraints and the agency of individual actors is fluid and complex, and cannot be captured without embedding politics in a broader social context. With a combination of approaches (taking into account both institutional pressures and actor agency), it is still possible to identify general trends, but they are always provisional and context-dependent. This section first discusses the existence of multiple European pressures and their interactions. The benefits of the combination of a top-down institutional approach and a bottom-up sociology of the EU are then further specified. Attention is then turned to the temporal dimension, which has proven to be crucial for the study of the Europeanization of CSOs.

1.1 A diversity of interrelated EU pressures

According to liberal democratic theory, CSOs' participation in politics occurs mainly at the decision-making stage of the policy process. Based on this assumption, most studies on the Europeanization of CSOs focus on collective action and participatory governance. Given this narrow focus, the degree of Europeanization of CSOs has often been underestimated. The European opportunities that matter the most for CSOs' daily activities are not necessarily the ones that have been most studied. When analysis focuses exclusively on access opportunities, the emerging picture is one of a consultation and lobbying process dominated by an elite of large EU-based CSOs, often—but not always—supported by the Commission. This presents the EU as an elitist system that is not very likely to empower the weak (Dür and Mateo 2012).

When a more diverse set of opportunities is observed and when attention is also turned to the national level, a different picture emerges. The EU offers access and funding opportunities not only to EU-based CSOs but also to other CSOs at several levels. EU funding opportunities at the national level are mainly directed to service providers. However, most CSOs are engaged both in service provision and in advocacy activities, and, more often than not, both types of activities are interconnected. Examples of multilevel access opportunities are the European Social Fund and consultation obligations deriving from EU-driven policy coordination instruments (Chapter 7). When a wide variety of multilevel opportunities is taken into account, national CSOs are shown to be much more Europeanized than is normally assumed. The use of EU funding opportunities in policy areas where they are available is quite widespread. CSOs are also involved in advocacy activities on EU issues at the domestic level or through the intermediation of European peak associations (chapters 3 and 7). It is true that this involvement has not always implied a very strong degree of Europeanization, but the potential Europeanizing effects of these memberships are, nevertheless, relevant.

Even if the participation of CSOs in the decision-making process were the only relevant issue, it would still be necessary to look at funding opportunities, since they indirectly affect participation. European opportunities reinforce each other. The Europeanization of CSOs' advocacy activities can be strengthened through the development of funding opportunities, even if access opportunities remain constant. EU funding opportunities—which are the most widely used opportunities—have often contributed to the development of advocacy activities, confirming the thesis that public support of CSOs enhances their advocacy activities (Chaves et al. 2004; Mosley 2012).

EU funding schemes have promoted advocacy activities through the support of EU peak associations (Chapter 3). These peak associations have played a role in the promotion of access opportunities at the national level. EU funds have also instigated an expansion process among many CSOs, especially humanitarian CSOs (Chapter 5), which have thus become relatively large organizations with substantial budgets. This in turn has enabled them to effectively engage in advocacy activities. CSOs less represented at the EU level have never been empowered by EU funding schemes (Chapter 2). And, even setting aside the issue of organizational capacity, CSOs that have been in contact with the Commission for funding purposes have also tended to engage more frequently in EU consultations and partnerships, because they have become familiar with EU policies and access opportunities.

EU funding can also indirectly improve the dynamics of participation. EU officials have closer relationships with the inner circle of EU peak associations that obtain Commission support (Wolff 2013). This trend has been negatively perceived by scholars and observers, who assume that there is a cozy relationship between EU peak associations and EU officials. According to my interviews, the receipt of EU funds confers a certain legitimacy and thus increases one's chances of being heard. When an organization has a contract with the EU or a partnership agreement, European institutions feel obliged to hear its input. In the words of one CSO representative, 'When you work with governments, dialogue is improved. When you get their money, they are obliged to listen to you. Public funds open doors for communication. We feel more legitimate in addressing them.'[1] In fact, large CSOs sometimes decide to apply for funding schemes not because they need them, but rather to improve their communication with government officials.[2]

1.2 Bringing together bottom-up and top-down approaches to Europeanization

The mainstream institutional approach to Europeanization studies has often been challenged for its determinist, top-down character (Palier and Surel 2007). The actor-centered bottom-up approach has also been criticized for its lack of relevance for theory building. The combination of these two approaches offers a reliable representation of the nuances of reality without neglecting the identification of general trends.

The EU has clearly made a difference for CSOs in Europe. As a general rule, the Europeanization of CSOs has been mainly EU-driven. The EU has contributed to the shaping of national voluntary landscapes, reinforcing some policy areas, such as humanitarian aid, at the expense of other policy areas, such as the protection of human rights within the EU. Without this impetus, the Brussels complex would be almost exclusively dominated by business interests and wealthy professional groups.

The social area provides an interesting case study since there is a multilevel system of access and funding opportunities. The EU's shaping of social CSOs is much more complex than for other types of CSOs, since the former depends on the willingness and the capacity of member states to implement EU obligations regarding consultation procedures and the provision of funds. Here Europeanization should not be understood as a zero-sum game, in which the Europeanization of CSOs comes at the detriment of their national sense of belonging. The creation of EU opportunities has often reinforced the national dimension of CSOs. For example, the EU has indirectly contributed to the structuring of national civil society landscapes, strengthening the links between local CSOs and national peak associations.

The importance of the EU in shaping CSOs is not only shown in institutional top-down analyses of EU opportunities; it is also seen in analyses of their usages. More often than not, usages *by* Europe have determined the outcomes of the Europeanization process. EU opportunities have been created and promoted by Commission officials according to their own specific preferences and interests (Chapter 4).

Even if the role of EU officials and European policy entrepreneurs has been crucial, they have not always been able to dominate the process once it has started. A sociological account emphasizes the interactive nature of politics. Europeanization is not an automatic and one-sided process and there is also some evidence of usages of Europe. EU officials have been proven to have little capacity to create CSOs from scratch or to use CSOs too bluntly for their own purposes. Many CSOs have refused the support of the Commission for internal reasons and have preferred to develop weaker forms of Europeanization. CSOs have also been active in the shaping of funding and access opportunities. Once in Brussels, EU-based CSOs successfully advocated for the inclusion of a legal basis for consultations in the treaties. Nonetheless, CSOs are still far from getting everything that they want, and, more often than not, their demands are discarded without explanation.

Comparison shows that the EU's role in the shaping of CSOs is far from being uniform across policy areas. When political opportunities are weaker or non-existent, the EU has contributed much less to the shaping of CSOs. Humanitarian aid stands out as the most Europeanized sector, whereas human rights CSOs working within the EU are much less Europeanized. In other policy areas, such as development aid, the Europeanization process has been moderate but still significant. In the social policy area it is difficult to identify a general trend since consultation procedures and the availability of EU funds depend on member states. Further research should assess to what extent EU opportunities reflect the needs and aspirations of EU citizens as well as which sectors are being excluded or neglected.

A detailed account of the Europeanization process also reveals that the EU does not have the same effects in different national or regional contexts. The degree of Europeanization depends on the usages of EU opportunities, and these usages are affected by many factors, including national opportunities. EU member states offer different opportunities, which affect the Europeanization strategies of their CSOs. More interestingly, even when member states offer similar opportunities, effects also differ depending on the national contexts and the capacities of the voluntary sectors, among other factors. For example, while in some countries, like the United Kingdom, the existence of generous funding opportunities has supported the Europeanization of CSOs (positive persistence hypothesis); in other countries such as Spain the existence of generous national opportunities has discouraged many CSOs from acquiring European funding skills (negative persistence hypothesis). In the absence of sufficient national opportunities, CSOs turn to the EU level in search of compensation (France) or remain inactive (Greece). This diversity reflects the context-dependent combination of multiple factors that lead the process (Chapter 4).

Unbalanced Europeanization across countries and policy fields raises questions about how EU priorities are defined and to what extent they are being effectively implemented by the Commission and member states. Choices about who to support should be transparent and subject to public scrutiny. The implementation process should be closely monitored and regularly reviewed to reduce implementation gaps.

1.3 The importance of the temporal dimension in Europeanization studies

Through the inclusion of a comparative analysis over a long time period, this book has addressed many of the methodological challenges in the empirical study of the Europeanization of interest groups (Saurugger 2005). This has shown that Europeanization is not a linear, infallible process. It depends on the long-term evolution of EU and national opportunities. For example, EU funding opportunities for external action expanded considerably during the 1980s and 1990s, which helped shape the European CSO landscape of the time (Chapter 3). The EU had less influence on the shaping of CSOs during the 2000s, when national funding opportunities were generally gaining relevance. Many CSOs that were highly dependent on EU funds during the 1980s and 1990s successfully diversified their public funding sources during the 2000s. In the social area, the Europeanization of CSOs has been encouraged through the implementation of European Community Initiatives and it peaked with the EQUAL program (2000–2006). After EQUAL, the involvement of CSOs in the social area has been increasingly left to member states. Thus, the Europeanization of CSOs today depends more than ever on member states' willingness and capacities. The temporal dimension also affects access opportunities and its Europeanizing effects (Chapter 7). For example, many national CSOs started to get involved in the EU policy process when they had the opportunity to comment on the national reports on social inclusion produced within the framework of the Open Method of Coordination. However, since the introduction of the Europe 2020 strategy, social CSOs' participation in the elaboration of national reform plans has been much more limited. This trend could also be related to factors such as the economic crisis and changes of government in several member states.

Analysis over a long period is necessary but not always sufficient. Europeanization studies often fail to differentiate the two different stages of political processes. The first stage of Europeanization is the decision to use European opportunities. The second stage consists of the ensuing transformations. When Europeanization concerns hierarchically organized public policies, these stages are not so significant, since national political actors cannot decide to just take or leave EU directives and regulations. However, distinguishing between these stages is crucial in the analysis of the Europeanization of CSOs and other non-state actors. Failing to distinguish between stages of political processes can limit the scope of research findings.

The distinction between these two stages is also valuable in clarifying the ongoing debate over top-down Europeanization studies versus the 'usages of Europe' approach. Usages of Europe is much more relevant for the first stage, where the motto 'no impact without usages' prevails. For this stage a broad understanding of usages, including 'usages by Europe' is also needed to fully grasp the Europeanization process.

In the second stage, actors are confronted with EU rules and constraints, and thus a better motto would be 'no usages without impact'. Europeanization can be seen as downloading, cross-loading or counterloading. When EU requirements are quite specific, for example, in mandating sound management, there is much more room for downloading and for a process of imposed convergence (Andersen 2004). However, the EU does not always provide clear rules, for example, concerning the promotion of EU values and identity building (Chapter 6). In these areas, the EU has made itself simply a facilitator; it encouraged certain procedures and ideas. It is much less clear that CSOs' perceptions and values were transformed, and uploading dynamics were much more likely.

The EU has also initiated Europeanization through cross-loading by promoting transnational cooperation. Here, the outcome depends on the degree and quality of interactions. The EU could certainly design better rules to ensure that partnerships are not merely superficial, but even if it did so, it would be difficult to predict a uniform outcome for the Europeanization process (Chapter 6).

A bottom-up analysis sheds some light on another dynamic in Europeanization: counterloading. CSOs without direct EU contact with the EU can still be Europeanized to a certain extent. They often focus on popular EU topics in order to gain media visibility or mobilize their members (Chapter 7). In a dynamic of counterloading, CSOs define their action repertoires in opposition to models preferred by EU institutions. Even if the distinction between different stages is relevant, movement from stage one to stage two is not linear and automatic. There seems to be a middle area in which CSOs confront EU requirements, which can result in a successful learning process or in the abandonment of the European path.

2 The shaping of CSOs: Legitimate and democratic?

Scholars' positions on the potential contribution of CSOs to democratic legitimacy in the EU are far from uniform, and range from hostile to optimistic (Greenwood 2007). This lack of consensus contrasts with the official position of the Commission, which has high expectations for the democratic potential of CSOs. CSOs are particularly relevant for the EU, since its constitutional structure imposes considerable limits on democratic representation (Kohler-Koch and Quittkat 2013). It is difficult to empirically assess CSOs' contributions to EU democracy since there are many different facets to the problem: different dimensions of democracy, different institutions and different processes for involving CSOs (Hüller and Kohler-Koch 2008). The assessment of CSOs' contributions to the democratic process also depends on how this contribution is assessed. For example, it is understandable to arrive at discouraging conclusions from a scenario where CSOs' participation is considered conducive to democracy only when equal political participation is ensured and policy effects are seen (Kohler-Koch 2013). When assessment is not based on such high normative standards, but rather on analysis of the modest but relevant contributions of CSOs to democratic governance (as in this book), the overall picture tends to be more optimistic.

The potential contribution of CSOs to democratic legitimacy has been challenged on many grounds, namely, for the imbalances in the interest-group system, the poor quality of deliberations, the risk of instrumentalization of CSOs by the Commission and the weak links between CSOs and citizens (Kohler-Koch and Quittkat 2013; Warleigh 2001). It is argued that while CSOs can enhance democracy under certain circumstances, the current EU system does not satisfactorily fulfill these circumstances (Friedrich 2007). Analysis of the Commission's practices tends to conclude that its technocratic approach has improved transparency and access, but public discourse has not necessarily been enhanced (Hüller and Kohler-Koch 2008). Focusing on the EU's role in shaping CSOs sheds new light on these topics and offers new dimensions for assessing the democratic potential of CSOs. This section first addresses the topics that have been most widely discussed: the representativeness and autonomy of CSOs. Then attention turns to a more original—and currently neglected—way of looking at the democratic process: participatory democracy at the policy implementation stage and CSOs' contributions to identity building.

2.1 Addressing imbalances in the system of interest representation

Most studies on the contribution of CSOs to representation focus on the internal representation of EU-based CSOs. But CSOs do not only contribute to the policy process through their ability to coordinate, aggregate and channel their members' views. They also redress imbalances in the interest-group system by representing excluded voices and supporting causes that are current in the international community, such as the protection of human rights and the environment. This view is in line with codifications of political representation that are not exclusively based on the representation of a defined constituency through electoral mechanisms (Johansson and Lee 2012). Representation can also be understood as a process of claim making where legitimacy is acquired if a claim is considered authentic by a significant audience. Legitimate representation could also just mean that different social perspectives are being brought into the public debate. Actually, excessive emphasis in calculating memberships could exclude a significant part of civil society. Within the CSO community, there is currently no agreement on what constitutes representativeness, or on whether only representative organizations should be consulted (Ruzza 2007).

A broad conception of representation has some similarities with the principles of associative democracy, according to which public authorities should redress imbalances in the system of interest representation and shape organizations to ensure that they fully contribute to the democratic process (Cohen and Rogers 1992). Political intervention should reduce bias in representation by including poorly resourced and excluded groups. The inclusion of the excluded in the policy process also helps improve the quality of deliberations.

The imbalance in the representation of social interests at the EU level has been identified as one of the main shortcomings of civil society participation (Kohler-Koch 2013). To address this problem, the EU is funding many citizen groups in a conscious attempt to manipulate the composition of the interest-group system (Mahoney 2004). The EU is primarily funding CSOs that represent the voices of excluded populations and of the general interest, and thus it is addressing imbalances in the system of interest representation (Sanchez Salgado 2014a). Without Commission support, only large, well-resourced organizations would be represented in the policy process. This conclusion is valid not only for CSOs but also for economic interests. For example, the coordination of small and medium enterprises (SME) at the EU level was not spontaneous; it was supported by the Commission (Coen and Dannreuther 2003). EU opportunities play a potentially democratic role in the engineering of CSOs, which is consistent with the role required of state authorities in the associative democratic model. This system is not without risks. As discussed above, while addressing imbalances, the EU can also shape the system of interest representation in a way that fits its bureaucratic interests. State agencies may support some groups at the expense of others. There are many examples of CSOs that are not effectively represented at the EU level due to a lack of public resources and support. Further research is needed to determine to what extent the Commission's constituency-building strategy undermines its capacity to promote an autonomous democratic force. Once the potential risks are better known, the existing problems could be reduced through the establishment of procedures that place bureaucratic policy choices under public scrutiny.

Associative democracy also values classical forms of representation, since public authorities are expected to support healthy characteristics among CSOs, including formal mechanisms for accountability. To this purpose, the EU provides specific support to peak associations for developing contacts, solidifying membership and strengthening exchanges among their members (Sanchez Salgado 2014a). The EU also supports capacity-building in national CSOs, thus giving them more opportunity to participate effectively in national consultation procedures and EU peak associations (Sanchez Salgado 2013). The launch of the European Citizens' Initiatives (ECIs) has also created new opportunities to bridge the gap between EU peak associations and the grassroots, as it fosters coordination between EU-based and national CSOs (Greenwood 2012).

In spite of these efforts, EU-based CSOs are often accused of being closer to the Commission than to the social actors that they are expected to represent (Buth and Kohler-Koch 2013; Giraudon 2000). The problem is not the absence of formal mechanisms of representation. Most, if not all, EU peak associations have a membership-based democratic election system. However, scholars criticize the existence of a trade-off between efficiency and democracy. The more a group is able to provide expertise—as encouraged by the Commission—the less it is able to represent its members (Saurugger 2006). While relevant, this trade-off should not just be criticized; it needs to be assessed in relation to internal representational barriers (Johansson and Lee 2012). There are indeed many obstacles to effective representation in peak associations, especially those composed of a great number of individual member organizations and characterized by a long chain of representation. Language barriers, ideological and cultural differences, lack of resources and expert knowledge and a low level of attention to European issues have often hampered members' active participation. Conflicts over identity, resources, goals and strategy are common currency within any kind of transnational movement network (Bandy and Smith 2005b). EU-based CSOs would still experience serious difficulties in ensuring internal representation even if the EU were not promoting an action repertoire based on the provision of expertise. It could even be argued that the politization of EU discussions would exacerbate ideological differences within the CSO community.

Empirical evidence shows that a few EU-based CSOs do better than others in the task of representing their members (Chapter 7). The EU supports all inclusive peak associations, which, paradoxically, encounter greater obstacles to effectively representing their members. The trade-off that is more relevant to the study of internal representation is that between inclusiveness and effective participation, in other words, a trade-off between descriptive representation (completeness of group membership) and formal representation (direct governance by members). EU-supported peak associations tend to score better in descriptive representation, since they represent more CSOs and have wide geographical coverage. But, for this very reason, it is much harder for them to ensure formal representation in practice. These difficulties seem to be primarily related to internal cohesion and size. In large, all-inclusive peak associations, national CSOs do not have much incentive to become involved, given the small chance of being heard. This finding suggests that the normative conditions for ensuring CSOs' internal representation are too ambitious and often in conflict.

2.2 The EU's shaping of CSOs: Putting their autonomy at risk?

Even if the EU plays a key role in the structuring of CSOs, this does not necessarily mean that their autonomy is curtailed. The extent of the danger depends on the specific funding and consultation arrangements and on the way public officials and CSO leaders interact within the framework of these arrangements. In other words, one should not assume that public funds or consultation procedures lead to CSOs' dependency without further investigation. Some institutional arrangements are more conducive to a loss of autonomy than others. At the EU level, the Commission has often supported CSOs to serve its own purposes, but once established, this relationship has become one of mutual dependency. 'Interdependence' is a much better term for it (Steen 1996). This conclusion is confirmed by recent studies that argue that government funding does not inevitably cause voluntary organizations to become instruments of the state (Roberts 2007: 30).

The EU's shaping of CSOs for democratic purposes is not without risks. As Hirst pointed out, 'The risks of the state acquiring too much power become too great—it shapes associations to its own purposes' (1994: 101). More specifically, the model of associative democracy, in insisting on the role of the state in the shaping of associations, presupposes excessive power in executive agencies, which use this power to pursue their own self-interests.

This supports some commentators' hypothesis of a circle of convenience (Boin and Marchesetti 2010). According to it, CSOs support the Commission in order to secure EU funding; both the Commission and CSOs promote their narrow interests to the detriment of the democratic process. However, it seems unlikely that a circle of convenience would effectively continue to run over the long term in a system with as many checks and balances as the EU. For example, Commission officials do not have the power to adopt the EU budget, and thus they cannot always impose their will on the Parliament and the Council. The Commission has contributed to the Europeanization process through 'project politics' as a strategy to avoid the treaties and the resistance of the member states (Kohler-Koch 2013). However, member states could put an end to this expansion and increase their supervisory powers (Chapter 3). The thesis of a circle of convenience is thus challenged by an analysis that takes into account the long term. Due to lack of staff and organizational capacity, even the Commission has tried to put the brakes on a process of expansion that it initiated itself.

EU-funded CSOs could also tend to promote European solutions, thus undermining the subsidiarity principle (Kohler-Koch 2013). However, the EU does not just support EU-based CSOs. It has also empowered national CSOs to participate in national dialogue processes on EU issues (Chapter 7). One would expect that these national CSOs propose primarily national solutions. When everything is taken into account, participation is much more multilevel than usually imagined. The degree of empowerment of national CSOs depends on the policy area. If more subsidiarity is wanted, the social area could serve as a model.

There are many ways in which the risk of bureaucratic politics can be addressed by EU institutions. Executive bodies have to act within the framework of detailed and specific mandates and follow transparent procedures. The EU could still promote certain civic values, such as civic engagement, tolerance, cultural diversity. Even if the promotion of these values shapes the preferences of a few CSOs, this evolution should not be seen as problematic. CSO leaders and members could just as well make a legitimate and autonomous decision to dedicate time and effort to those values and priorities that are widely supported in a democratic system. Thus, even if Commission officials and CSO representatives often share policy goals, even if they agree that 'working together' is the best way to go forward, it is not so clear whether this situation is endangering the democratic process. More interestingly, funding arrangements can also promote CSO autonomy. State agencies can promote the diversification of sources of funding, which reduces the risks of resource dependency. Measures in this direction have already been adopted by the Commission in the social area (Sanchez Salgado 2014a).

To avoid giving excessive power to state agencies, some of the functions currently performed by the Commission could also be directly assumed by citizens. For example, a system of vouchers would allow citizens to choose the associations that benefit from public funding (Schmitter 1995). However, giving such power to citizens is not without risks. The average citizen might lack knowledge about the underlying causes of poverty and exclusion, and be influenced by catchy slogans and simplistic statements. There is no reason to expect that citizens would support *civic* organizations; they could give their vouchers to *uncivic* organizations that promote racism, discrimination and even violence.

Last but not the least, loss of autonomy can also result from dependence on other sources of funding such as foundations, churches and commercial activities. The disadvantages of the receipt of public funding are often overestimated while the limits of alternative sources of funding are never noticed. CSOs linked to religious institutions receive instructions from religious leaders and tend to limit their public statements to what is currently accepted in their dogma.[3] Even CSOs that get funding directly from members and supporters should not be a priori free from criticism. There is no reason why the autonomy of member-based organizations should be taken for granted. It can be compromised when a single member intrumentalizes the organization for its own purposes (Eising 2009). Public marketing techniques used to attract member-contributors run the risk of falling into the 'poverty porn' trap, which leads to focus on oversimplified stories, sensationalism and a 'worst is best' attitude.[4]

2.3 Shaping CSOs, but not controlling them

Some authors think that the Commission exerts a considerable degree of control over EU-funded networks (Wolff 2013). Participation in the policy process would not be very valuable if CSOs' actions were controlled by EU officials. EU funding and access opportunities do indeed shape CSOs' behavior, as has been shown in this book. However, it is much less clear whether the EU's influence on CSOs should be seen as 'control'.

EU influence is not direct and automatic; it always requires the consent of CSOs. Funding requirements are often very detailed, providing specific priorities and detailed instructions about management rules, which has led to goal displacement and to the promotion of NPM techniques among CSOs (Chapter 5). Given these opportunities, CSOs decided to dedicate time and energy to meeting EU requirements, detouring their attention from other priorities and management styles. However, goal displacement only clearly occurred in a few CSOs that were highly dependent on EU funds (exclusive CSOs). Also, resource dependency is not necessarily everlasting. The study of an extended time period revealed that a few CSOs have successfully used EU funds to launch expansion. After a few years of resource dependency, these CSOs successfully diversified their funding and attained a reasonable degree of autonomy. Interestingly, if these CSOs had not used EU funds, they might never have been able to attain the degree of maturity and autonomy that they have today. Resource dependency may be a necessary step to launch a quick growth process, and, if used well, to become a large professional CSO that makes a substantial impact. While small CSOs are very vulnerable to governmental constraints, large CSOs can always develop strategies to reduce resource dependency and the problems related to it.[5] In these cases, public support is paradoxical; it implies resource dependency but it can also empower CSOs to become independent in the long term.

CSOs have also adapted their action repertoires to the Commission's 'working together' consensual framework (Chapter 7). They have engaged in patterns of interaction with EU officials that have led to more trust and understanding. This does not necessarily mean that CSOs have changed their overall goals or intentions to satisfy EU preferences. EU-based peak associations highly dependent on EU funds are often very critical of EU policies and institutions (Armstrong 2010; Sanchez Salgado 2014a). In the words of a Commission official, 'The Social Platform takes positions about what the European Commission is doing and they are often quite direct in recounting problems, even aggressively so.'[6] To date, CSOs may not be capable of securing radical policy shifts, but they are able to exert modest pressure to achieve policy adjustment (Cullen 2010). The mutual shaping of CSOs and EU institutions is an essential part of the policy process. Protest groups also adapt their agendas to the most salient topics at different levels of governance in order to gain media attention (Chapter 7). They adopt professionalized CSOs as a countermodel and thus their action repertoires and even their identities are affected.

Even if the priorities of CSOs and the government may tend to coincide due to goal displacement, this does not necessarily mean that CSOs' priorities are mere implementations of government policies. CSOs also perform lobbying activities that affect governmental priorities. EU priorities are dictated by many factors, such as public opinion, the media and some big member states. CSOs are also often consulted about specific cases and situations. And, sometimes, EU officials administering support for CSOs have previously worked for large CSOs, which makes it even less clear who is really controlling or influencing whom.

Interestingly, the existence of control is never acknowledged by the main actors in the field (Wolff 2013). Key EU officials say that they do not need remote-controlled networks. They perceive key networks as independent and say that they never try to use these actors as their agents. They also say that EU-based CSOs would not accept any attempts to control them. In a situation of mutual dependency, one would expect that subtle methods of instrumentalization are not reported because both sides are benefiting from the relationship. So there could be a cozy relationship between CSOs in privileged positions and EU officials. This argument, supported by CSOs with less EU access and funding, is difficult to verify. EU funding has created tensions between funded CSOs and those that are a poor fit for EU funding priorities (Cullen 2010).

Independently of what EU officials and CSOs say, the empirical evidence in this book shows that EU-funded CSOs have enough leeway to develop a life of their own; they network, generate expertise, gain support and perform functions that are beneficial for society. When EU-funded CSOs perform well, they acquire a degree of reputation and public support that can be used to maintain their independence from public institutions. The EU has often supported CSOs to serve its own purposes, but once these CSOs are well established, the EU has shown little capacity to control them. This explains why excessive dependency on EU funding does not lead to an absence of criticism. It also shows why the Commission has rarely been able to stop the activities of EU-based CSOs through the suppression of funding. CSOs highly dependent on the EU, such as the former CLONG, have survived funding crises, but only when they had sufficient public support (Chapter 4).

2.4 The service delivery function and participatory democracy

Service provision is a fundamental dimension of the democratic process. While discussing the democratic potential of CSOs, current studies suffer from an 'input fixation' (Pestoff 2009). According to liberal democratic theory, the contribution of CSOs to democracy has always been related to their participation in decision-making processes, that is, the input side of the policy process. EU-based CSOs are expected to contribute to output legitimacy, but still, it is always assumed that their contribution intervenes exclusively at the decision-making stage of the policy process. This is a very narrow conception of CSOs' democratic potential. Democracy *by* the people also means granting citizens the ability to implement public policies. This obviously raises questions about the conditions under which citizens should be allowed to perform this function.

Many state requirements on service delivery by CSOs reflect the legitimate need to account for the use of public funds. Sound management ensures probity in the use of public funds, while NPM is expected to improve CSOs' performance. Like many other public authorities, the EU is requesting market-style efficiency of CSOs. Efficiency and value for money are currently the most popular values among public administrations, at the expense of other values more typical of the voluntary sector. Again, it is important to keep in mind that 'the problem is not a contract itself, but what an CSO agrees to do under the terms of a contract' (Smillie 2000: 172).

Many CSOs have embraced a market logic without considering this process problematic for their basic values. Bureaucratization and professionalization are seen as a consequence of organizational growth, and not necessarily linked to the use of public funding schemes (Roberts 2007). This argument is consistent with the fact that many CSOs not receiving any kind of governmental or intergovernmental funding also become professional. For the majority of CSOs studied, voluntary life and political activism are inherent to their mission. As Table C.1 shows, CSOs tend to be committed to certain values, as clearly stated in their websites.

Table C.1 Values of some of the most EU-active CSOs

Association	Values
Médecins du Monde	Human dignity, impartiality, independence
Médecins sans Frontières	Medical ethics, independence, impartiality and neutrality, bearing witness and accountability
Oxfam	Human rights, gender justice, diversity, active citizenship, good governance, transparency, etc.
Amnesty International	Human rights
Social Platform	Human dignity, gender equality and equality for all, respect for diversity, solidarity, freedom, social justice, sustainability, transparency and participatory democracy
CONCORD*	Solidarity, human rights, justice and democracy
Greenpeace	Transparency and accountability

Note: * Confederation for Relief and Development.
Source: The websites of these CSOs.[7]

Many CSOs fear the potential negative impact of professionalization on their voluntary values. To address this problem, they have developed strategies to preserve voluntary life. For example, Médecins du Monde France (MDM-France), concerned about the possible negative impact of professionalization, ordered an external evaluation by academics at the end of the 1990s (MDM-France 1999) and introduced several changes to its internal rules based on the recommendations.

Efforts to preserve voluntary life would be more effective if government rules were adapted to the needs of the voluntary sector. Though the need to account for public money is legitimate, the promotion of market-style management techniques is not the only way to ensure accountability, and it is certainly not the best fit for the voluntary sector. Public authorities should develop specific criteria to assess CSOs, including, for example, the number of volunteers, members and supporters and the quality of voluntary life. However, public authorities have up until now been generally reluctant to take voluntary values into account in their evaluation procedures. Just to give an example, the EU has always been very hesitant to accept in-kind contributions as eligible in their requirements for matching of EU funds with funds from other sources. The EU says that 'it may be difficult to calculate the financial value of such contributions and to assess whether it has effectively been provided'.[8] However, in-kind contributions are typical of the voluntary sector because volunteers provide services free of charge. The need to take in-kind contributions into account is regularly raised by CSOs, as their members and supporters continue to offer services in lieu of cash. That said, the most recent EU financial regulation states that access to funding has to be facilitated for entities with limited administrative resources representing a priority target population. This regulation opens up the possibility of accepting in-kind contributions in support of low-value grants (European Parliament and Council 2012).

It is the responsibility of public officials to discern which CSOs are better placed as channels for public funds that will serve the interests of target populations. To ensure the quality of public services, public authorities should make more effort to take the values of the voluntary sector into account in their evaluation tools. On top of financial audits, or even social audits (as is typical of the corporate sector), why not perform civic audits? Holding CSOs accountable to the values they proclaim would make more sense than pure financial accountability. Financial accountability in the voluntary sector could be less strict. This can be justified with one of the basic principles of the voluntary sector: the non-distribution constraint. According to economic theory, since the profit element is absent from voluntary organizations, there is no incentive for them to neglect quality of service. The non-distribution constraint can act as an accountability mechanism and reduce the need for alternative forms of accountability.

2.5 Identity building through CSOs: A political system with multiple identities

CSOs—along with many other kinds of transnational groups—have often been considered an essential component of a political system (Deutsch 1968; Haas 1968). CSOs have supported the EU integration process through the promotion of EU values and topics, through communication activities and through transnational cooperation. All of these activities have been aimed at creating a positive opinion of Europe, a sense of belonging to Europe and the eventual development of a European identity. A common identity is also usually considered essential for the development of representative democracy.

On the one hand, EU efforts to mobilize CSOs for these purposes are considered by many observers as legitimate means for informing the public and engaging citizens in the policy process. CSOs are also expected to contribute to the formation of a European public sphere, thus contributing to the democratic process. On the other hand, other observers think that CSOs are being instrumentalized as cheerleaders. According to them, the Commission is only using CSOs to increase its legitimacy. Again, any assessment of the legitimacy or effectiveness of EU incentives in promoting identity building should be based on detailed analysis. The effects of transnational projects are seen in other situations where mobility is promoted within Europe, such as in the Erasmus program. Interestingly, while the funding of CSOs' transnational activities is sometimes considered a waste of time and money, the funding of the Erasmus program and of mobility activities in the field of research has always been seen as highly successful by observers and commentators, which raises many questions about the social construction of success.

This study shows that the EU is generally flexible when it comes to the promotion of EU values and transnationality, but that requirements are precise when it comes to communication activities. Given the general character of EU guidelines and the weak supervisory powers of the Commission, convergence toward an identity or a demos in the classical sense is unlikely. According to the classical conception, identity, nation or demos is constituted from a set of objective features (language, religion) and subjective features (social cohesion, common destiny, collective identity) that can be observed empirically (Weiler et al. 1995). This conception of identity can be related to heroic nationalism, referring to the capacity of individuals to sacrifice themselves for a European ideal (Smith 1995). Within this conception of identity, it is difficult to envision the coexistence of multiple identities.

The EU is only promoting specific, well-defined slogans and symbols in its communication activities. Like many public donors and private actors, the EU uses publicity to increase its popularity and visibility among EU citizens and around the world. As a general rule, it is never thought that political publicity alone can generate a sense of attachment to Europe in the classical sense. The only factor that may be contributing to a classical conception of identity is the diffusion of the EU flag and symbols. But again, the EU flag is often presented next to national flags, which cancels out the possibility of generating heroic nationalism. This study has also revealed the many obstacles to promoting EU visibility, especially the context of multiple donors and the lack of monitoring by the Commission (Chapter 6). The Commission has shown little capacity to enforce its provisions and rules in this area. Thus, even in those cases where the requirements are very specific, their implementation depends a lot on the goodwill of CSOs. They are only effective if CSOs find added value in engaging in this activity.

The EU is not promoting an identity in the classical sense, but it would be premature to conclude that its efforts at identity building through

CSOs have no effect whatsoever. EU initiatives have been implemented in a very flexible way, leading to multiple 'usages of Europe'. A few CSOs, on their own initiative, are contributing to the promotion of a classical conception of identity because this serves their own objectives or mandate. More interestingly, CSO representatives involved in transnational projects have changed their perception of the EU and of the European other. They have become more familiar with their EU neighbors and have identified common EU traits (Sanchez Salgado 2008). This classical identity is far from the only possible outcome. Many EU-supported CSOs just promote cultural diversity as one of the EU's core values. CSO representatives and members engaged in EU mobility projects have often experienced detachment from their own identity, which points toward a possible postnational type of identity.

A shared European identity in the classical sense may not be essential for an effective political system. Nationalism contributed to the rise of nations, but a political community could also eventually be based on cultural diversity (Gellner 1983). Contrary to what one would expect, the promotion of mobility and the diversity it entails could also be sources of European integration (Cram 2009b). The EU may be promoting a sort of banal Europeanism or constitutional patriotism. Constitutional patriotism postulates that a nation does not necessarily need to be based on objective cultural features (Habermas 2001). Banal Europeanism suggests that the EU could someday be inhabited by individuals who assume that the current situation is how things always were. It provides a context within which individuals make calculations about the contingent benefits of affiliation (Cram 2009b). The EU seems here to be presented as an impartial political system that provides a political space for nations to flourish.

This last view of identity and identity building, while interesting, is often considered naive and idealistic. Through the promotion of tolerance and diversity, the EU could be seen as promoting citizenship and identity with a clear Westernized cultural bias (Pollock 2001). A European postmodern identity, based on diversity, mobility, tolerance and intercultural exchanges, would not necessarily be the most reasonable and civilized way of belonging. It could lead to postmodern forms of exclusion, for example, the exclusion of non-mobile individuals who remain enclosed in their local environment. Given this bias, banal Europeanism could easily degenerate into banal state supranationalism. The possibility of coexistence among multiple identities has also been challenged. Belonging to different spaces is possible but the sense of attachment is not of the same quality for each one of them (Schmidt 1999).

The EU is a complex and flexible multilevel political system with many dimensions, implementing a wide variety of policies that vary considerably over time. While it is possible to identify some general trends, one needs to be extremely cautious, since it is not often possible to take into account all relevant dimensions at the same time. The EU is a system characterized by a variety of funding schemes, by a variety of forms of participation and by a variety of identity-building processes. Even if it is not always easy to identify its effects, there are certainly a wide variety of options available for those European citizens who are ready and able to seize them.

Appendix 1: Interviews

BABY, Marion, Europe for Citizens EU contact point, Paris, 2013.
BANGMA, Pieter, Développement DG, Brussels, 2005.
BARGE, Pierre, FIDH-AE and Ligue française de droits de l'Homme, Paris, 2001.
BEAUJOLAIS, Aurelie, Coordination Sud, Paris, 2013.
BERMEJO, Antonio, Medicos del Mundo, Spanish section, Madrid, 2001.
BIRO, Julie, Coordination Sud, Paris, 2001.
BLANCO GUTIERREZ, Maria José, Barcelone Active, Barcelona, 2005.
BÖCKERMAN, Gesa, DG Employment, Brussels, 2005.
BRACHET, Isabelle, FIDH EU-office, Paris, 2001.
CHAMPEIX, Claire, EAPN, Brussels, 2003.
DAVIES, Matt, ATD-4world UK, London, 2003.
DAVIDSON, Claire, BOND, London, 2003.
DE DOMINGO, José Jaime, MPDL, Madrid, 2001.
ELLMAN, Michael, Liberty, London, 2003.
FAZI, Elodie, Civil Society Contact Group (CSCG), Brussels, 2005.
FRAISSE, Laurent, Institut de recherche scientifique et technologique (IRST), Paris, 2005.
HEINRICH, Anne Kristin, Amnesty International EU office, Brussels, 2005.
HONNOCK, Tim, Amnesty International-London, 2003.
KAMAROTOS, Alexandre, Paris, F 2001.
LE GUEN, Philippe, Administrateur de la Maison Jean Monet, Paris, 2010.
LEVAILLANT, Michel, SOSRacisme Spain, Barcelona, 2005.
MARTINEZ, Pepa, Federacion Catalana de ONG por la paz, el desarrollo y los derechos humanos, Barcelona, 2013.
MAYCOCK, Joanna, Action Aid, Brussels, 2005.
MALDONADO, Andreu, MSF Spain, Barcelona, 2013.
MCDONELL, Idda, OECD, Issy, 2005.
MOLE, Muala, AIRE Centre, London, 2003.
MORENO, Ana, MPDL EU office, Brussels, 2001.
MORENO, Lupe, Catalan Agency for Development, Barcelona, 2005.
NAVARRO, Amalia, MSF and former member of CONGDE, Madrid, 2001.
NOI, Jordi, Alternativa solidaria Plenty, Barcelona, 2005.
ORIOL, Anne Charlotte, European Year of Citizens Alliance, Amsterdam, 2013.
PARRON, Nina, Medicos del Mundo, Madrid, 2001.
PELIER, Christophe, Conseil General Seine Saint Denis, Seine Saint Denis, 2009.
ROSA, Giorgianna, National Council For Voluntary Organisations—NCVO (mail interview in 2003).
RUFINI, Giovani, VOICE, Brussels, 2001.
SALERES, Carole, UNIOPSS, Paris, 2005.
STEINER, Caroline, former FIDH (EU office), 2001.
THYGUESSEN, Mette, ECHO, Brussels, 2001.
VATANEN Lea, Commission Secretariat-General, Brussels, 2003.

VEGUE I GISBERT, Nuria, Fondation FIAS, Barcelona, 2005.
VILA, Sonia, Oxfam EU office, Brussels, 2003.
VILIANI, Francesca, SOLIDAR, Brussels, 2003.
WELSH, James, Liberty, London, 2003.
ZARZOSO, José, DG External Relations, Brussels, 2001.

Table A.1 Interviews with CSOs and EU officials[1]

	Development	Humanitarian	Human rights	Social	Total
EU level	2	2	2	3	9
Spain	3	5	2	2	12
France	2	1	2	4	9
UK	1	2	1	3	7
	6	9	6	12	37 + 7

Notes

Introduction

1. These sociological approaches are not related to the constructivist turn in international relations.
2. In a search made on 22 May 2012 on the SSCI, there were a total of 1068 articles that had 'Europeanization' as a topic. Out of this total number of articles, only a few included 'interest groups' (35), civil society (35) or 'social movements' as a topic. Most of the articles tended to be in the three categories at the same time, indicating a low total number of studies on Europeanization and CSOs.
3. Eighteen out of 35 combining 'civil society' and 'Europeanization'.
4. A detailed definition of the term is given in Chapter 1.
5. A detailed description of these sectors is given in Chapter 1.

1 The Europeanization of CSOs—Institutional Impact or Strategic Action?

1. Most CSOs studied in this book are formally organized. However, in order to give a more complete picture of the EU shaping of CSOs, Chapter 7 also discusses the EU shaping of social movements.
2. For the sake of clarity, I do not use the term 'CSO' for organizations of organizations, but terms such as 'peak association', 'platform', 'umbrella organization' or 'euro group'.

2 Domestic Civil Society: National or European?

1. Transnational peak associations are CSOs usually comprising CSOs from different European states.
2. This is the case of the Mines Advisory Group or Medair in the United Kingdom, and of the Asociación Navarra Nuevo Futuro in Spain. In France, some examples of EU-funded CSOs not included in the study carried out by the Commission Coopération Développement are Telecom sans Frontières and Solidarités.
3. The dates of consultation of the websites are the following: for Spanish CSOs (members of CONGDE), March 2003; for French CSOs involved in the CCD, May 2004 and for British CSOs (members of BOND), March–April 2004.
4. This is the case of ABANTU for Development (2006), the African Families Foundation (2011) and Allavida (2010).
5. The data is available at http://ec.europa.eu/beneficiaries/fts/index_en.htm, consulted on 23 September 2013.

6. The number of humanitarian CSOs obtaining EU funds is smaller in Table 2.2 than in Table 2.3. This is explained because Table 2.3 corresponds to a single year. Also, many humanitarian CSOs also obtain funds from other DGs for raising awareness or humanitarian activities (see also chapters 3 and 4).
7. If humanitarian CSOs that implemented development activities were included in Table 2.4, the percentage of development CSOs that obtain EU funds would have been even higher.
8. To avoid repetition and an overestimation of the number of CSOs receiving EU funds, only development CSOs that are not involved in humanitarian aid are considered in this table.
9. This information is available on the Commission's website: http://ec.europa.eu/europeaid/work/funding/documents/application_statistics_2011.pdf, last consulted on 30 July 2013.
10. Only grants given by DEVCO/EuropeAid were considered. Public procurement, other expenditures and the European Development Fund were not included, since they often fund many other operators, not just CSOs.
11. Interview with a CSO representative, Paris, 2005.
12. Interview with a local government official in charge of the distribution of ESF, Seine Saint Denis, 2009.
13. Interview with a CSO representative, Barcelona, 2005.
14. Community grants offer up to 12,000 pounds to small and community organizations that reach out to disadvantaged and excluded people. More information available at http://www.dwp.gov.uk/esf/funding-opportunities/community-grants/, consulted on 9 October 2013.
15. Interview with a CSO representative, Pays de la Loire, 2007.
16. The Ligue Francaise des Droits de l'Homme has sporadically obtained a very small amount of EU funding from the program Europe for Citizens, but only for education on human rights.
17. Human rights CSOs can be funded by DG Justice, but only for very specific activities (see Chapter 3).
18. This information has been retrieved from the FTS, consulted on 23 September 2013.
19. Interview with a CSO representative, London, May 2003.
20. Interview with a CSO representative, Brussels, 2003.
21. Interview with a CSO representative, Brussels, 2001.
22. This figure excludes five organizations that obtained less than 500,000 euros (AGA Khan, Afghanaid, Bonn Agreement, Farm Africa and CONCERN).
23. In order to avoid an EU bias, only direct contacts with European peak associations have been considered. The websites of all CSOs have been analyzed and specific mentions of direct links with peak European CSOs have been taken as indicators of the existence of direct contacts. Thus, the transnationalization of CSOs is certainly underestimated. However, if the links of CSOs to their partners are not reflected in their websites, it is likely because these contacts are less valued.
24. Interview with a CSO representative, London, May 2003.
25. Interview with a CSO representative, Paris, 2013.
26. Ibid., 2005.
27. Interview with a CSO representative, Barcelona, 2013.

28. Two humanitarian CSOs in Spain were active members of European peak associations, but they had not obtained EU funds at the time of the survey (Asamblea de Cooperación por la Paz and Solidaridad con el Tercer Mundo). It is, however, possible that these two CSOs obtained EU funds during the 1990s (see Chapter 4 for details).
29. All in all, there are only a few large CSOs involved in CONGO (the Conference of NGOs in Consultative Relationship with the UN). This international association aims to promote the involvement of CSOs in the workings of the UN. Only a few large CSOs, such as Save the Children or ActionAid, are members of CONGO. It is surprising that most international CSOs under analysis and the large French humanitarian and development CSOs are not members under this umbrella. The full list of members is available at http://www.ngocongo.org/membership/full-members-listing/, consulted 11 March 2013.
30. Interview with a CSO representative, Barcelona, 2013.
31. Ibid.
32. Interview with a CSO representative, Brussels, 2005.
33. The LDH obtained EU funds during the 2000s, but it had started to deal with EU topics during the 1990s.
34. Interview with a CSO representative, Paris, 2005.
35. For some strange reason, Oxfam does not include the Partnership Programme Agreement that it has with DFID in the income that it receives from public donors. For 2011–2012, this is an additional 11.2 million euros.

3 A European Policy for CSOs? Exploring European Political Opportunities

1. There is no official version of the first EEC treaty in English.
2. The Treaty of Amsterdam is available at http://eur-lex.europa.eu/en/treaties/dat/11997D/htm/11997D.html#0133040028, consulted on 25 september 2013
3. Idem.
4. The original is in French: certain member states 'répugnent à permettre aux associations et fondations d'avoir accès aux programmes de financement européens spécifiques dans lesquels ils ont un pouvoir de décision'.
5. ECU stands for European Currency Unit, and MECUS refers to a million ECUs.
6. More information is available in the Commission's website: http://ec.europa.eu/justice/fundamental-rights/program/index_en.htm, last consulted on 25 September 2013.
7. As was the case at the EU level, in these first years, the amount of money channeled to CSOs was very limited. In France, between 1977 and 1980 the amount of funding available totaled 2.6 million euros. In Spain, only around 300,000 euros was available during the first years (1984 and 1985).
8. This information is available at http://www.afd.fr/home/AFD/nospartenaires/ONG/solliciter-une-subvention, consulted in October 2012.
9. (2013) 'François Hollande Fixe un Cadre à l'Aide au Développement', Le Monde, 02 March 2013.

10. Interview with a CSO representative, Paris, October 2013.
11. Ibid.
12. More information is available at http://www.iledefrance.fr/action-quotidienne/s-ouvrir-international, consulted on 5 November 2013.
13. The rate used is 1 pound = 1.252 euros, retrieved on 23 June 2014.
14. The Civil Society Challenge Fund is no longer open for applications. Some of its activities are now covered by the Global Poverty Action Fund. More information is available at https://www.gov.uk/civil-society-challenge-fund, consulted on 10 December 2013.
15. Information is available at http://icai.independent.gov.uk/wp-content/uploads/2011/11/Evaluation-of-DFIDs-Support-for-Civil-Society-Organisations-through-Program-Partnership-Agreements.pdf, consulted on 11 April 2013.
16. The budget cuts might have been less drastic with a socialist government, since Spanish conservative governments traditionally focus more on self-interested bilateral cooperation. Interview with a CSO representative, June 2013.
17. This information was available in the Database CONECCS, which is no longer available online, consulted on 7 December 2004.
18. More information about these dialogues is at the EU website: http://ec.europa.eu/social/main.jsp?catId=961&langId=en&moreDocuments=yes, consulted on 2 October 2013.
19. More information is available at http://ec.europa.eu/europeaid/who/partners/civil-society/structured-dialogue_en.htm (last consulted on 25 September 2013); and on the website http://ec.europa.eu/europeaid/who/partners/civil-society/palermo-process_en.htm (last consulted on 5 February 2014).
20. This sentence is available on the website of the Parliament: http://www.europarl.europa.eu/aboutparliament/en/00567de5f7/Agora.html, consulted on 18 April 2013.
21. The last agora took place in November 2013 and dealt with the topic of youth unemployment. More information about agoras is available at http://www.europarl.europa.eu/aboutparliament/en/00567de5f7/Agora.html, last consulted on 25 September 2013.
22. Information on the survey is available at http://www.act4europe.org/code/en/policy.asp?Page=265, consulted on 17 April 2013.
23. The name of the website was www.Predsedovanje.si, as stated in the document published by the CSCG available at http://www.act4europe.org/code/en/policy.asp?Page=265, consulted on 17 April 2013.
24. More information is available at http://www.associations.gouv.fr/1103-installation-du-haut-conseil-a-la.html, consulted on 15 April 2013.
25. More information at www.vie-associative.gouv.fr/interlocuteurs/autres_instances_nationales/cnva.htm, consulted on 12 January 2005.
26. The Dutch website is www.internetconsultatie.nl and the Canadian one is www.consultingcanadians.gc.ca, consulted on 17 April 2013.
27. The document is available at http://bswn.org.uk/resources/policy/compact-codes/Home%20Office%20Compact%20Code%20of%20Good%20Practice%20on%20Consultation%20and%20Policy%20Appraisal.pdf/view, consulted on 16 May 2013.

4 European Opportunities: Institutional Factors and Creative Usages

1. At the beginning of the 1990s, EU funds were much more important for Spanish CSOs. As an example, in 1995, they represented 19 percent of total CSO income. However, at the end of the 1990s, there was a clear trend in favor of subnational public funds.
2. Interview with a CSO representative, Barcelona, June 2013, June 2001.
3. Interview with a CSO representative, June 2001.
4. Interview with a CSO representative, London, May 2003.
5. Ibid.
6. Interview with a CSO representative, Brussels, May 2003.
7. More information is available at http://ec.europa.eu/europeaid/how/public-consultations/5240_en.htm, consulted on 20 May 2013.
8. Interview with a CSO representative, Brussels, June 2001.
9. Interview with a CSO representative, Spain, June 2013.
10. Interview with a CSO representative, France, October 2013.
11. This general trend applies more to some policy fields (for example, development, humanitarian aid, social policy) than to others (promotion of active citizenship).
12. Interview with a CSO representative, Extremadura, November 2005.
13. The original is in French: 'La Commission a tendu en somme a développer la base sociale de l'unification politique et à considérer que l'intégration privée peut être un soutien de l'intégration publique.'
14. Interview with a CSO representative, Brussels, 2003.
15. Ibid.
16. Ibid.
17. Ibid.
18. Interview with a CSO representative, Brussels, 2005.
19. Ibid.
20. Interview with a CSO representative, Brussels, 2003.
21. Interview with a CSO representative, Berlin, December 2002.
22. Interview with a CSO representative, Brussels, 2001.
23. In final interviews with RACINE representatives, they mentioned that the government wanted to be directly in charge of ESF technical assistance. RACINE no longer has an operative website so it is very likely that this independent body has now been suppressed.
24. More information on how the United Kingdom uses technical assistance is available at http://www.dwp.gov.uk/esf/resources/technical-assistance/, consulted on 11 October 2013.
25. Interview with a CSO representative, Brussels, June 2001.
26. Interview with a Commission official, Brussels, May 2001.
27. Some exceptions are highlighted in the following chapter.
28. Most of the demands of CSOs are available at http://ec.europa.eu/budget/library/consultations/fin_reg2009/contributions/O044_2009-12-17_Transparency_intl_%20Belgium_en.pdf, consulted on 15 May 2013.
29. Interview with a CSO representative, London, May 2003.
30. A possible exception is the European ombudsman, who has organized many events to promote his office among CSOs and other actors.

31. The only cases introduced by CSOs that have been considered admissible were indeed able to prove individual concern. For example, Movimundo and Internationaler Hilfsfonds have successfully launched judicial proceedings to challenge certain decisions of the Commission regarding the admissibility for receipt of EU funds and the management of such funds, but the cases only referred to their own funding applications.
32. Case C-115/09, available at http://eur-lex.europa.eu/LexUriServ/LexUriServ.do?uri=OJ:C:2011:204:0006:0006:EN:PDF, consulted on 2 October 2013.
33. Interview with a CSO representative, London, May 2003.
34. This information is available in the website of this organization: http://www.opensocietyfoundations.org/voices/community-not-confinement, consulted on 27 May 2013.
35. More information on the website of the Commission: http://ec.europa.eu/citizens-initiative/public/initiatives/ongoing, consulted on 28 May 2013.

5 EU Funding of CSOs: From New Public to New Civic Management

1. Interview by Florence Assouline and Philippe Petit published in Télérama, 12 October 1995.
2. Brief note in Le Monde, 10 June 1998.
3. Idem.
4. Information available directly in the website of this organization at http://www.gitanos.org/quienes_somos/historia_de_la_fsg.html.en, last consulted on 29 July 2013.
5. Information available directly in the website of this organization at http://www.gitanos.org/quienes_somos/financiacion_transparencia.html, last consulted on 29 July 2013.
6. Interview with a CSO representative, Barcelona 2005.
7. More information about this program is directly available at http://www.gitanos.org/publicaciones/memoriaacceder2007/estatal/index.html, last consulted on 29 July 2013.
8. It should be noted, however, that AI and its sections do occasionally accept grants from DFID, the EU and other public donors to support awareness-raising activities.
9. Interview with a CSO representative, Barcelona, April 2005.
10. Interview with a CSO representative, Barcelona, April 2005.
11. European Commission press release, published on 12 April 1983.
12. The first general conditions for CSOs were published in 1979, but they only concerned a few projects aiming to promote civic awareness in development cooperation.
13. More information available on this initiative at http://europa.eu/rapid/press-release_MEMO-97-98_en.htm, last consulted on 24 March 2014.
14. Interview with a CSO representative, Brussels, 2001.
15. Interview with a EU official, DG Employment, Brussels, 2005.
16. Interview with a CSO representative, Paris, 2005.
17. Interview with a CSO representative, London, May 2003.

226 Notes

18. More information is available at http://euronaid.net/archives/events/report_oxfam-10-2001.htm, last consulted on 4 June 2005.
19. Interview with a CSO representative, Brussels, 2001.
20. Interview with an EU official, Brussels, 2005.
21. More information on: http://www.bond.org.uk/resources/ec-funding-advice-line, consulted on 23 July 2013.
22. More information is available at http://www.bond.org.uk/learning-and-training.php?topic=Fundraising+and+finance, last consulted on 23 July 2013.
23. More information is available at http://www.coordinationsud.org/formation/gestion-contrat-europeaid-prag-2013/, last consulted on 23 July 2013.
24. This quote comes directly from South Research website. Available at http://www.southresearch.be/content/view/16/31/lang,english/, last consulted on 23 July 2013.
25. More information is available at http://www.ecbrussels.com/about/ last consulted on 23 July 2013.
26. More information is available at http://www.mdf.nl/company-profile/who-we-are/, last consulted on 23 July 2013.
27. More information is available at http://www.inprogressweb.com/, last consulted on 23 July 2013.
28. Interview with a CSO representative, Barcelona, 2005.
29. Interview with a CSO representative, Brussels, October 2005.
30. Interview with a CSO representative, Barcelona, 2005.
31. Lernes, C. (1995) 'Le Choc du Retour et les Bureaucrates de l'Humanitaire' in Le Monde, on 16 November.

6 CSOs and Identity Building: Cheerleaders for European Integration?

1. Data in this chapter derived from interviews have to be taken with great caution. One would expect that, as a general rule, CSOs are not very prone to admit that they do not follow the Commission requirements when it comes to the promotion of European values and EU visibility. However, as will be shown in this chapter, often CSOs do not hesitate to criticize EU requirements.
2. Speech to the churches on February 1992, quoted in the EU website http://ec.europa.eu/dgs/policy_advisers/archives/activities/dialogue_religions_humanisms/sfe_en.htm, last consulted on 25 July 2013.
3. In 1998, this aim was pursued by budget lines A-3024, which supported all kinds of projects advancing European ideas, and budget line A-3021, which covered core funding for organizations representing European interests.
4. Interview with a CSO representative, Paris, October 2013.
5. More information about the discussions at the European Parliament and the position of the Council and the Commission is available at http://www.europarl.europa.eu/sides/getDoc.do?secondRef=TOC&language=EN&reference=20131118&type=CRE, consulted on 13 January 2014.
6. Interview with a CSO representative, Paris, June 2010.
7. Interview with an EU official, Brussels, October 2005.

8. Interview with a national official, Nantes, 2007.
9. These grants run for longer periods (36 months) and can reach almost one million euros each. The list of beneficiaries for 2010 is available on the EU website https://webgate.ec.europa.eu/europeaid/online-services/index.cfm?ADSSChck=1375175161764&do=publi.detPUB&searchtype=AS&Pgm=7573847&zgeo=35590&debpub=&orderby=upd&orderbyad=Desc&nbPubliList=15&page=1&aoref=129493, last consulted on 30 July 2013.
10. Amnesty International also obtained an EU grant for awareness-raising activities this same year. The list of beneficiaries is available on the EU website https://webgate.ec.europa.eu/europeaid/online-services/index.cfm?ADSSChck=1375175161764&do=publi.detPUB&searchtype=AS&Pgm=7573847&zgeo=35590&debpub=&orderby=upd&orderbyad=Desc&nbPubliList=15&page=1&aoref=129493, last consulted on 30 July 2013.
11. This information is available on the Commission's website http://ec.europa.eu/europeaid/work/funding/documents/application_statistics_2011.pdf, last consulted on 30 July 2013.
12. This information is available at http://ec.europa.eu/europeaid/work/funding/documents/application_statistics_2010.pdf, last consulted on 30 July 2013.
13. One hundred eight projects were funded in 2007, 131 in 2008 and 127 in 2009 (ECORYS 2013).
14. Interview with a CSO representative, October 2013.
15. The role played by the contact point depends greatly on the member state and on the engagement and enthusiasm of the person and/or structure responsible for it. Interview with a CSO representative, October 2013.
16. The list of projects is available at http://eacea.ec.europa.eu/citizenship/funding/2009/selection/documents/list_selected_projects_action2_3.pdf, last consulted on 2 August 2013.
17. These figures are available on the Commission's website http://eacea.ec.europa.eu/citizenship/results_compendia/statistics_en.php, last consulted on 30 July 2013.
18. Interview with a CSO representative, October 2013.
19. Ibid.
20. Ibid.
21. Ibid.
22. Interview with a CSO representative, Paris, 2005.
23. Interview with a CSO representative, Paris, 2013.
24. Interview with an EU official, Brussels, 2005.
25. Interview with a CSO representative, Barcelona, 2005.
26. Community initiatives were also implemented by public authorities and even private firms. However, the statistics show that firms only took the lead for 70 projects (0.69 percent of the total). The database from which this data was retrieved, which is no longer available online, included projects in 25 member states. The category 'voluntary organization or charity' did not include trade unions, universities, training agencies or professional organizations. It is worth mentioning that this database did not always seem reliable. Sometimes professional organizations were considered non-profit groups while on other occasions they were considered enterprises. The

obsolete link to the database was http://europa.eu.int/comm/employment_social/equal/oldsite. This research was carried out on 23 June 2005.
27. However, only 10.5 percent of the total project leaders fell into the category of 'organization providing support and guidance for disadvantaged groups', which is much narrower. As mentioned earlier, this database is to be taken with a grain of salt. These data were available at the following link: http://equal.cec.eu.int/equal/jsp/index.jsp?long=fr, consulted on 23 June 2005.
28. Interview with an EQUAL project manager, Nantes, 2007.

7 The Europeanization of CSOs' Participation: Beyond the Brussels Consensus

1. (2010) 'Brussels Says First-Ever Citizens' Petition Does Not Count', EU Observer, 30 November 2010.
2. (2012) 'First Citizens' Petition Set to Be on Water', EU Observer, 21 March 2012.
3. (2010) 'EU Democracy Instrument Continues to Cause Headaches', EU Observer, 23 June 2010.
4. Interview with a CSO representative, Paris, October 2013.
5. Interview with a CSO representative, Brussels, October 2005.
6. Interview with a CSO representative, Brussels, 2001.
7. Interview with a CSO representative, Brussels, October 2005.
8. Interview with a CSO representative, Brussels, October 2003.
9. For example, the first annual Convention of the EPAP included presentations by EU officials form DG Justice, DG Education and Culture, DG Internal Market and Services and DG Health and Consumers Affairs. More information is available at http://ec.europa.eu/social/main.jsp?catId=961, last consulted on 24 February 2014.
10. More information on the stakeholders' dialogue and its participants is available at http://ec.europa.eu/social/main.jsp?langId=en&catId=88&eventsId=804&furtherEvents=yes, last consulted on 7 October 2013.
11. Similar patterns can be identified in other transnational newspapers such as *Euroactiv, European Voice, The Financial Times* and *The Economist*. Greenpeace has very high scores in all these newspapers (713, 423, 1104 and 1120, respectively, in October 2013) while EU-supported CSOs have fewer results.
12. According to this newspaper, there is no evidence that CONCORD has organized any symbolic or contentious activity since 2001.
13. Information retrieved in October 2013.
14. For example, EAPN-Europe and the EWL have supported many demonstrations organized by their members and ETUC, giving wide coverage in their website. More information for EAPN is available at http://www.eapn.eu/en/search?searchword=demonstration. The EWL also supports contentious action organized by its members and even organized a European demonstration in Brussels for the right to abortion in February 2014: http://www.womenlobby.org/spip.php?page=recherche&lang=en&recherche=demonstration, last consulted on 24 February 2014.

15. (2005) '50,000 Protesters to March Across Brussels', in EU Observer, 18 March 2005.
16. (2001) Federalist Stage Human Chain Protest, in EU Observer, 14 December 2001.
17. Interview with a CSO representative, Brussels, October, 2003.
18. (2009) 'Security Embarrassment', European Voice, 17 December 2009.
19. (2011) 'Greenpeace Stunt at European Business Summit', EU Observer, 25 August 2011.
20. The website of AI has an entire page dedicated to appeals for action, urging citizens to write letters (http://www.amnesty.org/en/how-you-can-help, consulted on 6 June 2013). The EU office does not offer such an option.
21. Interview with a CSO representative, Brussels, October 2005.
22. More information about this ECI is available at http://www.right2water.eu/, last consulted on 7 October 2013.
23. This information has been retrieved from an online presentation by Graciela Malgesini, a representative of EAPN-Spain. The document is available at http://www.eapn.eu/images/stories/docs/Events-docs-programmes/2012-policy-conference/presentations/2012-conference-EAPN-Spain.pdf, consulted on 7 October 2013.
24. Interview with a CSO representative, London, May 2003.
25. Idem.
26. More information is available in the presentation by Jonathan Zeitlin, 'How a Reformed EPAP Could Contribute to a More Participatory European Semester' at the Social Policy Working Group of the Social Platform on 24 June 2013.
27. As the Commission put it, 'Where the number of organizations interested—and hence the potential partnership—is particularly large, it might be appropriate for potential partners to establish coordination platforms and umbrella organizations and to designate a common representative (...)' (European Commission 2012b: 8).
28. Interview with a CSO representative, Brussels, October 2003.
29. Interview with a CSO representative, Paris, 2013.
30. Some examples are Action Aid, Care International, Handicap International, Oxfam, Plan International, Save the Children, Terre des Homes and World Vision.
31. CSOs funded exclusively by member contributions are strongly dependent on churches, such as the Association of World Council of Churches Related Development Organizations in Europe (APRODEV), the Adventist Development and Relief Agency (ADRA) and the International Alliance of Catholic Development Agencies (CIDSE). As may be expected, these organizations have specific views on development that are highly related to religion.
32. In 1993 there was only one person working on EU issues and in 2003 there were five. Interview with a CSO representative, London, May, 2003.
33. Interview with a CSO representative, Brussels, 2005.
34. Interview with a CSO representative, Paris, 2001.
35. SOLIDAR has 28 full members, 6 affiliates and 1 observer from 18 different countries. More information at www.solidar.org/doclist.asp?sectionID=3m, consulted on 14 December 2004.
36. Interview with a CSO representative, Brussels, October 2005.

37. Another example is the Spanish Human Rights League (Asociación Española Pro-Derechos Humanos, a very small organization with limited resources, and only a small number of members and volunteers). However, European topics have also been included occasionally in their agenda.
38. Interview with a CSO representative, London, May 2003.
39. Ibid.
40. Interview with a CSO representative, London, May, 2003.
41. The LDH has only been able to get small amounts of EU funds from DG Education and Culture. The LDH has supported transnational campaigns but they have not been very successful so far.
42. Analysis was made of 276 activities carried out during the ESF in Malmö. Only 41 out of 276 directly and explicitly targeted the EU (14.85 percent). However, the EU was much more present than other levels of governance (the EU was mentioned 136 times in the program), and other international organizations were mostly ignored (the United Nations (UN) is only mentioned ten times and the International Monetary Fund (IMF) and the World Bank (WB) only twice each). Some activities targeted national governments, but this was not very frequent either ('government' was only used 22 times). These movements seemed to be more affected by the EU agenda than by the agenda of other International Organizations, or even of specific member states.
43. It was not possible to find information about MEDEL (European Magistrates for Democracy and Freedom). Other organizations also were involved in EU activities, such as AEDH members from several European countries, Synaspismos from Greece and others from non-European countries (including Brazil, Venezuela, the United States).
44. According to Féron, around 15 percent of speakers at the ESF in Firenze come from the political milieu.

Conclusion: The Political Construction of European Civil Society: Legitimate and Democratic?

1. Interview with a CSO representative, June 2013.
2. Ibid.
3. During my work as a human rights activist, I had the opportunity to talk to some colleagues from church-supported organizations about these constraints.
4. http://www.fastcoexist.com/1679092/the-rise-and-fall-of-poverty-porn (blog) 'Has NGO advertizing gone to far?' Available at http://aidwatchers.com/2011/04/has-ngo-advertising-gone-too-far/, consulted on 22 July 2013.
5. For example, Médecins sans Frontières International (MSF International) has established a rule that institutional funding will not account for more than 15 percent of total funding. Independence, according to one representative of this CSO (this is not necessarily the official position of MSF), is having the capacity to return money to a donor if you do not agree with some of its requirements.
6. Interview with an EU official, October 2005, Brussels.

7. These values are usually clearly posted in these CSOs' websites under a headline 'about us'. Most CSOs have a specific section on values, a charter of principles or include some of their values in their mission statement. The websites were consulted on 12 September 2013.
8. This quote comes from the EU website http://ec.europa.eu/europeaid/work/procedures/faq/grants_en.htm, consulted on 12 September 2013.

Appendix 1: Interviews

1. It was often difficult to arrange interviews with some representatives of CSOs, especially in France and the United Kingdom. Organizations such as Oxfam UK, Christian Aid, Action Aid, MSF-France or CARE refused to give interviews due to lack of time.

References

Anderson, J. (2003) 'Europeanization in Context: Concept and Theory' in Dyson, K. and Goetz, K. (Eds.) *Germany, Europe and the Politics of Constraint*, (Oxford: OUP) pp. 37–53.

Andersen, S. (2004) 'The Mosaic of Europeanization: An Organizational Perspective on National Re-contextualization', *Arena Working Papers*, n° 4/11.

Archambault, E. (1996) *Le secteur sans but lucratif. Associations en Fondations en France*, (Paris: Economica).

Armstrong, K.A. (2010) *Governing Social Inclusion. Europeanization Through Policy Coordination*, (Oxford: OUP).

Armstrong, K.A. (2006) 'Inclusive Governance. Civil Society and the Open Method of Coordination' in Smismans, S. (Ed.) *Civil Society and Legitimate European Governance*, (Cheltenham: Edward Elgar) pp. 42–67.

Armstrong, K.A. (2002) 'Rediscovering Civil Society: The European Union and the White Paper on Governance' *European Law Journal*, 8:1, pp. 102–132.

Attanasio, P. (1994) 'Communauté européenne' in Smillie, I. and Helmich, H. (Eds.) *Organisations non gouvernementales et gouvernements: Une association pour le développement*, (Paris: OECD) pp. 319–338.

Bache, I. (2000) 'Europeanization and Partnership: Exploring and Explaining Variations in Policy Transfer' *Queen's Papers on Europeanization*, 8, 24 pages, Available at: http://www.qub.ac.uk/schools/SchoolofPoliticsInternational StudiesandPhilosophy/FileStore/EuropeanisationFiles/Filetoupload,38439,en.pdf.

Baiges, S., Mira, E., Dusster, D. and Viladomat, R. (1996) *Las ONG de desarrollo en España*, (Barcelona: Flor del Viento).

Balme, R., Chabanet, D. and Wright, V. (2002) *L'action collective en Europe*, (Paris: Presses de Sciences Po).

Balme, R. and Chabanet, D. (2008) *European Governance and Democracy*, (Plymouth: Rowman & Littlefield Publishing Group).

Balme, R. and Chabanet, D. (2002) 'Action Collective et gouvernance de l'Union européenne' in Balme, R., Chabanet, D. and Wright, V. (Eds.) *L'action collective en Europe*, (Paris: Presses de Sciences Po) pp. 21–122.

Bandy, J. and Smith, J. (2005a) 'Introduction: Cooperation and Conflict in Transnational Protest' in Bandy, J. and Smith, J. (Eds.) *Coalitions Across Borders. Transnational Protest and the Neoliberal Order*, (Oxford: OUP) pp. 1–17.

Bandy, J. and Smith, J. (2005b) 'Factors Affecting Conflict and Cooperation in Transnational Movement Networks' in Bandy, J. and Smith, J. (Eds.) *Coalitions Across Borders. Transnational Protest and the Neoliberal Order*, (Oxford: OUP) pp. 231–252.

Bartolini, S. (2006) 'Should the Union be "Politicised"? Prospects and Risks' *Notre Europe Policy Paper*, 19, pp. 29–50. Available at: http://www.notre-europe.eu/media/policypaper19-en.pdf?pdf=ok.

Besset, J.P. (1991) *Amnesty International. La conspiration de l'espoir. Trente ans au service des droits de l'Homme*, (Paris: Éditions du Felin).
Beyers, J. and Kerremans, B. (2007) 'Critical Resource Dependencies and the Europeanization of Domestic Interest Groups' in Coen, D. (Ed.) *EU Lobbying: Empirical and Theoretical Studies*, (New York: Routledge) pp. 128–149.
Beyers, J. (2004) 'Voice and Access. Political Practices of European Interest Associations' *European Union Politics*, 5:2, pp. 211–240.
Beyers, J. (2002) 'Gaining and Seeking Access: The European Adaptation of Domestic Interest Associations' *European Journal of Political Research*, 41:5, pp. 585–612.
Billet, S. (2007) 'The Theologies of Transparency in Europe: The Limits and Possibilities of "Fusion" in the EU Transparency Regime' *Journal of Public Affairs*, 7, 319–330.
Boin, C. and Marchesetti, A. (2010) *Friends of the EU. The Cost of a Taxpayer-Funded Green Lobby*, (London: International Policy Network).
Bomberg, E. and Peterson, J. (2000) 'Policy Transfer and Europeanization: Passing the Heineken Test?' *Queen's Papers on Europeanization*, 2, 43 pages. Available at: http://www.qub.ac.uk/schools/SchoolofPoliticsInternationalStudiesandPhilosophy/FileStore/EuropeanisationFiles/Filetoupload,38445,en.pdf.
Börzel, T. (2003) *Environmental Leaders and Laggards in Europe. Why There is (Not) a Southern Problem*, (Aldershot, Burlington, Singapore, Sydney: Ashgate).
Börzel, T. (2002) *States and Regions in the European Union. Institutional Adaptation in Germany and Spain*, (Cambridge: Cambridge University Press).
Börzel, T. and Risse, T. (2006) 'Europeanization: The Domestic Impact of European Union Politics' in Jørgensen, K.E., Pollack, M.A. and Rosamond, B. (Eds.) *Handbook of European Union Politics*, (London: Sage) pp. 483–504.
Börzel, T. and Risse, T. (2003) 'Conceptualizing the Domestic Impact of Europe' in Featherstone, K. and Radaelli, C.M. (Eds.) *The Politics of Europeanization*, (Oxford: Oxford University Press) pp. 57–82.
Bouwen, P. (2003) 'A Theoretical and Empirical Study of Corporate Lobbying in the European Parliament' *EIOP*, 7:11 17 pages. Available at: http://eiop.or.at/eiop/pdf/2003-011.pdf.
Bowden, M. (2005) 'Democratic Governance or Social Control? Networks Involving Civil Society Organizations, the State and Police' Paper Presented to EMES/ISTR Conference, Paris, April.
Brandsen, T., Pavolini, E., Ranci, C., Sittermann, B. and Zimmer, A. (2005) 'The National Action Plan on Social Exclusion. An Opportunity for the Third Sector?' *TSEP Working Paper*, n° 14, 40 pages. Available at: http://eprints.lse.ac.uk/29023/1/14TSEP.pdf.
Brehon, N.J. (1997) *Le budget de l'Europe*, (Paris: L.F.D.J).
Budke, A. (2008) 'Contacts Culturels et Identités Ethniques des Etudiants Erasmus en Allemagne' in Dervin, F. and Byram, M. (Eds.) *Echanges et Mobilités Academiques. Quel Bilan?* (Paris: L'Harmattan) pp. 43–64.
Bulmer, S. and Radaelli, C. (2004) 'The Europeanization of National Policy?' *Queen's Papers on Europeanization*, 1, 22 pages. Available at: http://www.qub.ac.uk/schools/SchoolofPoliticsInternationalStudiesandPhilosophy/FileStore/EuropeanisationFiles/Filetoupload,38405,en.pdf.
Buth, V. and Kolher-Koch, B. (2013) 'The Balancing Act of European Civil Society: Between Professionalism and Grass Roots' in Kohler-Koch, B. and

Quittkat, C. (Eds.) *De-Mystification of Participatory Democracy: EU-Governance and Civil Society*, (Oxford: OUP) pp. 114–148.
Callanan, M. (2011) 'EU Decision-Making: Reinforcing Interest Group Relationships with National Governments?' *Journal of European Public Policy*, 18:1, pp. 17–34.
Carbone, M. (2008) 'Theory and Practice of Participation: Civil Society and EU Development Policy' *Perspectives on European Politics and Society*, 9:2, pp. 241–255.
Casado, D. (1996) 'Visión Panorámica de las organizaciones voluntarias en el ámbito social' *Revista de estudios sociales y de sociología aplicada*, 103, pp. 263–280.
Casado, D. (1992) *Organizaciones voluntarias en España*, (Barcelona: Editorial Hacer).
Castellanet, C. (2003) 'Cycle des projets, cadre logique et efficacité des interventions de développement' *Traverses*, 13, October, 34 pages. Available at: http://www.groupe-initiatives.org/IMG/pdf/traverse_13.pdf.
Chabanet, D. (2002) ' Les marches européennes contre le chômage, la précarité et les exclusions' in Balme, R., Chabanet, D. and Wright, V. (Eds.) *L'action collective en Europe*, (Paris: Presses de Sciences Po) pp. 461–493.
Chalmers, A.W. (2011) 'Interest, Influence and Information: Comparing the Influence of Interest Groups in the European Union' *Journal of European Integration* 33:4, pp. 471–486.
Chaves, M., Stephens, L. and Galaskiewicz, J. (2004) 'Does Government Funding Suppress Nonprofits' Political Activity?'*American Sociological Review*, 69:2, pp. 292–316.
Checkel, J.T. (2001) 'Constructing European Institutions' in Schneider, G. and Aspinwall, G. (Eds.) *The Rules of Integration. Institutionalist Approaches to the Study of Europe*, (Manchester: Manchester University Press) pp. 19–40.
Cichowski, R. (2007) *The European Court and Civil Society: Litigation, Mobilization and Governance*, (Cambridge: Cambridge University Press).
Císař, O. and Vráblíková, K. (2012) 'Transnational Activism of Social Movement Organizations: The Effect of the European Union Funding on Local Groups in the Czech Republic' *European Union Politics*, 14:1, pp. 140–160.
Clarke, T. (2000) 'EC Support for Development NGOs' *The Courier N° 181*—June—July, 2000—Dossier: The New ACP–EU agreement, NGO Focus, pp. 51–54, Available at: http://aei.pitt.edu/39221/1/Courier.181.pdf.
Closa, C. (2001) *La Europeaización del sistema politico español*, (Madrid: Itsmo).
Coen, D. (2007) 'Empirical and Theoretical Studies in EU Lobbying' *Journal of European Public Policy*, 14:3, pp. 333–345.
Coen, D. (1998) 'The European Business Interest and the Nation State: Large-Firm Lobbying in the European Union and Member State' *Journal of Public Policy*, 18:1, pp. 75–100.
Coen, D. and Dannreuther, C. (2003) 'Differentiated Europeanization: Large and Small Firms in the EU Policy Process' in Featherstone, K. and Radaelli, C.M. (Eds.) *The Politics of Europeanization*, (Oxford: Oxford University Press) pp. 255–278.
Coen, D. and Richardson, J. (2009) *Lobbying the European Union: Institutions, Actors and Issues*, (Oxford: Oxford University Press).

Cohen, J. and Rogers J. (1992) 'Secondary Associations and Democratic Governance' *Politics & Society*, 20, pp. 393–411.
Cohen, J.L. and Arato, A. (1992) *Civil Society and Political Theory*, (Massachusetts: Mit Press).
Cowles, M.G., Caporaso, J. and Risse, T. (2001) *Transforming Europe: Europeanization and Domestic Change*, (Ithaca and London: Cornell University Press).
Cram, L. (2011) 'The Importance of the Temporal Dimension: New Modes of Governance as a Tool of Government' *JEPP*, 18:5, pp. 636–656.
Cram, L. (2009a) 'Introduction. Banal Europeanism: European Union Identity and National Identities in Synergy' *Nations and Nationalism*, 15:1, pp. 101–108.
Cram, L. (2009b) 'Identity and European Integration: Diversity as a Source of Integration' *Nations and Nationalism*, 15:1, pp. 109–128.
Cram, L. (1997) *Policy-Making in the European Union, Conceptual Lenses and the Integration Process*, (London: Routledge).
Crettiez, X. and Sommier, I. (2006) *La France rebelle. Tous les foyers, mouvements et acteurs de la contestation*, (Paris: Editions Michalon).
Cullen, P. (2010) 'The Platform of European Social NGOs: Ideology, Division and Coalition' *Journal of Political Ideologies*, 15:3, pp. 317–331.
Cullen, P. (2009) 'Pan-European NGOs and Social Rights: Participatory Democracy and Civil Dialogue' in Jutta, J. and Birgit, L. (Eds.) *Transnational Activism in the UN and the EU*, (London: Routledge) pp. 134–146.
Dacheux, E. (2004) *L'impossible défi. La politique de communication de l'Union européenne*, (Paris: Éditions CNRS).
Dahan, N. (2004) 'Le lobbying des "ONG"' *Après Demain*, 460–462, January–March, pp. 29–31.
Davis, F. (2009) 'Faith Advocacy and the EU Anti-Poverty Process: A Case of Caritas' *Public Money and Management* 29:6, pp. 379–386.
Debouzy, O. (2004) 'Le rôle du lobbying dans la démocratie technicienne' *Après Demain*, 460–462, January–March pp. 10–12.
De Crombrugghe, D. (1993) 'Le projet de statut pour l'association européenne' in Julien, C. (Ed.) *Citoyens et pouvoirs en Europe*, (Paris: Syros) pp. 141–150.
Degnbol-Martinussen, J. and Engberg-Pedersen, P. (2003) *Aid: Understanding International Development Cooperation*, (London: Zed Books).
Dehousse, R. (2005) *La fin de l'Europe*, (Paris: Flammarion).
Dehousse, R. (1997) *La Cour de Justice des Communautés européennes*, (Paris: Montchrestien).
Della Porta, D. and Caiani, M. (2009) *Social Movements and Europeanization*, (Oxford: Oxford University Press).
Della Porta, D, Peterson, A. and Reiter, H. (2006) *The Policing of Transnational Protest*, (Aldershot: Ashgate).
Della Sala, V. and Ruzza, C. (2007) *Governance and Civil Society in the European Union*, (Manchester: MUP).
De Schutter, O. (2002) 'Europe in Search of its Civil Society' *European Law Journal*, 8:2 pp. 198–217.
Deutsch, K.W. (1968) *The Analysis of International Relations*, (Prentice-Hall, Englewood Cliffs).
Dumon, G. (1994) 'La politique européenne de développement vue par les ONG' *Associations Transnationales*, 1 January–February, pp. 42–45.

Dür, A. (2009) 'Interest Groups in the EU: How Powerful Are They?' *West European Politics*, 31:6, pp. 1212–1230.
Dür, A. and De Bièvre, D. (2007) 'The Question of Interest Groups Influence' *Journal of Public Policy*, 27:1, pp. 1–12.
Dür, A. and Mateo, G. (2012) 'Who Lobbies the European Union? National Interest Groups in a Multi-level Polity' *JEPP*, 19:7, pp. 969–987.
Dyson, K. and Goetz, K.H. (2003) 'Living with Europe: Power, Constraint, and Contestation' in Dyson, K. and Goetz, Klaus H. (Eds.) *Germany, Europe and the Politics of Constraint*, (Oxford: Oxford University Press) pp. 3–36.
Eberwein, W. and Saurugger, S. (2009) 'Professionalization and Participation: NGOs and Global Participatory Democracy? A Research Agenda' Paper Presented at the IPSA Biannual Conference, Santiago, July.
Eder, K. (2001) 'Chancenstrukturen fur Burgerbeteiligung und Protestmobilisierung in der EU' in Kleinm, A., Koopmans, R. and Geiling, H. (Eds.) *Globalisierung, Partizipation, Protest*, (Opladen: Leske&Budrich) pp. 45–75.
Eising, R. (2009) *The Political Economy of State–Business Relations in Europe. Interest Mediation, Capitalism, and EU Policy-Making*, (London: Routledge).
Eising, R. (2007) 'Institutional Context, Organizational Resources and Strategic Choices. Explaining Interest Groups Access in the European Union' *European Union Politics*, 8:3, pp. 329–362.
EPPIE (2007), 'Introduction. Analyser l'européanisation des politiques publiques' in Palier, B. and Surel, Y. *L'Europe en action: l'européanisation dans une perspective comparée*, (Paris: L'Harmattan) pp. 13–86.
Evans, G. (2006) 'From Humanitarian Intervention to the Responsibility to Protect' *Wisconsin International Law Journal*, 24:3, pp. 101–120.
Exadaktylos, T. and Radaelli, C.M. (2009) 'Research Design in European Studies: The Case of Europeanization' *Journal of Common Market Studies*, 47:3, pp. 507–530.
Fagan, A. (2005) 'Taking Stock of Civil Society Development in Post-Communist Europe: Evidence from the Czech Republic' *Democratization*, 12:4, pp. 528–547.
Featherstone, K. and Radaelli, C.J. (2003) *The Politics of Europeanization*, (Oxford: Oxford University Press).
Féron, E. (2005) 'Les altermondialistes dans le mouvement social européen: entre participation et retrait' *Critique internationale*, 27, April–June, pp. 163–175.
Finke, B. (2007) 'Civil Society Participation in EU Governance' *Living Reviews in European Governance*, 2:2, 31 pages. Available at: http://europeangovernance.livingreviews.org/Articles/lreg-2007-2/download/lreg-2007-2Color.pdf.
Fligstein, N. (2008) *Euroclash. The EU, European Identity, and the Future of Europe*, (Oxford: Oxford University Press).
Fligstein, N. and Stone Sweet, A. (2001) 'Institutionalizing the Treaty of Rome' in Stone Sweet, A. Sandholtz, W. and Fligstein, N. (Eds.) *The Institutionalization of Europe*, (Oxford: Oxford University Press) pp. 29–55.
Flyvbjerg, B. (2006) 'Five Misunderstandings About Case-Study Research' *Qualitative Inquiry*, 12, pp. 219–245.
Fraisse, L. (2002) 'S'organiser en réseau: une mutation de l'espace public associatif' in Haeringer, J. and Traversaz, F. (Eds.) *Conduire le changement dans les associations d'action sociale et médico-sociale*, (Paris: Dunod) pp. 117–134.

Freyss, J. (2004) 'La Solidarite' internationale, une profession?' *Révue tiers monde*, 180, pp. 735–772.
Friedrich, D. (2007) 'Old Wine in New Bottles? The Actual Potential Contribution of Civil Society Organisations to Democratic Governance in Europe' *RECON Online Working Paper*, 4, 19 pages, Available at: http://www.reconproject.eu/main.php/RECON_wp_0704.pdf?fileitem=50511929.
Furtak, F. (2001) *Nichtregierungsorganisationen (NGOs) im politischen System der Europäischen Union*, (München: Tuduv).
Geddes, M. (2000) 'Lobbying for Migrants Inclusion in the European Union: New Opportunities for Transnational Advocacy?' *JEPP*, 7:4, pp. 623–649.
Gellner, E. (1983) *Nations and Nationalism*, (Oxford: Basil Blackwell).
Geyer, R. (2001) 'Can European Union (EU) Social NGOs Cooperate to Promote EU Social Policy?' *Journal of Social Policy*, 30:3, pp. 477–493.
Giraudon, V. (2000) 'L'espace sociopolitique européen, un champ encore en friche?' *Culture et Conflits*, 38–39, pp. 7–37.
Giraudon, V. and Favell, A. (2009) 'The Sociology of the EU' *European Union Politics*, 10:4, pp. 550–576.
Glennerster, H. (1995) *British Social Policy Since 1945*, (Oxford: Blackwell Publishers).
Gómez Gil, C. (2005) *Las ONG en España. De la apariencia a la realidad*, (Madrid: Catarata).
Goodwin, J. and Jasper, J. (2004) *Rethinking Social Movements. Structure, Meaning and Emotion*, (Oxford: Rowman & Littlefield Publishers).
Granda Alva, G., Guzman, G. and Rama, R. (1987) *Nuevas formas de cooperación para España*, (Madrid: CIDEAL).
Grande, E. (2003) 'How the Architecture of the EU Political System Makes it Difficult for Business Associations' in Greenwood, J. (Ed.) *The Challenge of Change in EU Business Associations*, (Basingstoke: Palgrave Macmillan), pp. 45–59.
Gray, E. and Statham, P. (2005) 'Becoming European? The Transformation of the British Pro-Migrant NGO Sector in Response to Europeanization' *JCMS*, 43:4, pp. 877–898.
Graziano, P. and Vink, M. (2007) *Europeanization. New Research Agendas*, (Houndmills: Palgrave).
Graziano, P. Jacquot, S. and Palier, B. (2011) 'Domestic Recontiliation Policies and the Usages of Europe' *European Journal of Social Security*, 12:1, pp. 3–24.
Greenwood, J. (2012) 'The European Citizens' Initiative and EU Civil Society Organizations' *Perspectives on European Politics and Society*, 13:3, pp. 325–336.
Greenwood, J. (2007) *Interest Representation in the European Union*, London: Macmillan.
Greenwood, J. and Dreger, J. (2013) 'The Transparency Register: A European Vanguard of Strong Lobby Regulation?' *Interest Groups and Advocacy*, 2:2, pp. 139–162.
Greenwood, J. and Halpin, D. (2007) 'The European Commission and the Public Governance of Interest Groups in the European Union: Seeking a Niche Between Accreditation and Laissez-Faire' *Perspectives on European Politics and Society*, 8:2, pp. 190–211.
Grossman, E. (2009) 'Interest Groups in France and Europe' in Perrineau, P. and Rouban, L. (Eds.) *Politics in France and Europe*, (Houndmills: Palgrave) pp. 87–104.

Grossman, E. and Saurugger, S. (2006) 'Les groupes d'intérêt au secours de la démocratie?' *Revue française de science politique*, 56:2, pp. 229–321.

Grote, J. and Lang, A. (2003) 'Europeanization and Organizational Change in National Trade Associations: An Organizational Ecology Perspective' in Featherstone, K. and Radaelli, C.M. (Eds.) *The Politics of Europeanization*, (Oxford: Oxford University Press), pp. 225–254.

Haas, E. (1968) *The Uniting of Europe: Political, Social, and Economic Forces: 1950–1957*, (Stanford: Stanford University Press).

Habermas, J. (2001) *The Postnational Constellation: Political Essays*, (Cambridge: Polity Press).

Hanke, K. (2012) *Promoting Democracy via the Web? NGOs Use of the Internet at the National and the European Level*, UvA Master Thesis. Amsterdam: UvA.

Harlow, C. (1992) 'Towards a Theory of Access for the European Court of Justice' *Yearbook of European Law*, 12, pp. 213–248.

Harris, M. and Rochester, C. (2001) *Voluntary Organizations and Social Policy in Britain*, (Houndmills: Palgrave).

Harris, M, Colin, R. and Halfpenny, P. (2001) 'Voluntary Organizations and Social Policy: Twenty Years of Change' in Harris, M. and Rochester, C. (Eds.) *Voluntary Organizations and Social Policy in Britain*, (Houndmills: Palgrave) pp. 1–20.

Harvey, B. (1993) 'Lobbying in Europe: The Experience of Voluntary Organizations' in Mazey, S. and Richardson, J. (Eds.) *Lobbying in the European Community*, (Oxford: Oxford University Press) pp. 188–200.

Hassenteufel, P. (2005) 'De la comparaison internationale à la comparation transnationale. Le déplacement de la construction d'objets comparatifs en matière de politiques publiques' *Revue française de Science Politique*, 55:1, pp. 113–132.

Hassenteufel, P. and Surel, Y. (2000) 'Des politiques publiques comme les autres? Construction de l'objet et outils d'analyse des politiques européennes' *Politique Européenne*, 1:1, pp. 8–24.

Haverland, M. (2005) 'Does the EU Cause Domestic Developments? The Problem of Case Selection in Europeanization Research' *EIOP*, 9:2, 14 pages. Available at: http://eiop.or.at/eiop/pdf/2005-002.pdf.

Hayes-Renshaw, F. (2009) 'Least Accessible But Not Inaccessible: Lobbying the Council and the European Council' in Coen, D. and Richardson, J. (Eds.) *Lobbying the European Union. Institutions, Actors and Issues*, (Oxford: OUP) pp. 70–88.

Heinelt, H. and Niederhafner, S. (2008) 'Cities and Organized Interest Intermediation in the EU Multi-Level System' *European Urban and Regional Studies*, 17:1, pp. 173–187.

Héritier, A., Kerwer, D., Knill, C., Lehmkuhl, D., Teutsch, M. and Douillet, A.C. (2001) *Differential Europe: The European Union Impact on National Policymaking*, (New York: Rowman & Littlefield).

Hilson, C. (2002) 'New Social Movements: The Role of Legal Opportunity' *JEPP*, 9:2, pp. 238–255.

Hirst, P. (1994) *Associative Democracy: New Forms of Economic and Social Governance*, (Cambridge: Polity Press).

Hood, C. (1998) *The Art of the State. Culture, Rhetoric, and Public Management*, (Oxford: Clarendon Press).

Hours, B. (1998) 'ONG et idéologies de la solidarité' in Deler, J.P., Fauré, Y.A., Piveteau, A. and Roca, P.J. (Eds.) *ONG et Développement*, (Paris: Karthala).
Hüller, T. and Kohler-Koch, B. (2008) 'Assessing the Democratic Value of Civil Society Engagement in the European Union' in Kohler-Koch, B., De Bièvre, D. and Maloney, W. (Eds.) *Opening EU-Governance to Civil Society. Gains and Challenges*, Connex Repport Series 5. pp. 145–181. Available at: http://www.mzes.uni-mannheim.de/publications/books/connex_report_5.html#Inhaltsverzeichnis.
Imig, D. and Tarrow, S. (2001) *Contencious Europeans. Protest and Politics in an Emerging Polity*, (Lamham, MD: Rowman & Littlefield).
Imig, D. and Tarrow, S. (1999) 'The Europeanization of Movements? A New Approach to Transnational Contention' in Della Porta, D., Kriesi, H. and Rucht, D. (Eds.) *Social Movements in a Globalizing World*, (London: Macmillan) pp. 113–133.
Ion, J. (1997) *La fin des militants?* (Paris: Les éditions de l'Atelier).
Jacquot, S. and Woll, C. (2004) 'Usage et travail politiques: une sociologie compréhensive des usages de l'integration européenne' in Jacquot, S. and Woll, C. (Eds.) *Les usages de l'Europe, acteurs et transformations européennes*, (Paris: L'Harmattan) pp. 1–27.
Jacobsson, K. and Johansson, H. (2009) 'The Micro-Politics of the Open Method of Coordination: NGOs and the Social Inclusion Process in Sweden' in Heidenreich, M. and Zeitlin, J. (Eds.) *Changing European Employment and Welfare Regimes*, (Abingdon: Routledge) pp. 173–191.
James, A. (2012) *Fundraising from Institutions*, (London: BOND).
Jas, P., Wilding, K., Wainwright, S., Passey, A. and Hems, L. (2002) *The UK Voluntary Sector Almanac 2002*, (London: National Council for Voluntary Organisations publications).
Johansson, H. (2012) 'Whom Do They Represent? Mixed Modes of Representation in EU-Based CSOs' in Kröger, S. and Friedrich, D. (Eds.) *The Challenge of Democratic Representation in the European Union*, (Palgrave: Macmillan) pp. 74–91.
Johansson, H. (2007) 'Europeanization from Bellow. The OMC Process on Social Inclusion in the Swedish Welfare State' in Hvinden, B. and Johansson, H. (Eds.) *Citizenship in Northern Welfare States: Dynamics of Choice, Duties and Participation in a Changing Europe*, (London: Routledge) pp. 125–139.
Johansson, H. and Lee, J. (2012) 'Bridging the Gap: How Do EU-Based Civil Society Organizations Acquire their Internal Representation?' *Voluntas*, DOI 10.1007/s11266-012-9343-4.
Jordan, G., Halpin, D. and Maloney, W. (2004) 'Defining Interests: Disambiguation and the Need for New Distinctions? *BJPIR*, 6, pp. 195–212.
Jutta, J. and Dembinski, M. (2012) 'A Contradiction in Terms? NGOs, Democracy and European Foreign and Security Policy' *JEPP*, 18:8, pp. 1151–1168.
Keane, J. (1998) *Civil Society: Old Images, New Visions*, (Cambridge: Polity Press).
Keck, M. and Sikkink, K. (1998) *Activist Beyond Borders: Advocacy Networks in International Politics*, (Ithaca: Cornell).
Kelemen, R.D. (2003) 'The EU Rights Revolution: Adversarial Legalism and European Integration' in Börzel, T. and Cichowski, R. (Eds.) *The State of the European Union: Law, Politics and Society*, (Oxford: Oxford University Press) pp. 221–234.

Kendall, J. (2009) *Handbook of Third Sector Policy in Europe: Multi-Level Processes and Organized Civil Society*, (Chentelham: Edward Elgar).
Kendall, J. and Anheier, H. (1999) 'The Third Sector and the European Union Policy Process: An Initial Evaluation' *Journal of European Public Policy*, 6:2, pp. 283–307.
Kendall, J. and Fraisse, L. (2005) 'The European Statute of Association: Why an Obscure But Contested Symbol in a Sea of Indifference and Scepticism?' *Third Sector European Policy Working Papers*, 11. 30 pages. Available at: http://eprints.lse.ac.uk/29018/1/11TSEP.pdf.
King, R. and Ruiz-Gelices, E. (2003) 'International Student Migration and the European "Year Abroad": Effects on European Identity and Subsequent Migration Behaviour' *International Journal of Population Geography*, 9: 229–252.
Klingberg, S. (1998) 'Le sans-frontierisme et l'intégration planetaire' *L'homme et la Société*, 129, July, 29–46.
Klüver, K. (2010) 'Europeanization of Lobbying Activities: When National Interest Groups Spill Over to the European Level' *European Integration*, 32:2, pp. 175–191.
Knill, C. and Lehmkuhl, D. (1999) 'How Europe Matters. Different Mechanism of Europeanization', *EIOP*, 3:7, 19 pages.
Kohler-Koch, B. (2013) 'Civil Society and Democracy in the EU. High Expectations Under Empirical Scrutiny' in Kohler-koch, B. and Quittkat, C. (Eds.) *De-Mystification of Participatory Democracy*, (Oxford: OUP) pp. 2–6.
Kohler-Koch, B. (2010) 'Civil Society and EU democracy: 'Astrofurf' Representation?' *JEPP*, 17:1, pp. 100–116.
Kohler-Koch, B. (2003) 'Interdependent European Governance' in Kohler-Koch, B. (Ed.) *Linking EU and National Governance*, (Oxford: Oxford University Press) pp. 10–23.
Kohler-Koch, B. (2001) 'The Commission White Paper and the Improvement of European Governance' *Jean Monnet Working Papers*, 6/01.
Kohler-Koch, B. and Eising, R. (1999) 'Network Governance in the European Union' in Kohler-Koch, B. and Eising, R. (Eds.) *The Transformation of Governance in the European Union*, (London: Routledge), pp. 3–13.
Kohler-Koch, B. and Finke, B. (2007) 'The Institutional Shaping of EU–Society Relations: A Contribution to Democracy via Participation?' *Journal of Civil Society Studies*, 3:3, pp 205–221.
Kohler-Koch, B. and Quittkat, C. (2013) *De-Mystification of Participatory Democracy: EU-Governance and Civil Society*, (Oxford: OUP).
Kollman, K. (1998) *Outside Lobbying: Public Opinion and Interest Group Strategies*, (Princeton: Princeton University Press).
Kramer, R.M. and Grossman, B. (1987) 'Contracting for Social Services: Process Management and Resource Dependencies' *Social Service Review*, 61:1, pp. 32–55.
Kreppel, A. (2012) 'The Normalization of the European Union' *Journal of European Public Policy*, 19:5, pp. 635–645.
Kriesi, H., Tresch, A. and Jochum, M. (2007) 'Going Public in the European Union. Action Repertoires of Western European Collective Political Actors' *Comparative Political Studies*, 40:1, pp. 48–73.
Kröger, S. (2007) 'The End of Democracy as We Know It? The Legitimacy Deficits of Bureaucratic Social Policy Governance' *Journal of European Integration*, 29:5, pp. 565–582.

Kröger, S. and Friedrich, D. (2012) *The Challenge of Democratic Representation in the European Union*, (Palgrave: Macmillan).

Kutay, A. (2012) 'Europeanisation of Civil Society Through the Sponsored European Publics' *Javnost-The public*, 19:1, 19–34.

Lang, J. (2003) 'Policy Implementation in a Multi-Level System: The Dynamics of Domestic Response' Kohler-Koch, B. (Ed.) *Linking EU and National Governance*, (Oxford: Oxford University Press) pp. 154–174.

Lascoumes, P. and Le Galès, P. (2007) *Sociologie de l'action publique*, (Paris: Armand Colin).

Lascoumes, P. and Le Galès, P. (2004) 'L'action publique saisie par les Instruments' in Lascoumes, P. and Le Galès, P. (Eds.) *Gouverner par les instruments*, (Paris: Presses de Sciences Po) pp. 11–44.

Lehmann, W. (2009) 'The European Parliament' in Coen, D. and Richardson, J. (Eds.) *Lobbying the European Union*, (Oxford: OUP) 39–69.

Lewis, D. (2001) 'International Development NGOs: Policy Conflict and Convergence' in Harris, M. and Rochester, C. (Eds.) *Voluntary Organisations and Social Policy in Britain*, (Houndmills: Palgrave) pp. 141–153.

Lernes, C. (1995) 'Le Choc du Retour et les Bureaucrates de l'Humanitaire' in Le Monde, on 16 November.

Lewis, O. (2001) *NGOs as Social Service Providers in Europe. A Review of Literature*, (Brussels: Solidar).

Liebert, U. (2009) 'The Contentious Role of Civil Society in Reconstituting Democracy in the European Union' *Policy and Society*, 28:1, pp. 71–86.

Liebert, U. and Trenz, H.J. (2010) *The New Politics of European Civil Society*, (Abingdon: Routledge).

Liebert, U. and Trenz, H.J. (2009) 'Civil Society and the Reconstitution of Democracy in Europe: Introducing a New Research Field' *Policy and Society*, 28:1, pp. 1–9.

Lucarelli, S. and Radaelli, C.M. (2004) 'The European Convention: A Process of Mobilization?'*South European Society & Politics*, 9:1, pp. 1–23.

Mahoney, C. (2004) 'The Power of Institutions: State and Interest Group Activity in the European Union' *European Union Politics*, 5:4, pp. 441–466.

Mahoney, C. and Beckstrand, M. (2011) 'Following the Money: European Union Funding of Civil Society Organizations' *JCMS*, 49:6, pp. 1339–1361.

Mahoney, J. and Goertz, G. (2006) 'A Tale of Two Cultures: Contrasting Quantitative and Qualitative Research' *Political Analysis*, 14, 227–249.

Mair, P. (2010) 'Concepts and Concept Formation' in Della Porta, D. and Keating, M. (Eds.) *Approaches and Methodologies in the Social Sciences: A Pluralist Perspective*, (Cambridge: Cambridge University Press) 177–197.

Majone, G. (2010) 'Transaction-Cost Efficiency and the Democratic Deficit' *JEPP*, 17:2, pp. 150–175.

March, J.G. and Olsen, J.P. (2005) 'Elaborating the New Institutionalism' *Arena Working Papers*, 11, 28 pages. Available at: http://web.iaincirebon.ac.id/ebook/moon/PoliticalScience/wp05_11%20on%20institusionalism.pdf.

Marks, G. and McAdam, D. (1999) 'On the Relationship of Political Opportunities to the Form of Collective Action: The Case of the European Union' in Della Porta, D., Kriesi, H. and Rucht, D. (Eds.) *Social Movements in a Globalizing World*, (London: MacMillan Press) p. 97–111.

Marks, G. and McAdam, D. (1996) 'Social Movements and the Changing Structure of Political Opportunities in the European Union' *West European Politics*, 19:2, pp. 249–278.

Mastenbroek, E. and Kaeding, M. (2006) 'Beyond the Goodness of Fit: Domestic Politics on the Forefront' *Comparative European Politics*, 4:4, pp. 331–354.

Mazey, S. and Richardson, J. (2006) 'Interest Groups and EU Policy-Making: Organizational Logic and Venue-Shopping' in Richardson, J. (Ed.) *European Union: Power and Policy-making*, (London: Routledge) pp. 247–265.

Mazey, S. and Richardson, J. (2002) 'Pluralisme ouvert ou restreint? Les groupes d'intérêt dans l'Union européenne' in Balme, R., Chabanet, D. and Wright, V. (Eds.) *L'action collective en Europe*, (Paris: Presses de Sciences Po) pp. 123–161.

McAdam, D., Mc Carthy, J. and Mayer, Z. (1996) 'Introduction: Opportunities, Mobilising Structures, and Framing Processes-Towards a Synthetic, Comparative Perspective on Social Movements' in McAdam, D., Mc Carthy, J. and Mayer, Z. (Eds.) *Comparative Perspectives on Social Movements*, (Cambridge: Cambridge University Press) p. 1 à 20.

McCauley, D. (2011) 'Bottom-Up Europeanization Exposed. Social Movements Theory and Non State Actors in France' *Journal of Common Market Studies*, 49:5, pp. 1019–1042.

Meyer, D.S. (2004) 'Protest and Political Opportunities' *Annual Review of Sociology*, 30, pp. 125–145.

Meyer, D.S. and Minkoff, D.C. (2004) 'Conceptualizing Political Opportunity' *Social Forces*, 82:4, pp. 1457–1492.

Meynaud, J. and Sidjanski, D. (1969) *Les groupes de pression dans la Communauté européenne*, (Montreal: Université de Montreal).

Michalowitz, I. (2007) 'What Determines Influence? Assessing Conditions for Decision-Making Influence of Interest Groups in the EU' *Journal of European Public Policy*, 14:1, pp. 132–151.

Michalowitz, I. (2005) 'DG Trade's Formal Civil Society Dialogue: Fostering a European Public Space?' Paper Presented to the Institutional Shaping of EU–Society Relations, Mannheim, October.

Michel, H. (2005) 'The Lobbyist and the Consultation on the White Paper: Objectivization and Institutionalisation of Civil Society' Paper Presented to the Institutional Shaping of EU–Society Relations, Mannheim, October.

Morris, S. (2000) 'Defining the Non-Profit Sector: Some Lessons from History' *Civil Society Working Paper*, 3, 21 pages. Available at: http://eprints.lse.ac.uk/29032/1/cswp3.pdf.

Mörth, U. (2003) 'Europeanization as Interpretation, Translation and Editing of Public Policies' in Featherstone, K. and Radaelli, C.M. (Eds.) *The Politics of Europeanization*, (Oxford: Oxford University Press) pp. 159–169.

Mosley, J. (2012) 'Keeping the Lights On: How Government Funding Concerns Drive the Advocacy Agendas of Nonprofit Homeless Service Providers', *Journal of Public Administration Research and Theory Advance Access* 22, pp. 841–866.

Obradovic, D. (2009) 'Regulating lobbying in the European Union' in Coen, D. and Richardson, J. (Eds) *Lobbying the European Union: Institutions, Actors and Issues*, (Oxford: Oxford University Press) pp. 298–334.

Olsen, J.P. (2002) 'The Many Faces of Europeanization' in *JCMS*, 40:5, pp. 921–52.

Olson, M. (1965) *The Logic of Collective Action: Public Goods and the Theory of Groups*, (Cambridge: Harvard University Press).
Palier, B., Erhel, C., and Mandin, L. (2005) 'The Leverage Effect. The Open Method of Coordination in France' in Zeitlin, J. and Pochet, P. (Eds.) *The Open Method of Coordination in Action*, (Brussels: P.I.E.-Peter Lang) pp. 217–248.
Palier, B. and Surel, Y. (2007) *L'Europe en action. L'europeanisation dans une perspective comparée*, (Paris: L'Harmattan).
Panebianco, S. (2000) *Il lobbying Europeo*, (Milano: Giuffrè).
Pasquier, R. and Weisbein, J. (2004) 'L'Europe au microscope du local. Manifeste pour une sociologie politique de l'integration communautaire' *Politique européenne*, 12:1, pp. 5–21.
Perez-Solozarno Barragan, N. (2007) 'The Convention Experience: Between Rhetoric and Participation' *Journal of Civil Society*, 3:3, pp. 271–286.
Perri 6 (1992) 'European Competition Law and the Non-Profit Sector' *Voluntas*, 3:2, pp. 215–246.
Pestoff, V. (2009) *A Democratic Architecture for the Welfare State*, (London: Routledge).
Peugeot, V. (1997) 'Des Initiatives Citoyennes' *La Tribune Fonda*, 126, July.
Pierson, P. (1996) 'The Path to European Integration. A Historical Institutionalist Analysis' *Comparative Political Studies*, 29:2, pp. 123–163.
Piveteau, A. (1998) 'Pour une analyse économique des ONG' in Deler, J.P., Fauré, Y.A., Piveteau, A. and Roca, P.J. (Eds.) *ONG et Développement*, (Paris: Karthala) pp. 271–292.
Pollock, G. (2001) 'Civil Society Theory and Euro-Nationalism' *Studies in Social & Political Thought*, 4, March 2001, pp. 31–56.
Pollack, M.A. (1997) 'Representing Diffuse Interests in EC Policy-Making' *Journal of European Public Policy*, 4:4, pp. 572–590.
Princen, S. and Kerremans, B. (2008) 'Opportunity Structures in the EU Multi-Level System' *West European Politics*, 31:6, pp. 1129–1146.
Queinnec, E. and Ingalens, J. (2004) *Les organisations non gouvernementales et le management*, (Paris: Vuibert).
Quittkat, C. (2013) 'New Instruments Serving Democracy. Do Online Consultations Benefit Civil Society' in Kohler-Koch, B. and Quittkat, C. (Eds.) *De-Mystification of Participatory Democracy: EU-Governance and Civil Society*, (Oxford: OUP) pp. 85–113.
Quittkat, C. (2011) 'The European Commission's Online Consultations: A Success Story?' *JCMS*, 49:3, pp. 653–674.
Radaelli, C.M. (2006) 'Europeanization: Solution or Problem?' In Cini, M. and Bourne, A. (Eds.) *European Union Studies*, (Basingstoke: Palgrave) pp. 56–76.
Radaelli, C.M. (2003) 'The Europeanization of Public Policy' in Featherstone, K. and Radaelli, C.M. (Eds.) *The Politics of Europeanization*, (Oxford: Oxford University Press) pp. 27–56.
Rhodes, R.A.W. (1999) 'Foreword: Governance and Networks' in Stoker, G. (Ed.) *The New Management of British Local Governance*, (London: Macmillan Press) p. xii–xxvi.
Richardson, J. (1993) 'Government and Groups in Britain: Changing Styles' in Clive, S.T. (Ed.) *First World Interest Groups, A Comparative Perspective*, (London: Greenwood Press) pp. 53–66.
Rieff, D. (2002) *L'humanitaire en crise*, (Paris: Le serpent à Plumes).

Roberts, J. (2007) 'Partners or Instruments: Can the Compact Guard the Independence and Autonomy of Voluntary Organizations?' *Voluntary Sector Working Papers*, 8, 40 pages. Available at: http://eprints.lse.ac.uk/29246/1/VSWP8_Roberts.pdf.

Rouault, S. (2001), 'De l'insertion professionnelle à la valorisation du capital humain: un changement de paradigme accompagné par l'UE?' *Politique européenne*, 2, pp. 49–66.

Rüb, U. (2002) *European Governance. News from the UK on Democracy, Participation and Policymaking in the EU*, (London: The Federal Trust).

Ruiz Olabuénaga, J.L. (1995) *El Tercer sector en España*, (Madrid: Fundación BBV).

Rumford, C. (2002) *The European Union. A Political Sociology*, (Oxford: Blackwell Publishing).

Ruzza, C. (2011) 'Social Movements and the European Interest Intermediation of Public Interest Groups' *Journal of European Integration*, 33:4, pp. 453–469.

Ruzza, C. (2007) 'Advocacy Coalitions and the Participation of Organized Civil Society in the European Union' in Della Salla, V. and Ruzza, C. (Eds.) *Governance and Civil Society in the European Union. Volume 2: Exploring policy issues*, (Manchester: MUP) pp. 47–71.

Ruzza, C. (2004) *Europe and Civil Society. Movements Coalitions and European Governance*, (Manchester: Manchester University Press).

Ryfman, P. (2004) *Les ONG*, (Paris: La Decouverte).

Sabel, C. and Zeitlin, J. (2008) 'Learning from Difference: The New Architecture of Experimentalist Governance in the EU' *European Law Journal*, 14:3, pp. 271–327.

Salamon, L.M. and Anheier, H.K. (1997) *Defining the Nonprofit Sector. A Cross-National Analysis*, (Manchester: Manchester University Press).

Salinas Ramos, F. (2001) *La evolución del tercer sector hacia la empresa social*, (Madrid: Plataforma para la promoción del voluntariado en España).

Sanchez Salgado, R. (2014a) 'Rebalancing EU Interest Representation? Associative Democracy and EU Funding of Civil Society Organizations' *Journal of Common Market Studies*, 52:2, pp. 337–352.

Sanchez Salgado, R. (2014b) 'Europeanization of CSOs in Times of Crisis: Exploring Coping Strategies of Humanitarian and Development CSOs' Paper Presented to the Conference of the ECPR Standing Group on the European Union, June.

Sanchez Salgado, R. (2013) 'From "Talking the Talk" to "Walking the Walk": The Contribution of Structural Funds to the Implementation of European Employment Priorities' *EIOP*, 17:2, 26 pages. Available at: http://eiop.or.at/eiop/index.php/eiop/article/view/2013_002a/247.

Sanchez Salgado, R. (2011) 'La Société Civile européenne: Les usages d'une fiction' *Raisons Politiques*, 44:4, pp. 201–226.

Sanchez Salgado, R. (2010) 'NGOs Structural Adaptation to Funding Requirements and Prospects for Democracy: The Case of the European Union', *Global Society*, 24:4, pp. 507–527.

Sanchez Salgado, R. (2009) 'Les effets des programmes européens sur les associations du secteur social: Une influence à des niveaux multiples' *Pôle Sud, revue de Science politique de l'Europe méridionale*, 31, pp. 41–56.

Sanchez Salgado, R. (2008) 'Les projets transnationaux européens: Analyse d'une expérience de travail européanisante' *Politique européenne*, 26, pp. 53–74.

Sanchez Salgado, R. (2007a) *Comment l'Europe construit la société civile*, (Paris: Dalloz).
Sanchez Salgado, R. (2007b) 'Giving a European Dimension to Civil Society Organizations' *Journal of Civil Society Studies*, 3:3, pp. 253–269.
Sanchez Salgado, R. (2006) Civil Society in Spain, Research report written for the project *Civil Society Mapping Study*, Notre Europe, Paris.
Sanchez Salgado, R. and Parthenay, K. (2013) Fostering Regional Democracy Through Civic Organizations' *Journal of European Integration*, 32:2, pp. 151–168.
Sanz Corella, B. and Van Goey, A. (2012) Report on the Key Results of the On-line Consultation on the Issues-Paper 'CSO in Development Cooperation' Brussels: Europeaid/129783/C/SER/multi.
Saurugger, S. (2008) 'Une sociologie de l'Integration européenne' *Politique européenne*, 25, pp. 5–22.
Saurugger, S. (2007) 'Differential Impact: Europeanizing French Non-State Actors' *Journal of European Public Policy*, 14:7, pp. 1079–1097.
Saurugger, S. (2006) 'The Professionalisation of Interest Representation: A Legitimacy Problem for Civil Society and the EU?' in Smismans, S. (Ed.) *Civil Society and Legitimate European Governance*, (Cheltenham: Edward Elgar) pp. 260–276.
Saurugger, S. (2005) 'Europeanization as a Methodological Challenge: The Case of Interest Groups' *Journal of Comparative Public Analysis, Research and Practice*, 7:4, pp. 291–312.
Saurugger, S. (2003) 'Les groupes d'interet entre démocratie associative et mecanismes de contrôle' *Raisons politiques*, 10, pp. 151–169.
Saurugger, S. (2002) 'Analyser les modes de representation des interest dans l'Union européenne: Construction d'une problematique' *Questions de Recherche*, 6, 49 pages. Available at: http://www.sciencespo.fr/ceri/sites/sciencespo.fr.ceri/files/qdr6.pdf.
Schmidt, V. (2004) 'Europeanization and the Mechanics of Economic Policy Adjustment' in Lequesne, C. and Surel, Y. (Eds.) *L'intégration européenne. Entre emergence institutionnelle et recomposition de l'Etat*, (Paris: Presses de Sciences Po) pp. 185–216.
Schmidt, V. (1999) 'National Patterns of Governance Under Siege. The Impact of European Integration' in Kohler-Koch, B. and Eising, R. (Eds.) *The Transformation of Governance in the European Union*, (London: Routledge) pp. 155–172.
Schmitter, P. (1995) 'The Irony of Modern Democracy and the Viability of Efforts to Reform its Practice' in Cohen, J. and Rogers, J. (Eds.) *Associations and Democracy*, (London: Verso), pp. 167–183.
Schmitter, P. (1979) 'Still the Century of Corporatism?' in Lehmbruch, G. and Schmitter, P. (Eds.) *Trends Towards Corporatist Intermediation*, (London: Sage) pp. 7–53.
Schmitter, P. and Streeck, W. (1981) *The Organization of Business Interests: A Research Design to Study the Associative Action of Business in the Advanced Industrial Societies of Western Europe*, (Berlin: WZB).
Schneider, G. and Aspinwall, M. (2001) 'Moving Beyond Outworn Debates: A New Institutionalist Research Agenda' in Schneider, G. and Aspinwall, M. (Eds.) *The Rules of Integration. Institutionalist Approaches to the Study of Europe*, (Manchester: Manchester University Press) pp. 177–187.
Sfez, P. and Sherlock, K. (2008) General Evaluation of Actions to Raise Public Awareness of Development Issues in Europe, Report Ordered by the

Commission. Available at: http://ec.europa.eu/europeaid/what/civil-society/documents/de-ar_evaluation2008.pdf, Last Consulted on 5 August 2013.

Shapiro, M. (1998) 'The European Court of Justice: Of Institutions and Democracy' *Israel Law Review*, 32:1, pp. 3–50.

Sigalas, E. (2010) 'Cross-Border Mobility and European Identity: The Effectiveness of Intergroup Contact During the ERASMUS Year Abroad' *European Union Politics*, 11:2, pp. 241–265.

Smillie, I. (2000) *The Alms Bazaar: Altruism Under Fire: Non-Profit Organizations and International Development*, (Ester: ITP).

Smillie, I. (1994) 'United Kingdom' in Smillie, I. and Helmich, H. (Eds.) *Organisations non gouvernementales et gouvernements: une association pour le développement*, (Paris: OECD) pp. 282–300.

Smismans, S. (2006) *Civil Society and Legitimate European Governance*, (Cheltenham: Edward Elgar).

Smismans, S. (2002) 'Civil Society in European Institutional Discourses' *Cahiers européens de Sciences Po*, 4, 25 pages. Available at: http://www.cee.sciences-po.fr/erpa/docs/wp_2002_4.pdf.

Smith, S.R. and Lipsky, M. (1993) *Nonprofits for Hire. The Welfare State in the Age of Contracting*, (London: Harvard University Press).

Smith, A. (1995) *Nations and Nationalism in a Global Era*, (Cambridge: Polity Press).

Sommer, J.G. (1977) *Beyond Charity: US Voluntary Aid for a Changing Third World*, (Washington: Overseas Development Council).

Soulet, J.F. (2001) *La revolte des citoyens*, (Toulouse: Éditions Privat).

Souto, O.M. and McCoshan, A. (2006) *Survey of the Socio-economic Background of Erasmus students DG EAC 01/05*, (Birmingham: ECOTEC Research and Consulting Limited).

Stangor, C., Jonas, K., Stroebe, W. and Hewstone, M. (1996) 'Influence of Student Exchange on National Stereotypes, Attitudes and Perceived Group Variability' *European Journal of Social Psychology*, 26, pp. 663–675.

Steen, O.I. (1996) 'Autonomy or Dependency? Relations Between Non-Governmental International Aid Organizations and Government' *Voluntas*, 7:2, pp. 147–159.

Stone Sweet, A. and Sandholtz, W. (1997) 'European Integration and Supranational Governance' *JEPP*, 4:3, pp. 297–317.

Trenz, H.J. (2007) 'A Transnational Space of Contention? Patterns of Europeanisation of Civil Society in Germany' in Della Sala, V. and Ruzza, C. (Eds.) *Governance and Civil Society in the European Union*, (Manchester: MUP) pp. 89–112.

Vallaeys, A. (2004) *Médecins Sans Frontières, La biographie*, (Paris: Fayard).

Vanhala, L. (2009) 'Anti-Discrimination Policy Actors and their Use of Litigation Strategies: The Influence of Identity Politics' *JEPP*, 16:5, pp. 738–754.

Vayssade, M.C. (2001) "Le statut d'association européenne' in *Les associations et l'Europe en devenir*, (Paris: La Documentation francaise) pp. 113–114.

Vayssière, B. (2002) *Groupes de Pression en Europe*, (Toulouse: Privat).

Vedelago, F. Valéau, P. and Quéinnec, E. (1996) 'Les conflits des valeurs au sein des ONG et des organisations de solidarité: portée et signification pour le management' in Queinnec, Erwan and Ingalens, Jacques (Eds.) *Les organisations non gouvernementales et le management*, (Paris: Vuibert).

Venables, T. (2007) *Tips for the Would-be European Lobbyist*, (Brussels: ECAS).
Verdier, D. and Breen, R. (2001) 'Europeanization and Globalization' *Comparative Political Studies*, 34:3, pp. 227–262.
Walzer, M. (1995) *Towards a Global Civil Society*, (Oxford: Bergham Books).
Ward, S. and Lowe, P. (1998) 'National Environmental Groups and Europeanization: A Survey of the British Environmental Lobby' *Environmental Politics*, 7:4, p. 155–165.
Warleigh, A. (2001) 'Europeanizing Civil Society: NGOs as Agents of Political Socialization' *Journal of Common Market Studies*, 4:7, pp. 155–165.
Webster, R. (2000) 'What Drives Interest Groups Collaboration at the EU Level? Evidence from the European Environmental Interest Groups' *European Integration Online Papers*, 17, 22 pages. Available at: http://eiop.or.at/eiop/pdf/2000-017.pdf.
Weiler, JHH, Haltern, F. and Mayer, F. (1995) 'European Democracy and its Critique. Five uneasy Pieces' *Jean Monnet Papers*, 1. Available at: http://www.jeanmonnetprogram.org/archive/papers/95/9501ind.html.
Weisbein, J. (2001) 'Le militant et l'Expert: Les associations civiques face au système politique européen' *Politique Européenne*, 4: pp. 105–118.
Wolff, C. (2013) *Functional Representation and Democracy in the EU*, (Colchester: ECPR Press).
Woll, C. (2012) 'The Brash and the Soft-Spoken. Lobbying Styles in a Transatlantic Comparison' *Interest Groups & Advocacy*, 1:2, pp. 193–204.
Woll, C. (2007) 'Leading the Dance? Power and Political Resources of Business Lobbyists' *Journal of European Public Policy*, 27:1, pp. 57–78.
Woll, C. and Jacquot, S. (2009) 'Using Europe: Strategic Action in Multi-Level Politics' *Comparative European Politics*, 8, pp. 110–126.
Wonka, A., Baumgartner, F., Mahoney, C. and Berkhout, J. (2010) 'Measuring the Size and Scope of the EU Interest Group Population', *European Union Politics*, 11:3, pp. 463–476.
Zeitlin, J. (2010) 'Towards a Stronger OMC in a More Social Europe 2020: A New Governance Architecture for EU Policy Coordination' in Marlier, E. and Natali, D. (Eds.) *Europe 2020: Towards a More Social EU?* (Brussels: Peter Lang) pp. 253–273.

Government & EU policy papers

CCD (2003) *Argent et Organisations de Solidarité Internationale 2000–2001* (Paris: Commission Coopération Développement).
CCD (2000) *Résultats de l'enquête sur les ressources et les dépenses des OSI en 1998 et 1999* (Paris: Commission Coopération Développement).
Council of Ministers (1998) Règlement (CE) No 1658/98 du Conseil du 17 juillet 1998 relatif au cofinancement avec les organisations non gouvernementales de développement (ONG) européennes d'action dans le domaine intéressant les pays en développement» OJ L213.
Court of Auditors of the European Communities (1991) Annual Report Concerning the Financial Year 1990 Together with the Institution's Replies, OJ C324, Brussels.
DGCID (2001) Organisations de solidarité Internationale et Pouvoirs Publics en Europe (Paris: Ministère des Affaires étrangères).

ECHO (2000) ECHO, Rapport Annuel 1999, Luxembourg: Office des publications des Communautés européennes.

EESC (2010) Opinion on 'Civil Society Organisations and the EU Council Presidency'—Ref. CES 464/2010.

EESC (2006) Opinion on 'The Representativeness of European Civil Society Organisations in Civil Dialogue'—Ref.: CES 240/2006.

EESC (1999) Opinion on 'The Role and Contribution of Civil Society Organisations in the Building of Europe, CES 851/99, Brussels, on the 22nd September.

European Commission (2014) The European Code of Conduct on Partnership, Luxembourg: Publications Office of the European Union.

European Commission (2013) Amended Proposal for a Regulation (...) Laying Down Common Provisions on the European Regional Development Fund, the European Social Fund, the Cohesion Fund, the European Agricultural Fund for Rural Development and the European Maritime and Fisheries Fund Covered by the Common Strategic Framework and Laying Down General Provisions on the European Regional Development Fund, the European Social Fund and the Cohesion Fund and Repealing Council Regulation (EC) No 1083/2006, COM(2013) 246 Final, Brussels.

European Commission (2012a) Standing Up for your Right(s) in Europe, Available at: http://www.europarl.europa.eu/committees/en/juri/studiesdownload.html?languageDocument=EN&file=75651, Consulted on 27 May 2013.

European Commission (2012b) The Partnership Principle in the Implementation of the Common Strategic Framework Funds—Elements for a European Code of Conduct on Partnership, Commission Staff Working Document, SWD (2012) 106 Final, Brussels.

European Commission (2012c) 2011 Annual Activity Report DG for Humanitarian Aid and Civil Protection, Available at: http://ec.europa.eu/atwork/synthesis/aar/doc/echo_aar_2011.pdf, Last Consulted on 27 March 2014.

European Commission (2011) PROGRESS Annual Performance Monitoring Report 2010 (Luxembourg: Publications Office of the EU).

European Commission (2010a) Communication and Visibility Manual for European Union External Actions, Available at: http://ec.europa.eu/europeaid/work/visibility/documents/communication_and_visibility_manual_en.pdf, Last Consulted on 26 July 2013.

European Commission (2010b) The European Platform Against Poverty and Social Exclusion: A European Framework for Social and Territorial Cohesion, SEC(2010) 1564 Final.

European Commission (2010c) Call for Proposals VP/2010/012, Establishment of 3-Year Framework Partnership Agreements with EU-level NGO Networks, Brussels.

European Commission (2009a) Visibility, Information and Communication in the European Commission's Humanitarian Aid, Available at: http://ec.europa.eu/echo/files/partners/humanitarian_aid/toolkit_for_partners_sept_09_en.pdf, Last Consulted on 25 March 2014.

European Commission (2009b) Framework Partnership Agreement with Humanitarian Organizations, Available at: http://ec.europa.eu/echo/files/partners/humanitarian_aid/fpa/2010/FPA_en.pdf, Last Consulted on 25 March 2014.

European Commission (2006) Green Paper European Transparency Initiative, COM(2006) 194 final, Brussels.

European Commission (2004a) Project Cycle Management Guidelines, Brussels: EuropeAid Cooperation Office.
European Commission (2004b) EQUAL, Libre Circulation des bonnes idées. Combattre les discriminations et les inégalités en Europe, Luxembourg: Office des publications officielles des Communautés européennes.
European Commission (2002a) Towards a Reinforced Culture of Consultation and Dialogue—Proposal for General Principles and Minimum Standards for Consultation of Interested Parties by the Commission, COM (2002) 704 Final.
European Commission (2002b) Participation of Non-state Actors in EC Development Policy, COM(2002) 598 Final.
European Commission (2001a) European Governance: A White Paper, COM (2001) 428 Final.
European Commission (2001b) A new Framework for Co-operation on Activities Concerning the Information and Communication Policy of the European Union, COM (2001) 354 final.
European Commission (2000a) The Commission and Non-Governmental Organisations: Building a Stronger Partnership, Discussion Paper, Available at: http://ec.europa.eu/transparency/civil_society/ngo/docs/communication_en.pdf, Last Consulted on 3 February 2014.
European Commission (2000b) The European Commission and the Liaison Committee of Development Non-Governmental Organisation to the EU, Press Release Reference: IP/00/1485, Available at: http://europa.eu/rapid/press-release_IP-00-1485_en.htm, Last Consulted on 8 May 2013.
European Commission (1998a) Vade-mecum on Grant Management, Available at: http://www.kulturpont.hu/letolt/vm/shortvad-en.pdf, Last Consulted on 23 July 2013.
European Commission (1998b) Rapport de la Commission sur la coopération avec les organisations non gouvernementales de développement (ONGD) européennes dans les domaines intéressant les pays en voie de développement (exercice 1996), COM (1998) 127 Final.
European Commission (1998c) Guide des Initiatives Communautaires 1994–1999, Luxembourg: Office des Publications Officielles des Communautés européennes.
European Commission (1997) Communication from the Commission on promoting the role of voluntary organisations and foundations in Europe, COM (1997) 241 Final.
European Commission (1996a) Répertoire des groupes d'intérêt (Luxembourg: ECPO).
European Commission (1996b) Communication on Evaluation, SEC (96) 659, Bruxelles.
European Commission (1996c) 'Communication 96/C 200/05 aux États membres portant fixation des directives modifiées applicables aux programmes opérationnels, ou aux subventions globales que les États membres sont invités à soumettre dans le cadre de l'initiative communautaire Adapt, visant à promouvoir l'emploi et l'adaptation de la main-d'oeuvre au changement industriel, in JOCE, No C200/7, July.
European Commission (1995) Informe sobre la aplicación de las acciones de fomento de los derechos humanos y de la democraticación para el año 1994, COM (95) 191 Final.

European Commission (1994a) Rapport de la Commission sur la coopération avec les organisations non gouvernementales de développement (ONGD) européennes dans les domaines intéressant les pays en voie de développement (exercice 1993), COM (94) 468 Final, Bruxelles.

European Commission (1994b) Rapport de la Commission sur la coopération avec les organisations non gouvernementales (ONGD) européennes dans des domaines intéressant les pays en voie de développement (exercice 1992), COM (94) 7 Final.

European Commission (1992a) Rapport de la Commission sur la Coopération avec les organisations non gouvernementales de développement (ONGD) européennes dans les domains intéressant les pays en voie de développement (exercice 1991), SEC (92) 1921 Final.

European Commission (1992b) An Open and Structured Dialogue Between the Commission and Special Interest Groups, OJ 93 C63/02.

European Commission (1991) Emergency Humanitarian Aid: A Unified Framework and the European Office for Emergency Humanitarian Aid, SEC (91) 1957/6, Bruxelles.

European Commission (1988) Conditions Générales pour le cofinancement d'actions réalisées dans les pays en voie de développement (PVD) par les ONG, VIII/764/87/FR.

European Parliament and Council (2013) Regulation (EU) No 1304/2013 on the European Social Fun, OJEU, L347/470.

European Parliament and Council (2012) Regulation (EU, EURATOM) No 966/2012 of 25 October 2012 on the Financial Rules Applicable to the General Budget of the Union and Repealing Council Regulation, OJEU, L298/1.

European Parliament and Council (2002) Décision établissant un programme d'action communautaire pour la promotion des organisations non gouvernementales actives principalement dans le domaine de la protection de l'environnement, OJ l 75/1.

European Parliament (2014) Report on the Modification of the Interinstitutional Agreement on the Transparency Register, PE 528.034v02-00, Available at: http://www.europarl.europa.eu/sides/getDoc.do?pubRef=-%2f%2fEP%2f%2fTEXT%2bREPORT%2bA7-2014-0258%2b0%2bDOC%2bXML%2bV0%2f%2fEN&language=EN.

European Parliament (2013) Draft Annual Report of the Activities of the Committee of Petitions, Available at: http://www.europarl.europa.eu/sides/getDoc.do?pubRef=-//EP//NONSGML+COMPARL+PE-508.200+01+DOC+PDF+V0//EN&language=EN.

European Parliament (2012) Draft Annual Report of the Activities of the Committee of Petitions. Available at: http://www.europarl.europa.eu/committees/en/peti/draft-reports.html?linkedDocument=true&ufolderComCode=PETI&ufolderLegId=7&ufolderId=11542&urefProcYear=&urefProcNum=&urefProcCode=#menuzone

European Parliament (2011) Decision of 11 May 2011 on Conclusion of an Interinstitutional Agreement Between the European Parliament and the Commission on a Common Transparency Register, 2010/2291(ACI)), Available at:. http://www.europarl.europa.eu/sides/getDoc.do?pubRef=-//EP//TEXT+TA+P7-TA-2011-0222+0+DOC+XML+V0//EN.

European Parliament (1986) Rapport sur la coopération entre la Communauté européenne et les ONG dans le domaine de la coopération au développement, document A2-185/86.
ICISS (2001) The Responsibility to Protect, Available at: http://www.iciss.ca/report-en.asp.
National Audit Office (2006) Working with Non-governmental and Other Civil Society Organizations to Promote Development, LONDON: The Stationery Office, Available at: http://www.nao.org.uk/wp-content/uploads/2006/07/05061311.pdf.
OECD (2002) Civil Society and the OECD-November 2002 Update, Policy Brief, OECD, Available at: http://www.oecd.org/development/pcd/2367485.pdf, Last Consulted on 15 April 2013.
OECD (1988) Voluntary Aid for Development. The Role of Non Governmental Organisations, Paris: OECD.
Senat (2005) Rapport d'information N46, Paris: Sénat, Available at: http://www.senat.fr/rap/r05-046/r05-0461.pdf, Last Consulted on 10 April 2013.
World Bank (1996) The World Bank's Partnership with Nongovernmental Organizations, Washington: The International Bank for Reconstruction and Development.

NGO, Press Articles & Consultancies Papers:

Alter-EU (2012) Dodgy Data. Time to Fix the EU Transparency Register', Brussels: Alter-EU.
Alter-EU (2009) The Commission's Lobby Register One Year On: Success or Failure? Brussels: Alter-EU.
Amnesty International (2010a) Report and Financial Statement for the Year Ended 31 March 2010, Available at: http://www.amnesty.org/en/library/asset/FIN40/013/2010/en/1efe033e-9922-4495-b4f7-36198a545a0f/fin400132010en.pdf, Last Consulted on 22 July 2013.
Amnesty International (2010b) Integrated Strategic Plan 2010 to 2016, April, Available at: http://www.amnesty.org/sites/impact.amnesty.org/files/POL%2050_002_2010%20Public%20ISP.pdf, Last Consulted on 24 July 2010.
Amnesty International (1998) Amnesty et l'Union européenne' La Chornique d'Amnesty, February.
BOND (2011) Influencing the European Union. An Advocacy Guide, Available at: http://www.bond.org.uk/data/files/Influencing_the_EU_an_Advocacy_Guide.pdf.
Caritas Europe (2011) Europe 2020 Shadow Report, Available at: http://www.caritas.eu/sites/default/files/shadowreporteurope2020-nov2011.pdf.
Caritas Europe (2002) Strategic Organizational Development Approach (SODA), Discussion Paper, March, Available at: http://www.caritas-europa.org/module/FileLib/SODApaperApril22002.pdf, Last Consulted on 23 July 2013.
CCFD (2013) Rapport Annuel 2012, Paris: CCFD, Available at: http://ccfd-terresolidaire.org/qui-sommes-nous/rapports/rapport-annuel-2012/, Last Consulted on 18 July 2013.
CEDAG (2003) Statut d'Association européenne: Etat des lieux, Bruxelles: CEDAG.

CLONG (2001) Commentaires relatifs aux conclusions de l'évaluation des modalités de cofinancement de la CE (B7-6000) et recommandations pour les activités de suivi, Brussels: CLONG.
CLONG (1999) Bulletin des ONG de l'UE engagées dans l'action Nord-Sud, No 451, December and January.
CLONG (1997a) Bulletin des ONG de l'UE engagées dans l'action Nord-Sud, No 29, October.
CLONG (1997b) Bulletin des ONG de l'UE engagées dans l'action Nord-Sud, No 25.
CLONG (1996) Bulletin des ONG de l'UE engagées dans l'action Nord-Sud, No 19.
CONCORD (2013) Annual Report 2012. Concord Europe, Brussels: CONCORD, Available at: http://www.concordeurope.org/publications/item/241-annual-report-2012, Last Consulted on 24 March 2014.
CONCORD (2012) Annual Report 2011. Concord Europe, Brussels: CONCORD Available at: http://www.concordeurope.org/85-annual-report-2011, Last Consulted on 8 May 2013.
CONCORD (2011) Lessons Learnt from the SAG (Stakeholders Advisory Group), Presentation During the Structured Dialogue Follow up Conference, November, Brussels.
CONCORD (2009) Concord contribution to the Review of the Financial Regulation, available at: http://ec.europa.eu/budget/library/consultations/fin_reg2009/contributions/Compilation_Organisations.pdf, last consulted on 24 July 2014.
CONGDE (2013) Memoria de Actividades 2012, Madrid: CONGDE, Available at: http://www.congde.org/contenidos.html?search[tag_taggings_tag_name_contains]=Memorias, Last Consulted on 31 July 2013.
CONGDE (2012) Memoria de Actividades 2011, Madrid: CONGDE, Available at: http://www.congde.org/contenidos.html?search[tag_taggings_tag_name_contains]=Memoria+2011, Last Consulted on 20 August 2013.
CONGDE (2005) Informe de la CONGDE sobre el sector de las ONG 2004, Madrid: CONGDE, Available at: http://www.congde.org/CONGDE2004.pdf, Last Consulted on 10 May 2006.
Coordination Sud (2012) Rapport Annuel 2012, Paris, Available at: http://www.coordinationsud.org/wp-content/uploads/RA-2012-Coordination-SUD-Web.pdf, Last Consulted on 25 March 2014.
EAPN (2013) Widening the Gap. EAPN Assessment of the National Reform Programmes 2013, Document Available at: http://www.eapn.eu/images/stories/docs/NRPs/2013-EAPN-NRP-Report.pdf, Last Consulted on 7 October 2013.
EAPN (2012) Breaking Barriers. Driving Change. Case Studies of Building Participation of People Experiencing Poverty, Available at: http://www.eapn.eu/images/stories/docs/eapn-books/2012-participation-book-en.pdf, Last Consulted on 7 October 2013.
EAPN (2010) Building Security. Giving Hope. EAPN Assessment of the National Strategic Reports on Social Protection and Social Inclusion (2008–2010), Available at: http://www.eapn.eu/images/stories/docs/EAPN-position-papers-and-reports/napreport2008-en.pdf, Last Consulted on 7 October 2007.
EAPN (2009) The Contribution of Cohesion Policy to Social Inclusion. What Role for Social NGOs? EAPN Mid-Term Assessment of the Current Programing Period

and Perspective for Post-2013, Available at: http://www.eapn.eu/images/docs/policy%20paper_social%20inclusion%20survey_05%2010%2009final.pdf, Last Consulted on 11 October 2013.

ECORYS (2013) Interim Evaluation of the Europe for Citizens Programme 2007–2013, Available on: http://ec.europa.eu/citizenship/pdf/doc1227_en.pdf, Last Consulted on 1 August 2013.

EESC and Notre Europe (2003) Dialogue sociale européen et dialogue civile, differences et complementarités, Available at: http://www.eng.notre-europe.eu/media/Semi19-fr_02.pdf, Last Consulted on 17 April 2013.

EUCLID (2012) Easier, Faster Routes to EU Grant Funding for Civil Society Organisations and Social Enterprises are Opening Up, Available at: http://euclidnetwork.eu/news-and-events/sector-news/815-easier-faster-routes-to-eu-grant-funding-for-civil-society-organisations-and-social-enterprises-are-opening-up.html, Last Consulted on 15 May 2013.

EurActiv (2011) Journalistic Spoof Traps MEPs in Bribery Affair, Available at: http://www.euractiv.com/en/future-eu/journalistic-spoof-traps-meps-bribery-affair-news-503281.

EuronAid (2007) EuropeAid to Cease Operational Activities by December 2007, Brussels: EuropeAid, Available at: http://www.euronaid.net/index.html?id=290200000074, Last Consulted on 8 May 2013.

Evalua (2004) Evaluation de la ligne budgétaire A3024-Rapport Final, R4129B, Available at: http://europa.eu.int/comm/dgs/education-culture/association/evalreport.pdf, Last Consulted on 11 July 2005.

Evaluation Partnership (2007) Evaluation of Communication, Information and Visibility Actions in Humanitarian Aid, Available at: http://ec.europa.eu/echo/files/evaluation/2007/communication.pdf, Last Consulted on 24 March 2014.

Fundacion Vives (2006) Los Fondos Estructurales 2007–2013. La participación de las ONG, Available at: http://www.fundacionluisvives.org/servicios/publicaciones/detalle/3818.html.es, Last Consulted on 9 October 2013.

Green 10 (2009a) Issue for Commission Designated Hearings: Weakening of DG Environment, Open Letters Available at: http://www.green10.org/, Last Consulted on 15 May 2012.

Green 10 (2009b) Green 10 Working Group Answer to the EC Online Consultation Reg the Review of the Financial Regulation, Available at: http://ec.europa.eu/budget/library/consultations/fin_reg2009/contributions/Compilation_Organisations.pdf, Last Consulted on 15 May 2013.

LDH (2001) Rapport Annuel 2000, Paris: Ligue des droits de l'Homme.

LDH (1999) Hommes et Libertés, n104, Paris: LDH.

LDH (1992) Hommes et Libertés, n66, Paris: LDH.

LDH (1977) Hommes et Libertés, n5, Paris: LDH.

MDM-France (1999) Rapport Moral 1998, Paris: MDM.

MDM-France (1997) Rapport Moral 1996, Paris: MDM.

MDM-France (1994) Rapport Moral/Rapport Financier. Rapport d'activités 1993–1994, Paris: MSF.

MDM-Spain (1999) Informe de Actividades, Madrid: MDM.

MSF-France (1989) Rapport Moral 1988–1989 Presented by Rony Braumman, Paris: MSF.

Oxfam (2012) Oxfam Annual Reports and Accounts, London: Oxfam UK.

Social Platform (2010a) How to Establish and Effective Dialogue Between the EU and Civil Society Organizations, Available at: http://www.socialplatform.org/wp-content/uploads/2013/07/20100201_SocialPlatform_EffectiveCivilDialogue.pdf, Last Consulted on 24 March 2014.

Social Platform (2010b) Social Platform Response to the EU Finantial Regulation Consultation, Available at: http://cms.horus.be/files/99907/Media Archive/Policies/Participatory_democracy/091218_%20Social%20Platform%20response%20EU%20Financial%20Regulation.pdf, Last Consulted on 13 May 2013.

South Research, IDPM, INTRAC, Particip GmbH and Prospect (2000) Evolution of Co-financing Operations with European Non Governmental Development Organisations Budget Line B7-6000, Leuven (Belgique), Available at: http://europa.eu.int/comm/europeaid/projects/ong_cd/fichiers/pvd_eval_2000_en.pdf, Last Consulted on 14 March 2006.

The Economist (2004) A Rigged Dialogue with Society, Available at: http://www.economist.com/node/3308986, Last Consulted on 15 April 2013.

The Economist (2000) Sin of the Secular Missionaries, Available at: http://www.economist.com/node/276931, Last Consulted on 9 July 2012.

VOICE (2004) Partners in Humanitarian Aid. The FPA Consultation as a Model of EC Partnership with NGOs, VOICE Briefing Paper, Brussels, Available at: http://www.ngovoice.org/documents/VOICE_FPA_Briefing_December_2004.pdf.

Index

Aarhus Convention, 116
access opportunities, 3, 12–13, 23, 69, 83, 85–6, 89–92, 99–100, 102, 105, 110, 113, 117, 169, 189, 198–202, 210
accountability, 30, 133, 136, 141, 143, 145, 152, 197, 206, 213–14
action aid, 33, 57–8, 61, 188, 229, 231
advocacy activities, 9, 24, 42, 58, 61, 67–8, 96, 100–2, 107, 111, 123, 132, 180, 183, 185, 189, 197, 199
AECI, 82
Agence Française pour le Développement, 81
agency
  actors, 8, 198
  of individual, 94, 103, 198
agriculture, 86
AIDCO (EuropeAid Cooperation Office), 51–2, 87, 106, 139
alter-globalization, 158, 194–5
Amnesty international, 35, 57, 67, 90, 111, 115, 131, 142, 176, 187, 213, 227
analysis
  institutional, 3, 7–8, 14, 19–21, 36
  sociological, 7, 22, *see also* approach, sociological
Anti-Counterfeiting Trade Agreement, 118, 176
approach
  institutional, 17, 198, 200, *see also* analysis, institutional
  sociological, 2–3, 8, 18, 21, 25, 198, 220
audit, 110, 135, 154, 214
Austria, 155
autonomy, 13, 24, 62, 145, 185, 187–8, 196–7, 205, 207–10
awareness-raising, 9, 13, 32, 99, 103, 118, 142, 148, 151, 153–6, 161–2, 166, 175, 225, 227

Belgium, 80
best practices, 61, 180
Blair, Tony, 92, 99
British Overseas NGOs for Developmenet (BOND), 44, 61, 100, 139, 172, 183, 220
bureaucratic politics, 74, 209
business groups, 84, 86, 112, 117, 173

campaigns, 33, 127, 171, 175, 187
church/es, 70, 72, 126, 130, 186, 209, 229–30
citizenship, 1, 143, 149, 153, 213, 224
civic engagement, 9, 153, 209
civil dialogue, 86, 90, 114
Civil Society Contact Group, 89, 114
civil society (defined), 28
CLONG-UE, 87, 107, 110–11, 139, 173, 183–4, 186, 212
community
  international, 32, 88, 205
  political, 158, 166, 216
competition/competitiveness, 22, 72, 109, 163, 172, 188
CONCORD, 60, 100–2, 111, 113, 173–6, 183–5, 193, 213, 228
CONGDE, 44, 62, 83, 101, 140, 220
constituency-building strategy, 24, 104–6, 206
constructivism, 18
consultation procedures, 5, 42, 56, 59, 64, 85, 87, 113, 174, 178, 180, 182, 200, 206, 208
convention on the future of Europe, 5, 89, 176, 180
Council of Europe, 90
Council of Ministers, 73, 75, 78, 149
counter-loading, 27–8, 189, 203–4
Court
  of Auditors, 78, 81, 108, 128, 134
  of Justice of the EU, 72, 77, 116–17, 170, 189

cross-loading, 16, 27, 28, 123, 148, 152, 162, 189, 203
cultural diversity, 149, 209, 216
Czech Republic, 96

decision-making, 1, 8, 108, 114, 137, 172, 198, 199, 212
Delors, Jacques, 149
democracy
　participatory, 205, 212, 213
　representative, 1, 71, 214
democratic
　deficit, 1, 192, 194
　legitimacy, 3, 13, 88, 204
Denmark, 77, 80, 95, 155
dependency, 24, 174, 208, 209, 210–12
development
　aid, 32–3, 73, 79–80, 98, 100, 201
DFID, 66, 82, 99, 131, 139, 222
DG
　Competition, 106
　DEVCO, 47, 51–2, 58, 73, 78, 86–7, 105–6, 133, 148, 153–4, 162–3, 173–4
　ECFIN, 105
　ECHO, 10, 45, 47–9, 58, 86, 134, 139, 150, 159, 161, 174
　Employment, 53–5, 74, 86–7, 105–6, 134–5, 139, 151, 161, 174, 193
　Environment, 86, 105–6, 113
　Justice, 56, 77, 79
　trade, 107, 173
discrimination (non-), 31, 129, 179, 183, 209
downloading, 15–17, 26–8, 123, 133, 148, 189, 203

effectiveness, 2, 24, 33, 76, 119, 135, 137, 139, 142–3, 146, 151, 156, 160, 180, 197
elite/tist system, 56, 59, 198
EPAP, 174, 228–9
EQUAL, 55, 152, 157, 163, 202
Erasmus, 73, 165, 215
EuronAid, 111, 138
Europe
　for Citizens Programme, 149, 153–8
　2020, 179–80, 182–3, 203

European
　Anti-poverty Network (EAPN), 106–7, 110, 174, 176, 178, 181–4
　Citizen Initiative, 118, 171, 206
　Citizenship, 1, 149, 153
　Convention on Human Rights, 116
　Council, 89, 114, 151, 175–6
　Court of Human Rights, 63, 189
　Economic and Social Committee, 70–1, 86, 89–90
　Economic Community, 69–70, 80, 90, 108, 123, 127, 147, 188, 222
　Identity, 24, 148–9, 152, 164–6, 197, 214, 216
　Initiatives, 77
　Integration, 1, 3–4, 11, 13, 15–16, 26–7, 104, 106, 147–50, 153, 158, 166
　Ombudsman, 117, 224
　Parliament, 73, 78, 85–6, 88, 100, 103, 111–12, 117–18, 133, 170, 175–6, 182, 194, 214
　Pressures, 12, 17, 19–20, 26, 27, 53, 67, 198
　Refugee Fund, 53
　Social Forum, 27, 170, 191–5
　Social Fund, 53, 74, 110, 128, 150, 157, 179, 199
　Statute of Association, 5, 45
　Trade Union Confederation, 176, 228
　Values, 147–9, 153, 166
　Women's Lobby (EWL), 107, 176, 184, 228
Europeanization
　bottom-up perspective, 19, 21, 25–6, 41–2, 115, 156, 189
　degree of, 12, 25, 41–3, 65, 187, 198–9, 201
　top down perspective, 17, 20–1, 26–7, 198, 203
Euro skeptics, 171
expertise, 23, 85–6, 88, 105, 119, 144, 161, 170–5, 189–90, 192, 195, 207, 211
externalization, 25, 28, 42, 47, 56, 65, 67, 190

FIDH, 35, 51, 57
foundations, 49, 74, 80, 87, 128, 175, 209
Framework Partnership agreement (FPA), 86, 174
funding opportunities, 22–4, 28, 53, 72–81, 87, 92, 95–9, 102–3, 107–9, 112, 123–4, 126, 132–3, 151, 156, 198, 200, 202

general interest, 4, 5, 46, 70–1, 112, 118, 206
Germany, 7, 33, 70, 71, 74, 77, 81, 155
goal displacement, 13, 129, 131, 210–11
goodness of fit, 17–18, 99
good practices, 10, 152, 155, 158
governance
    multilevel, 160
    network governance, 152
    participatory governance, 88, 171, 198
grassroots, 59, 73, 104, 145, 171, 172, 177, 183, 206
Greece, 81, 101, 202

health, 34, 89, 106–7, 129
Hollande, Francois, 81, 101, 222
homophobia, 77
humanitarian aid, 9, 31, 45, 47, 75–6, 99, 124, 136, 150, 160, 200–1, 221, 224
Human Rights
    protection, 10, 55, 190
    violations, 35, 75
Human Rights Watch, 35, 57, 67, 111
Hungary, 155

identity
    building, 13, 147–9, 151, 153, 155, 157, 159, 161–5, 203, 205, 214–17
    Common, 164, 214
    European, *see* european
Ile de France, 82, 193
implementation, 29, 33, 55, 72, 74, 76, 79, 85–8, 151–2, 157, 160–3, 179–82, 187, 202, 205, 211, 215
innovation, 73, 85, 134, 151, 152

institutional
    analysis, *see* analysis
    approach, *see* approach
instrumentalization, 106, 147, 153, 166, 204, 211
intercultural
    dialogue, 153
    exchanges, 148–9, 165, 216
interdependence, 26, 152, 208
interest groups system, 83
internalization, 28, 43, 59–60, 63–5, 68, 189
international
    CSO, 33–5, 45, 82, 89, 91, 118, 170, 183, 186, 188, 193, 222
    Organization, 22, 33, 35, 53, 57, 65, 67, 90–1, 230
Ireland, 74, 95, 182

Kouchner, Bernard, 101

learning, 20, 137, 138, 141, 172–4, 204
legitimacy
    deficit, 107
    democratic, *see* democratic
leverage effect, 19
Lisbon strategy, 182
litigation, 9, 42, 115–17, 193
lobbying
    activities, 83–4, 96, 101, 211
    practices, 114, 171
local
    authorities, 67, 82–3, 97
    government, 10, 82, 95, 100
Luxembourg, 115, 155, 156

Medecins du Monde, 49, 125, 136, 187–8, 213
Medecins Sans Frontieres, 49, 62, 66–7, 108, 123, 126–7, 188
media, 22, 148, 150, 159, 161, 170–1, 175–7, 191–3, 199, 201, 211
micro-sociological approach/of the EU, 8, 14, 20, 21, 25, 36
Miterrand, François, 91
monitoring, 115, 128, 134–6, 157, 161, 166, 180, 182, 215

multi-level
  governance, *see* governance
  system, 3, 177, 195

neo-corporatism/st, 60, 80, 86, 90
neo-functionalism/st, 3, 6, 104, 148
Netherlands, 155
networking, 101, 109, 149
neutrality, 31, 108, 213
New Civic Management, 123, 142, 145–6
New public management, 124, 133, 147, 170, 197
Norway, 79–80

Open Method of Coordination (OMC), 5, 20, 179, 180, 202
opportunities
  access, *see* access
  funding, *see* funding
Organization for Economic Cooperation and Development (OECD), 53–4, 80–1, 91, 135
Oxfam, 31, 33, 37, 45, 49, 51–2, 57–8, 61, 66, 82, 130–1, 136, 138, 154, 176–7, 186, 194, 213

participation, 1, 3–6, 10, 13, 22–3, 27, 29, 36, 43, 47, 55–62, 67, 70–1, 84–9, 91, 100–1, 104, 107, 133, 143, 146, 147, 150, 154–5, 157, 161, 169–96, 198–9, 203–5, 207, 209–10, 212, 217, 228
partnership principle, 77, 155, 182
petition, 115, 117–18, 175, 177–8
pluralism, 1, 4, 8, 59, 79, 125
Poland, 96, 155
policymaking, 1, 106, 112, 148, 158, 172, 193
political
  opportunities, *see* opportunities
  parties, 126
  sociology, 7, 8
politization, 172, 207
Portugal, 101
poverty, 33–4, 74, 77, 86, 174, 181, 183, 191, 209–10
preliminary ruling procedure, 116

professionalisation, 123–4, 129, 141–2, 145, 192, 212–13
project cycle management, 135–6, 139, 140
public
  authorities, 7, 53, 56, 67, 74, 76, 91, 101, 113, 142, 163, 179–81, 205–6, 212–14
  donors, 29, 67, 103, 126, 130, 132, 136, 142, 215
  groups, 13, 23, 27, 67, 191, 196, 211
  interest, 10, 29, 115–16
  marketing, 126, 210
  opinion, 11, 104, 175, 211
  space, 170, 191

racism, 56, 77, 132, 192, 209
rational choice, 18
Red Cross, 30–1, 45–6, 62, 66, 91, 103
representativeness, 13, 90–1, 195, 205
resources
  distribution of, 124, 133, 145

Save the Children, 31, 49, 51–2, 66, 82
service
  delivery, 9, 30, 32, 107, 145, 158, 212
  directive, 64, 72, 176
Single European Act, 4, 71, 83, 190
Single Market, 70–2
Slovenia, 89
Small and Medium Enterprises (SME), 112, 206
social
  action, 29, 34, 37, 45, 58, 81
  dialogue, 86, 114
  inclusion, 5, 55, 100, 152, 179, 181, 183, 202
  movement, 5–6, 13, 18, 21–3, 29, 42, 191, 194, 196, 220
  platform, 43, 60, 86, 89, 113–14, 118, 175–6, 178, 183, 193, 213
socialization, 20, 137–8, 175
sociological
  analysis, *see* analysis
  approach, *see* approach
  comparative approach, 9, 12, 14, 28
solidarity, 29, 143, 148, 159, 164, 166, 175, 187, 192, 213

sound management, 109, 134, 136, 143, 145, 203, 212
stakeholders, 5, 86–7, 104, 137, 143, 172, 174–5, 179, 180, 182, 192, 228
structural funds, 77, 110, 113, 118, 179, 180, 182
subsidiarity, 52, 151, 208–9
summit & countersummit, 69, 176, 191, 193
supranational, 11, 27, 43, 105, 165
Sweden, 7, 80, 155

temporal dimension, 25, 198, 202
territorial interests, 95
Thatcher, Margaret, 99
Third sector, 4, 72, 87
Trade Union, 69, 118, 176, 195, 227
transnational
  cooperation, 13, 25, 148, 151–2, 154, 162–6, 190, 203, 214
  dimension, 152, 161, 163
transnationalization, 25, 43, 59, 65, 190
transparency, 84–5, 89, 117, 133, 136, 142–3, 171, 185, 205, 213
  initiative, 84, 114
  transparency register, 85, 114–15
Treaty
  of Amsterdam, 70, 222
  of Brussels, 73
  establishing a Constitution for Europe, 71, 89
  of Lisbon, 71, 93, 113–14, 118
  of Maastricht, 4, 70, 72
  of Nice, 71
  of Rome, 72, 147

United Nations, 35, 67, 90, 230
United States of America, 131, 138, 230
usages
  creative, 94–5, 224
  by Europe, 11, 20, 28, 94, 103, 107, 112, 201, 203
  of Europe, 18–20, 25, 94, 112, 118, 159, 161, 201, 203, 216
  strategic, 21

voluntary
  Organizations in Cooperation in Emergency, 45, 86, 107
  sector, 10, 13, 30–1, 70–1, 124, 142–3, 145–6, 197, 201, 212–14

welfare state, 10, 30, 79
White paper on European Governance, 5, 88
women, 42, 77, 107, 176, 183, 194
World
  Bank, 91, 230
  Social Forum, 88
  Trade Organization, 88

xenophobia, 56, 77, 192

young people, 77, 156
youth organizations, 69